'This book packs an extraordinary amount of insight into a deceptively small space' Stephanie Flanders, *Financial Times*

'Mr Kay is a brilliant writer.' *Wall Street Journal*

'It will probably be the cheapest and most valuable investment IFAs can make, both for themselves and for their clients.' Russell Taylor, *Money Management*

'Beautifully written and immensely readable.' Jeremy Peat, formerly chief economist, Royal Bank of Scotland.

'I am in awe' Andrew Hilton, Director, CSFI

'John Kay is one of the most engaging and accessible writers on economics in Britain today' *Morning Star*

JOHN KAY is 'both a first-class economist and an excellent writer' (*Financial Times*). He is a visiting professor at the London School of Economics, a Fellow of St John's College, Oxford and director of several public companies. He contributes a weekly column to the *Financial Times*. He chaired the UK government review of Equity Markets which reported in 2012 recommending substantial reforms. He is the author of many books including *Obliquity* [9781846682896] and *Other People's Money* [9781781254455] both published by Profile Books.

the long and the short of it

a guide to finance and investment for normally intelligent people who aren't in the industry

Second Edition

John Kay

P

PROFILE BOOKS

This second edition published in Great Britain in 2016 by
PROFILE BOOKS LTD
29 Cloth Fair
London EC1A 7JQ
www.profilebooks.com

Typeset in Minion by MacGuru Ltd
Printed in United States of America

A CIP catalogue record for this book is available from the British Library.

ISBN 978 1 78125 677 0
eISBN 978 1 78283 269 0

Contents

8: A WORLD OF UNKNOWNS

9: MODERN DEVELOPMENTS IN FINANCIAL MARKETS

10: THE CONVENTIONAL INVESTOR

11: THE INTELLIGENT INVESTOR'S STRATEGY

12: INTELLIGENT INVESTMENT CHOICES

13: THE CUSTOMERS' YACHTS

Preface

The purpose of this book is to give you the information you need to be your own investment manager. It is a natural companion to *Other People's Money* (Profile and Public Affairs, 2015), which analyses the process of financialisation that culminated in the global financial crisis of 2008. The critique of the finance sector developed in *Other People's Money* raises two questions: what should be done to protect the public interest, and what should I do to protect my own interests? The concluding chapters of *Other People's Money* attempt to answer the first of these questions. *The Long and the Short of It* attempts to answer the second. In one respect, my task here is easier. To reform the financial sector, we need to persuade politicians, regulators and the public. To reform your financial affairs, the only person I need to persuade is you.

In this book I'll describe the investment options available, and the institutions that will try to sell them to you. I'll explain the principles of sound investment, and introduce you to the research that supports these principles. Sound investment is based on the returns from productive assets, and in a modern economy these are mostly owned by companies. So I'll describe how businesses succeed, and fail, in generating value for their shareholders, and how to distinguish fact from fiction in what they tell you.

Profitable investment involves risk, and the returns from investment are uncertain. Amateurs and professionals alike are bad at managing investment risks, although for different reasons. I'll discuss why, and explain the theories that try to clarify how we assess risks and the evidence that provides partial, but only partial, justification for these theories. I'll go on to develop a practical investment strategy for the intelligent investor, based on three fundamental principles – pay less, diversify more and resist conventional thinking – and give you the specific information you need to implement that strategy.

I'll describe the sophisticated innovations of the modern financial system. The same innovations that led directly to the global financial crisis of 2008. The world I will describe is complex and sophisticated, but greedy, cynical and self-interested. The only way to cope is to acquire your own knowledge and form your own judgement. You cannot, unfortunately, trust people who offer financial advice. If you can trust me, it is because the only product I am trying to sell you – this book – is one you have already bought. Even so, I need to insert the caveat that I am not offering advice that is specific to your circumstances, that I am not recommending any particular investment or investment product to you and that I accept no liability whatever for the consequences of your investment decisions. When they work out badly – and some of them will – it will be your fault, and when they work out well – and I hope some of them will also – you will certainly take the credit. I will explain that even a decision that works out badly may have been a good decision. But that is not a proposition that ambulance-chasing lawyers, crusading journalists or politicians wise after the event find easy to accept. So I am not going to offer advice, only suggest how you should make your own decisions.

Most investment books advise you how to trade; I suggest you trade as little as possible. Most investment books advise you to get to know the mind of the market; I suggest you think for yourself instead. Most investment books take for granted that your search for new investments is a search for stocks that are likely to go up. While I'm certainly not going to dissuade you from that, I suggest you give equal weight to a different question: is this investment different in character from those I already own?

In this book I shall describe the principles of intelligent investment that lead to these, and other, unconventional conclusions. But you will probably want to begin with a more conventional stance, and I would encourage you to do so. The conventional investor follows the average of what professional investors do. The power of conventional thinking in the City is so pervasive that this is, in reality, what the vast majority of professional investors do themselves. But you can follow that consensus with the aid of publicly available information and the properties of efficient markets. Instead of paying heavily for conventional thinking, you can use conventional thinking for free.

The conventional investor is in awe of those who have a deep understanding of what the market thinks. He should be: he is typically paying enough for the privilege. The education of the conventional investor begins with forming a sceptical view of financial market expertise. The intelligent investor doesn't care what 'the market thinks', save to the extent that its mistakes and irrationalities create opportunities. For the conventional investor, risk is being out of step; for the intelligent investor, risk is losing money.

But it is uncomfortable to be out of step. And the conventional investor will do as well as the average of professional investors, which isn't bad, and better than the vast majority of retail investors. The strategy I recommend is that you begin as a conventional investor, and as you gain experience and confidence, you devote an increasing fraction of your portfolio to intelligent investment. The intelligent investor has a mind of his or her own, can take a sceptical view of market wisdom and make his or her own risk evaluation. Such detachment enables the intelligent investor to earn better returns with less risk of loss.

The term 'intelligent investor' originates with Benjamin

Graham, who wrote a book with that title. Graham's modern disciple is Warren Buffett, the most successful investor in history. He has claimed that

> Observing correctly that the market was frequently efficient, they (the academics – and many investment professionals and corporate managers) went on to conclude incorrectly that it was always efficient. The difference between these propositions is night and day. (Cunningham, quoting Buffett, 2002)

I'll paraphrase Buffett's remark by saying that markets are 80 per cent efficient, but the profits from investment are mostly to be found in the 20 per cent that is not.

There is more to this comment – a lot more – than meets the eye. Your immediate, and understandable, reaction might be to ask 'tell me about the 20 per cent'. But I want first to raise the more general philosophical issue. What does it mean to say that a theory is 80 per cent true? We're used to the idea that theories are either true or false. There isn't room for theories that are partly true, or mostly true.

But we have to find room. The world of business and finance is comprehensible only with the aid of theories, such as market efficiency, which are illuminating but not true. It would be easy to pursue this issue into the philosophy of science, but this is intended to be a practical book. I shall simply make the pragmatic assertion that you cannot be an intelligent investor if you believe either that markets are always efficient or that they are not mostly efficient – if you believe that the efficient market hypothesis is true, or if you believe it is false. The same is true of two other theories – the capital asset pricing model and the approach to risk analysis that I describe as 'subjective expected utility' – theories that are central to modern finance theory and to the risk control models widely used in financial institutions.

The 80/20 per cent hypothesis – that the world of business

and finance is best understood with the aid of models that are partly true, partly false, is at the heart of this book. You need to understand both the 80 per cent and the 20 per cent. It is necessary both to be familiar with the ideas of efficient markets and subjective expected utility, and yet not to take either notion too seriously. Intelligent laypeople, who approach finance and investment without preconceptions, may find this easier to accept than professionals who have been forced to take one side or another in a debate.

The target readers of this book have to deal with issues of finance and investment because they have been successful in some other, unrelated, activity. These readers expect the same level of intellectual seriousness as from a book of popular science or popular history, and that is the level at which this book is written.

Many issues of finance and investment are, necessarily, technical, and their explanation involves jargon. I've provided at the end of the book a Glossary, which offers quick definitions of many terms that may be unfamiliar. The jargon is the language of the financial professional. No apology for jargon should be required if the explanation of its meaning needs to be a good deal longer than the word or phrase itself. There is one conspicuous exception to that principle – the use of the term 'high-net-worth' for 'rich'. I hope there is none of the jargon of the management world, in which new terms are coined to conceal emptiness of thought.

But this book is not an academic monograph. I have kept references to a minimum. I give references to enable the reader to check the sources of claims made. In a final section on bookmarks and bookshelves I have indicated some books and web sites that readers can use to pursue issues further. I have not thought it necessary to provide links to the commercial web sites of product providers – these are very easy to locate – but I have included details of some useful web sites that provide information or comparisons useful to intelligent investors

Acknowledgements

Many people assisted in the preparation of this book. I would like to thank those who have helped me understand the financial services industry over the past twenty-five years. This book is critical of that industry, and of what it offers to small customers. Yet while there are people in the sector whose ethics and behaviour are beyond contempt, there are also many who consistently display exceptional intelligence and unquestionable integrity. I have been privileged to work with, and learn from, some of them.

I am grateful to Robert Metz and Liz Bates for research assistance on this edition, and to Jo Charrington, who has not only organised the process from first draft to finished book but who has also, by keeping my life in order, made the whole venture possible. And an especial thank you to Mika Oldham. She suggested the idea of such a volume in the first place and has been a source of encouragement throughout.

1

Sense and the City

Can you be your own investment manager?

Many people think that successful investment is about hot tips. If someone rings you with a hot tip, ask yourself, 'Why is he calling me?' and put down the phone. If you act on a hot tip from a friend, you may lose a friend and some money. If you act on a hot tip from a stranger, you will just lose some money.

Books tell you how to become rich from stocks. Software programs and training courses claim to help you trade successfully. Their authors assert that, with their assistance, you can make a comfortable living playing the market. Before you succumb, ask the following question: if I had a system that held the secret of lazy riches, would I publicise it in a book from which I will earn only modest royalties? Writing a book is hard work, believe me.

You might already have asked a similar question: why would anyone who could write a book like this one choose to do so? I am one of a minority, perhaps eccentric, who find the study of financial markets intellectually engaging. And I enjoy writing, and hope that you enjoy reading this book as much as I have enjoyed writing it.

My target reader wants to make good returns on investments without worry. He or she probably thinks that managing money is a chore, and that people obsessed by the stock market are sad.

My target reader's financial objective is to have sufficient financial security not to have to worry about money. My target reader would be happy to go on holiday, even for months, and not look at his or her portfolio. My target reader is willing to take risks, but only with small amounts.

My target reader is a private investor, a term by which I simply mean someone who is investing his or her own money, or would like to do so. The purpose of this book is to help such a reader become an intelligent investor who can be his or her own investment manager. If you are hesitant about taking on that responsibility, you should, by the end of this book, be able to ask penetrating questions of anyone who offers you financial advice. This book is not for people who want to become professional traders, but for those who want to sleep securely in the knowledge that their portfolio is in the most trustworthy of hands – their own.

A book that told you how to be your own doctor or lawyer would be an irresponsible book. 'The man who is his own lawyer has a fool for a client.' Is it possible to be your own investment manager? The financial services industry attracts many smart people, and certainly employs many of the best-paid people in the world. Financial centres accommodate thousands of professionals. Traders spend long days dealing in securities, with access to unlimited computing power and extensive data resources. How can you compete with them? You can't, and you shouldn't. But you can hold your own in their world. There are reasons why DIY investing is possible, even necessary, unlike DIY law or DIY medicine.

An obvious and depressing reason for relying on your own judgement is that most people who offer financial advice to small and medium investors aren't much good. A doctor or lawyer may not always get it right, but you can be confident that their opinions are based on extensive knowledge derived from a rigorous training programme with demanding entry requirements. You can also expect that the doctor or lawyer will have real concern for your interests, not just his or her own.

Traditionally, financial advisers were neither expert nor disinterested. People who called themselves financial advisers were salesmen (overwhelmingly they were men) remunerated by commissions and selected for bonhomie and persuasiveness rather than financial acumen. They were financial advisers in the same sense that car dealers are transport consultants. Most of these financial advisers knew little that their customers did not know – except one piece of information which they did not share: how much the adviser would be paid to make a sale.

In some ways, things are getting better. Regulation has driven many ill-equipped financial advisers from the market. The large conglomerates that dominate the finance sector spend billions of dollars on training and regulatory compliance. But at the same time they have been obliged to pay billions of dollars in fines and compensation to people whose trust they have abused. The Dodd–Frank legislation in the United States, and the consequent establishment of the Consumer Financial Protection Bureau, have given new emphasis to the interests of customers, although these measures have been vigorously resisted by industry lobbyists. In Europe, however, the extensive new rules introduced since the global financial crisis of 2007–8 are as much aimed at protecting established financial institutions as at protecting their customers.

So there is still a long way to go. A 'bias to activity' is intrinsic to the processes of financial advice; few people will pay much to be told to do nothing, even though that is often wise counsel. Training and compliance are largely concerned with the process of selling and the mechanics of regulation rather than financial economics. After reading this book, you will understand the principles of investment better than most people who offer financial advice to retail investors. You do not have to worry about 'knowing your customer' if you are your own customer.

You need not fear that the advice you give yourself will be biased by the prospect of a fat commission.

You can also benefit from the wider set of opportunities the internet has given the individual investor. Financial services can not only be bought and sold electronically, but can also be delivered electronically. From home or office, you can now obtain a wide range of information, buy and sell securities very cheaply, and access many investment products that did not exist two decades ago. Comparison sites enable you to scan a range of providers.

The internet will never replace the truly skilled intermediary, just as it will never replace the doctor or lawyer, though it may change the roles of these intermediaries. But the search engine and the comparison site can now do much of what intermediaries would once have done. Unfortunately, the search engine and the comparison site are also corruptible. Like the sales people, they are paid by product providers. What these sites display may not be comprehensive; what they highlight is not necessarily what is best for you.

The divergence between your interests and the interests of those who would sell you financial products is pervasive. One of the oldest anecdotes in the financial world tells of a visitor to Newport, Rhode Island, weekend home of American plutocrats, who is shown the symbols of the wealth of financial titans. There is Mr Morgan's yacht, and there is Mr Mellon's yacht. But, he asks, where are the customers' yachts? The question is as pertinent today.

A sideshow of the global financial crisis was the exposure of some of the largest frauds in history. Bernard Madoff and Allen Stanford, who had each stolen billions of dollars from their customers, ended up facing extended terms of imprisonment. Such crude theft is, fortunately, rare in the financial services industry, although many practices came close to what an ordinary person might describe as robbery. But the lawful earnings of many people in the industry seem ludicrous to an ordinary person, and are. In the course of this book you will learn how activities of little social value are so profitable for the individuals engaged in them.

No complex analysis is required to see that every penny that people take home from finance is derived from fees, commissions and trading profits obtained from outside finance. This is a simple matter of accounting. You and I, and people like us around the world, pay the large salaries and bonuses of people who work in the financial sector. We do so in our various roles as investors, as prospective pensioners, as customers of financial institutions and as consumers of the products of businesses that use financial services.

The massive rewards available in financial services are sometimes defended as the result of competition to attract talented people. The observation is true. Finance recruits many of the cleverest graduates from leading universities. In my experience, only a few top academics and lawyers rival the best minds in finance for raw intelligence. The mechanism that achieves this result is indirect. Massive rewards attract greedy people. If the number of greedy people is large, then financial services businesses can select the most talented among them. Within finance you find many who are greedy and talented, many who are greedy and untalented but few who are talented but not greedy. Interest in ideas is generally secondary to interest in money. That is why these people are in finance. So it is, unfortunately, necessary to be suspicious of the motives of everyone who offers you financial advice.

There are people in the financial world whose concerns are primarily intellectual. You will find some in the finance departments of universities and business schools. Others are behind the scenes in banks and financial institutions, where they are described as 'quants' or 'rocket scientists'. Modern financial markets are sufficiently complex, and the relevant analytic tools sufficiently sophisticated, for some people to find observation of these markets interesting for its own sake.

The good news is that the private investor can take a free ride on all these skills and activities. You can be a beneficiary of the efficiency of financial markets. Efficiency has both a wide and a narrow interpretation. Financial markets, though costly and imperfect, proved to be a more effective mechanism for promoting economic growth than central direction of production and investment. But in investment circles market efficiency has a specific technical meaning.

That meaning relates to the 'efficient market hypothesis' (EMH), the bedrock of financial economics. Much of this book will be concerned with the implications of that hypothesis, and its limitations. The professional expertise of everyone in financial markets is focused on the value of stocks and shares, bonds, currencies and properties, and on advising on when to buy and sell. Market prices reflect a consensus of informed opinions. The information that Apple builds great products or that the economy of Venezuela is in a mess is known to everyone who trades Apple stock or Venezuelan bolivars.

The efficient market hypothesis posits that all such information is absorbed in the market-place – it is 'in the price'. The market is a voting machine in which the opinions of all participants about the prospects of companies, the value of currencies and the future of interest rates are registered, and the result is publicly announced. The corollary of the efficient market hypothesis is that the results of the painstaking research of everyone in the financial sector are available to you for free.

If that conclusion seems startling, and it should, then imagine going to an auction – a fine-wine auction, for example – dominated by professionals. At first, you might be intimidated by the assembled expertise. But if you behave prudently, the dominance of professionals ensures you can't go too far wrong, because their bids will be the main influence on the price you pay.

You may not be convinced by this analogy. You may fear that there will be collusion among the dealers at the auction, that the market is rigged against the little guy. You may well be right. Fifty years ago, you would have been justified in having similar suspicions about securities markets. But, over recent decades, extensive public resources have been devoted to securing the integrity and transparency of financial transactions.

These regulatory provisions don't work perfectly, and never will. When you trade, your broker must normally get you the best price available in the market. The reality is that a bank dealing on its own account will often do better. But not so much better. The edge that the skilled and experienced buyer may have can be more than offset by the advantages you have in trading for yourself. You have greater knowledge of your own needs; you know that you can trust yourself. Best of all, you don't have to pay yourself. Your bonus is already in your pocket.

From gentlemen to players

The efficient market hypothesis describes how the market handles information. Information has always been the life-blood of markets, but the manner in which information is handled has changed. Finance was once based on relationships: the community bank manager, the locally based insurance agent and the gentlemanly stockbroker knew their clients, often socially as well as professionally. Investment bankers nurtured a long-term association with big and small companies, investing time in acquiring knowledge of the business, in the expectation that they might occasionally be rewarded by commission on a new issue or fees on an acquisition.

The atmosphere of today's financial markets is very different. Most stock exchanges no longer have a trading floor where buyers and sellers meet. Now, the large investment banks have their own raucous trading floors, which may contain hundreds of desks, each linked to the market via a screen. The visual display has several parts, designed to convey the impression of an unmanageable flow of new information.

The modern financial institution encompasses a mixture of people and approaches: the urbane sophistication of the investment bankers who plan new issues and plot mergers and acquisitions; the rocket scientists and the quants – frequently intellectually sophisticated but often lacking in common sense; the traders – some of them graduates of leading business schools, some with no higher education at all – demonstrating the aggression and ethics of the market stall. The organisations that combine these functions are an explosive mix which frequently does detonate. The overall change is from benign amateurism, much of it based on what would now be called insider trading, to specialised professionalism, based on sophisticated analytic tools.

Technology, product innovation, globalisation and changes in regulation drove this transition. The development of quantitative techniques in investment analysis goes back more than a century. The first index of stock prices – an average of the prices of twelve leading stocks – was created in the US in 1896 by Charles Dow. A few years later the Frenchman Louis Bachelier presented a thesis on the mathematics of securities prices that is generally celebrated as the foundation of mathematical finance. Bachelier encountered resistance, both from practitioners, who ignored his work, and from his examiners, who gave it the modest accolade of 'honourable' – insufficient to enable the author to pursue an academic career. For half a century his work would be ignored.

Other seminal contributors to quantitative finance – such as Harry Markowitz, Fischer Black and Myron Scholes – would also initially encounter negative reactions. I'll describe their theories and these responses in later chapters. Their work, like that of Bachelier, is now fundamental not just to the analysis but also to the operation of modern financial markets. Much of this work originated at the University of Chicago, and the city of Chicago was also where new derivative markets were first established. Both the graduates and the techniques were taken up by Wall Street.

All kinds of financial institution – retail banks, investment banks, insurance companies – have broadened the range of their activities. Retail banks have become financial conglomerates, with a wide range of investment products as well as their traditional roles of providing payment services for large and small customers and lending, both to households and to corporate clients. The rationale of such conglomeration lies in cross-subsidy and cross-selling. Cross-subsidy involves selling some products below cost to enhance the sales of other more profitable lines; cross-selling involves use of the customer list for one group of products to promote others. Both practices generally operate to the long-term, and frequently immediate, disadvantage of customers. I'll discuss the conflicts of interest between investment banking and retail banking, and advise you to resist cross-selling.

Many commentators have anticipated the consolidation of retail banks into a smaller number of global firms, and the demise of the bank branch. Both of these developments will probably happen, but more slowly than has been generally supposed. The traditional bank manager was an independent financial adviser. He was an active participant in the local community, to which he would usually be attached for many years.

Personalised banking is today prohibitively costly for a mass market. While the cost of processing transactions has fallen with the development of information technology, the cost of employing knowledgeable people to handle them has risen rapidly; the scope of the financial services industry has become such that people of mediocre abilities now command large salaries. A vestige of relationship-based advice survives in private banking for high-net-worth individuals. But the modern bank branch is a shop and, like other shops, is staffed by pleasant sales assistants with limited knowledge and training. The physical environment has been remodelled accordingly.

Despite the efforts of designers, the bank branch is less inviting than most shops – security precludes too inviting a display of the goods. Few products are more suited to online retailing than financial services, and that is how I suggest you buy them. Still, the branches remain busy, as you discover if you try to visit one at lunchtime. Many people dislike dealing with money and managing financial services and need personal reassurance when they do. And more than a few readers will continue to feel this need for reassurance at the end of this book. Take advice, then, but do not pay much for it. Adopt the same sceptical attitude towards your advisers as you would towards a sales assistant in a shop.

While the passing of amateur finance was inevitable, there were losses as well as gains. The old world of finance was characterised by a certain rigid integrity. It wasn't exactly that people wouldn't steal from or cheat each other, rather that they would do so only in certain well-defined and tolerated ways. This carefully modulated self-regulation could not survive the globalisation of financial markets. Globalisation, professionalisation and the rise of financial conglomerates made new and different forms of regulation of financial services inevitable.

Although regulation of financial services is extensive, even intrusive, regulation has plainly not served consumers such as the readers of this book well. Individual savers, and the institutions through which they invested, suffered in the New Economy bubble in the 1990s. The promotion of complex packaged securities in the years after 2003 was followed by a near-meltdown in the global financial system following the collapse of the market for these products in 2007. The reckless lending of financial institutions in the north of Europe to borrowers in the south has created economic tensions that threaten social stability and the very survival of the European project. The common characteristics of all these episodes has been that individuals who promoted them became very rich and the public at large – taxpayers and users of financial products – was left poorer.

The fundamental reason for the repeated – and continued – failure of regulation to meet the needs of private investors is the prevalence of what economists characterise as 'regulatory capture'. Regulation operates, in large part, in the interests of the firms which are regulated rather than the customers of these firms. This is not because regulators are corrupt; most of the administrators engaged in the regulatory process are honest people performing a difficult job to the best of their abilities. In the United States, the degradation of the political process by the mechanisms of campaign funding is the primary cause of regulatory failure. In Europe, the problem is more an instinctive corporatism which tends to equate the national interest with the interests of large national firms. We have held, and continue to hold, unrealistic expectations of what regulation might achieve.

Scepticism and wariness are needed in dealing with even the most apparently reputable financial institutions. The intelligent investor needs to develop his or her own strategy. This book is intended to help the intelligent investor do that.

2

Basics of Investment

Before you begin

I'll start with preliminaries that you should consider before you even think about investment principles or investment options. Compile a list of your financial assets and liabilities. Do it with your spouse or partner. Whether you manage your financial affairs separately or collectively, plan together. The amount by which your assets exceed your liabilities is your net worth. 'High-net-worth' is the new euphemism for rich, but what people mean by 'high-net-worth' varies. You are well off, it is often said, if you earn more than your brother-in-law. Many people will find that their house, with the associated loan, dominates the calculation. I suggest that you put this in a separate column.

But don't put house and mortgage out of your mind altogether. A housing loan is the only form of borrowing appropriate for anyone planning an investment portfolio.

Later in this chapter I will suggest you aim for a target rate of return of 8 per cent, before tax and inflation. Even if you fall short of this, mortgage borrowing is so cheap that it is realistic to expect to earn more on your investment portfolio than the cost of the loan. Many conservative people want to reduce their mortgage as quickly as they can, but such a strategy isn't necessarily wise.

Although the mortgage is a product widely sold in all advanced countries, there are considerable differences internationally in the form of the typical mortgage contract. For example, US mortgages generally have interest rates fixed for the whole term of the mortgage, but the borrower has an option to repay, and even for someone who does not move house, refinancing may be attractive if rates have fallen. A German mortgage also has a fixed rate, but repayment may entail a penalty reflecting the difference between historic and current interest rates. Most British mortgages, by contrast, normally have variable rates of interest which the lender can raise or lower according to market conditions. Mortgage interest is tax deductible in some countries – the US and the Netherlands, for example – but not in most. American mortgages are generally 'non-recourse' – the borrower can 'hand back the keys' and walk away from the debt – but in most European countries the lender can pursue the borrower for any outstanding amount even after repossessing the house and selling it.

You will often be better off if you re-mortgage your property, and you should certainly take the opportunity to find out what deals may be available to you. You may be able to increase the amount of the debt, and this may be worth considering as you establish an investment portfolio. This option is particularly attractive in countries such as the Netherlands and the United States, where interest is tax deductible. The net cost of the mortgage is then significantly less than the return you can reasonably hope to earn on your investments. However, most countries no longer allow such tax deductions. In any event, before taking out any home loan be clear what the upfront fees are, what the rate of interest is and what the mechanism is through which the debt will be repaid.

If you have any debts other than a mortgage, repay them before you undertake any investment. In particular, repay outstanding credit card balances. The interest rate on almost all credit cards is well above 8 per cent, and certainly above the return you can realistically expect on your investments.

You will pay income tax on the yield from your portfolio. The rate will depend on the country in which you live and your personal circumstances. Work out the marginal rate of tax you pay – the proportion of any extra money you earn that will be levied in income tax. In many countries there is a difference between tax rates for dividends or other savings income and the rates which apply to earnings. You may also be liable for capital gains tax. Most countries also have gift or inheritance taxes. Take the opportunity to clarify these tax issues.

In particular, you will want to consider how your assets are distributed between yourself and your spouse or partner, whether you want to make gifts to your children and whether you are taking full advantage of reliefs for pension savings and any other tax concessions for investment. A financial adviser can help you with this but will almost certainly take advantage of the opportunity to sell you products. If you need assistance, I strongly recommend you nevertheless undertake your own internet research first. As I will show below, tax can have a very substantial impact on the value of your investment portfolio.

You need a current bank account, a savings or money market account, a payment (credit or debit) card and a mortgage. Many people buy all or most financial products from the same firm and have been with the same provider for years. This is usually a mistake. Financial institutions rely on inertia and often give introductory incentives to buy what later become uncompetitive products. The problem originates with consumers rather than with institutions. Banks or insurers who provide everyday good-value pricing find their customers drift away to the introductory bargains offered by other companies.

If you are willing to be a 'rate tart', sitting regularly at your computer pursuing the best deals, you can benefit permanently from introductory incentives. Most readers have better things to do. I would prefer to find a provider who offers competitive terms and good service, and so, I suspect, would you.

The best buys are often from 'monoliners' – firms that specialise in a single product group – because their future depends on their reputation in these products. Financial services conglomerates, especially the major banks, will try to cross-sell you products. They are not very successful at this, but they emphasise this business strategy to themselves and their shareholders. The products they cross-sell are rarely competitive, and the sales pitch will waste your time.

Since the modern bank branch is a shop selling products you probably don't want to buy, you do not need to pay fees – in the form of charges for a branch-based current or savings account – to go there. An internet account will operate on the platforms of the major banks so that processing of everyday transactions should proceed in exactly the same way. Many banks seeking new current accounts now offer services designed to make switching accounts easy.

The benefits of getting these preliminaries of banking arrangements and mortgages right are so large that anyone who fails to do so isn't serious about managing money. This exercise is likely to be the best paid few hours' work you will undertake in your lifetime. Obtaining a better deal may involve moving away from an established high-street provider (although frequently moving to a subsidiary of an established high-street provider). You don't need to be a rate tart; a comprehensive review of your arrangements every few years will be enough.

Review financial risks outside your investment portfolio

Households generally cover some risks by insurance – risks such as domestic fire or theft, car accidents, travel disruption. I'll come back to insurance in Chapter 11, after discussing the ways people think about risk. Most people take out insurances they shouldn't, and fail to take out insurances they should. Here are a few preliminary pointers.

If you have dependent children, you should consider insurance on the life of both parents. The low take-up of such policies is a legacy of the sale of life assurance, costly savings products with a small element of life insurance, by sales people on commission. The policyholders could rarely afford the premiums, so most policies lapsed, leaving children without protection and creating a well-founded perception that life insurance was expensive.

A more appropriate form of insurance – life insurance that has no savings component but lasts for the period of the child's dependency – is cheap, since young parents rarely die, although the financial consequences can be extremely serious if they do. Policies that cover costs and loss of earnings from long-term illness or disability are also worth considering, although far from cheap.

Do not buy insurance from someone who offers it when you are buying something else. You will be invited to purchase extended warranties on domestic appliances and to take out travel insurance when you buy a holiday. Because the purchaser has little opportunity to compare prices, or even to consider the purchase carefully, these policies are usually expensive. In Britain, payment protection insurance, pressed by banks on customers who took loans from them, was such scandalously bad value that its sale was effectively banned. When you refuse these policies, you are, unfortunately, depriving the sales person of income, since he or she receives large commissions for selling these policies. That is why the policies are expensive and the seller is persistent. If you want such insurance – mostly you don't – buy it elsewhere.

Insurance can cover some of the financial risks of everyday life: accidents at home and on the road, theft, sudden death.

But the most serious financial risks that most households face come from redundancy and unemployment, old age and chronic illness, marriage and relationship breakdown. Such risks cannot be insured effectively and can be mitigated only through careful money management and successful investment. That's the main subject of this book.

Investment choices

When people discuss investment in bars and lunch rooms, they generally mean investment in securities – stocks and shares, bonds and deposits. But investment finds another meaning in the creation of the physical infrastructure of the economy.

Companies invest in plant and machinery. They must finance inventories and pay for work in progress. They operate from offices and shops. The government invests in schools and hospitals, bridges and roads. People used to make a sharper distinction than they do now between savings – putting money aside for later – and investment – putting that money to use. But, perhaps significantly, these words have lost this differentiated meaning. I'll talk instead about financial investment and productive investment. The return on financial investment must, ultimately, be generated by the return on productive investment. The quest for financial perpetual motion machines is unending, but the basic principle of bookkeeping – money that goes out equals money that comes in – is as immutable as the natural laws of thermodynamics. Financial investments fund physical investments, and the two principal means by which they do so are shares and loans.

A stock or share (an equity) gives you a portion, for better or worse, of earnings and realisations from the productive activities of a company. A secured loan – such as a mortgage – gives the lender the right to seize some or all of the borrower's assets if the borrower fails to pay agreed interest and the original money lent.

Unsecured loans give the lender only a legal claim against the borrower for payment, and that claim will be met only after secured creditors have realised the value of the assets pledged to them.*

Physical objects, such as offices and machinery, are not the only productive assets. Many of the assets of modern companies are intangible. Companies own brands, and build reputations. They acquire licences and intellectual property, and they invest in internal systems and organisational structures. These assets earn a return, just as plant and buildings earn a return; many such assets can be bought and sold, and can even provide security for loans.

Some financial assets are not directly associated with productive assets. Governments discovered – hundreds, even thousands, of years ago – that they could borrow to finance wars and profligate consumption because lenders knew that states could raise taxes to repay the loans. (This did not always mean they would, as lenders continue to rediscover.) Individuals can, more modestly, borrow to spend now on the strength of their ability to earn income in future. So some investments are rewarded by what economists coyly call 'time preference' – the premium that impatient or hard-pressed people will pay to spend now rather than later.

Lending to government, or a credit card borrower, must compete with lending to a company. So the returns you can earn on these financial investments are ultimately governed by what productive investments can earn. None of the complexity of modern financial markets, which package and repackage

---

* The distinctions between shares, equities and secured and unsecured loans have become much less clear-cut than formerly as a result of financial innovation. A non-recourse loan gives the lender rights over the asset on which the borrowing is secured, but not over the other assets of the borrower. Junior, mezzanine or subordinated debt will be paid only after other lenders have been repaid. Such debt may, in recompense, enjoy some share of the profits.

securities in ever more elaborate ways, can alter that essential truth. A loan that is tradable is called a bond.

While investors mostly hold indirect claims on productive assets, through shares and loans, investors can also own a direct claim on the productive investments of businesses, governments and households. They sometimes do so by owning the buildings – shops, offices, warehouses, factories and houses – from which businesses, governments and households operate. Or they may lease equipment to them.

Shares, loans and property are the main investment choices. Most investors will also require some cash for immediate needs, and to exploit investment opportunities as they arise. In gloomy economic circumstances, cash may be an investment class in its own right.

What choices should you make? The strategy I will propose in Chapters 10 to 12 is that you should begin as a conventional investor – relying on the illumination of efficient markets to provide you with the assembled wisdom of the financial services industry. Recognising that this efficient market theory is only illuminating, not true, you will want, over time, to become an intelligent investor, employing your own judgement – to pay less, diversify more and take contrarian stances.

Conventional investment strategies

The conventional investor follows the average of what professional investors do. The power of conventional thinking in the finance sector is so pervasive that this is, in reality, what the vast majority of professional investors do themselves. You can follow that consensus with the aid of publicly available information and the properties of efficient markets. Instead of paying heavily for conventional thinking, you can use conventional thinking for free.

What do conventional investors do? One starting point is to look at the largest investment portfolios in the world. These funds publish their strategies in considerable detail. At the end of 2015 three of the biggest funds were the Norwegian government oil fund, with assets of around \$900 billion, the Dutch pension fund ABP (\$400 billion) and the California Public Employees' Retirement Scheme (CalPERS), which has built up a portfolio worth \$300 billion.

All of these funds have long time horizons, and their scale gives them access to whatever investment advice they feel they need. The Norwegian fund is managed directly by Norges Bank Investment Management (NBIM), a division of Norway's central bank. ABP uses both in-house and external expertise. The assets of the Californian fund are distributed among hundreds of asset managers, each responsible for part of the fund and utilising their specialist expertise. Table 1 below describes how the three schemes invested their money.

Table 1: **Percentage distribution of net assets by long-horizon funds, 2015**

	NBIM (Norway)	ABP (Netherlands)	CalPERS (State of California)
Listed shares	61	28	51
Bonds	36	43	26
Property	3	10	9
Hedge funds	0	6	0
Private equity	0	5	9
Cash	0	0.2	3
Other	0	8	2

Source: NBIM Government Pension Fund Global Annual Report (at 31 December, Table 8), ABP Quarterly Report (at end-Q3) and CalPERS Comprehensive Annual Report (at 30 June, pp. 55 and 101).

For each, shares are the largest asset class, with the equity component (including private equity) ranging from 28 per cent at ABP to 61 per cent for NBIM. The Californian scheme has about one quarter of its assets in bonds, but for both the Dutch and Norwegians the figure is closer to 40 per cent. ABP has a particularly large commitment to inflation-linked securities (I will explain these further in the next chapter). CalPERS and ABP each have around 10 per cent of their assets in real estate.

If you were to take the average of the three asset allocations of these global investors, you would put 51 per cent in shares, 35 per cent in bonds, 7 per cent in real estate and have 7 per cent available for liquidity and other opportunities. That is typical of the asset allocation strategy a prudent, conventional adviser would recommend for a long-term investor, and that is how these funds came to adopt these policies.

There are other options. Some large educational endowments in the United States – particularly Harvard and Yale Universities – pioneered the use of a wider range of investment categories to diversify their holdings. Yale's investment manager, David Swenson, attracted a following, first in the United States and then internationally, for an innovative approach which eschewed bonds and emphasised 'alternatives', notably hedge funds and private equity – which I will describe in Chapter 9. After the New Economy bubble burst in 2000, many investors, having learned that shares do not always go up, also turned their attention to alternative investment possibilities.

What was the next new thing? If you couldn't rely on equities any more, what was the new source of easy wealth? This search would be the dominant investment theme of the first years of the twenty-first century. Like a caravan of prospectors huddled together for mutual support and security, investment institutions moved from one asset class to another, bidding up each – property, minerals, emerging market bonds, energy and foodstuffs – to new highs. An older meaning of the term 'alternative investment' also described investments in objects such as fine art, vintage cars or wine, and in commodities such as gold, copper or coffee. The most widely favoured alternative assets today are private equity (shares not quoted on a stock exchange, which few institutions supported before the 1990s) and hedge funds.

These alternative asset classes were supported partly for their novelty and partly in the belief that a wider range of investment classes provided greater diversification and security of return. But after the global financial crisis of 2008 almost all these asset categories fell in value. Panicked investors, desperate to secure cash and deprived of access to funding, sold what they could sell almost regardless of the underlying character or value of the investment. And the golden reputations of the Harvard and Yale endowment managers lost much of their glister.

Realistic expectations

An earlier generation of investors was taught (in some cases compelled) to match their spending to their income – the interest and dividends they received each year from their portfolio. But when, as in the 1970s, inflation rates were much higher than interest rates, anyone who spent their income was eroding the real value of their capital. Conversely, if your investments have a low yield but continue to generate capital gains – as with many investments in the last two decades – then it may be sensible to treat some of that growth as available for current expenditure.

A modern maxim is 'Think total return', which means regarding both income and capital gain as part of the return on your investment. The CalPERS fund has a target total return of 7.5 per cent and over the last twenty years has achieved a total return of 8.5 per cent per annum. With inflation in the US averaging 2.4 per cent over the last twenty years, this corresponds to a total return in real terms of 6.0 per cent.

Some readers will think such figures are disappointing. They have heard many stories about people who have made a killing on the stock market through hot tips and inspired timing. If you click on internet bulletin boards, you will read about the search for 'ten and twenty baggers' – stocks that will rise, or have risen, to ten and twenty times their initial value. If you open an online stock-broking account – and you should – you will soon be seduced by bulletin boards and offered hot tips. The stocks promoted there may be 'concept stocks', based on unproven technologies or bright ideas. Penny shares are priced so low that any movement seems to have a large effect on the wealth of the holders.

When you begin investing, you may be inclined to back some of these tips, and I wouldn't discourage new investors from doing so with a very small proportion of their available funds. It is a cheap means of beginning to learn about the mechanics and the psychology of the market. A few people, possessed of ill-founded self-confidence or books or courses on how to trade, set out to make a fortune in this way. The New Economy bubble saw the emergence of 'day traders', who bought and sold stocks several times a day. Stockbrokers established offices to service them.

As with many forms of professional gambling, there do seem to be small numbers of people who are good at it. To good luck they add exceptional psychological insight and rigorous self-control. But surveys of day traders show that after a few months most give up, or are obliged to do so by their families. Not all. Besides the few who develop successful careers, a larger group of people become addicts, whose financial stability and family lives may be destroyed by their obsession.

Financial innovations, especially in derivative markets, have greatly increased the opportunities and risks of market-related gambling for both amateurs and professionals. In securities markets many people are in a position to gamble, legally, with their employers' money.

Some become hooked; a few corporate and municipal treasurers have lost large sums, and a personal tragedy has become an expensive disaster for shareholders or taxpayers. The most sophisticated punters are managers of hedge funds and operators in the proprietary trading operations – 'prop desks' – of investment banks. Even there, there is a heady mix of real skill, addiction, obsession and self-delusion on the part of both individuals and organisations – a self-delusion which in 2008 brought some of the largest and longest-established financial institutions in the world – Royal Bank of Scotland, Union Bank of Switzerland and Citigroup – to the point of collapse. If you are tempted to make a living from stock market speculation, this is not the book for you. There are many other books aimed at the seekers after twenty baggers. The target reader of this book is concerned, as are the global investment funds in Table 1, with the careful and responsible stewardship of assets. They are responsible investors of other people's money. You are a responsible investor of your own.

Benchmarking performance

Table 2 looks in more detail at CalPERS' performance. The data is a warning that, even over a five-year time horizon, returns can be volatile.

CalPERS' earnings on its global equity portfolio in the five years from 2004 to 2009 were virtually zero, and this was also true of its real estate holdings between 2009 and 2014. Shares were the best performer in the second period and the worst in the first; for property the opposite was true. And when I wrote the first edition of this book, slightly more than five years ago, this statement was precisely reversed. There is a marked tendency for periods of underperformance to be followed by periods of outperformance, and vice versa. I will come back to this phenomenon, called mean reversion, in Chapter 4.

You could have become rich by holding shares in the 1990s and

Table 2: **CalPERS returns by asset class (% p.a.)**

(Total return including income, rents, dividends) (%)

	2004–9	2009–14	2004–14	Benchmark
Global equity	0.2	15.6	7.6	7.9
Private equity	8.1	18.7	13.3	15.4
Fixed income	5.1	9.2	7.0	6.3
Real estate	6.7	0.8	3.7	9.1
Inflation linked	–	6.2	–	5.4

Source: CalPERS, author's calculations

disposing of them to buy property in 1999, selling that property in 2007 and putting your wealth back into shares in 2009. But neither you nor I, and not even the well-advised folk at CalPERS, had the foresight which hindsight now tells us would have been so rewarding. Most people thought the opposite, which is why prices moved as they did; shares were in fashion in the 1990s, and property unappreciated. In that new virtual world of 1999, economic power would lie with the young titans who had been the first to 'get it', and bricks and mortar would play a minor role in commerce. When this fantasy was dispelled, or at least postponed, it was obvious to all that low and falling interest rates and readily available finance for property purchases meant that real estate values would always rise. Until they didn't. Conventional wisdom dominates asset prices, but you would have been better off – over the long run – with a sceptical stance.

Over a longer period, returns are less volatile, as the ten-year CalPERS figures show. (CalPERS' real estate performance is wretched because the fund made some big and unsuccessful transactions in residential development during the US housing bubble.) But in other asset categories, CalPERS has performed pretty much in line with its benchmarks, ahead of them in the two categories of bond and behind in equities.

What are these benchmarks? Benchmarks play a central role in the lives of professional investors. These investors are judged relative to the performance of their peers, and therefore tend to focus not on absolute return but on relative return. It is not enough to have earned 20 per cent if the benchmark index has returned 25 per cent (as it often will, over a short period, and as it did over longer periods in the 1990s). It is defensible (even if uncomfortable) to have lost 15 per cent if the benchmark has lost 20 per cent. The manager can blame 'the market' for his poor performance.

These benchmarks are indices designed to measure the overall performance of an asset class and are widely – almost obsessively – used by asset managers and investment consultants. Despite the plethora of advice available to a fund the size of CalPERS, it has not done significantly better than its benchmarks. Nor is this true on a sustained basis for other, similar funds. How could such funds outperform, since these funds dominate the markets from which the benchmarks are compiled?

Large funds do not do better than their benchmarks, but most retail investors do worse – much worse. Charges are part of the explanation. Mutual fund investors pay not only management fees but also trading costs within the funds they hold, and may suffer a spread of prices when they buy and sell, which they do too often. But the principal explanation is bad timing. Retail investors buy high and sell low. They are late into fashionable sectors and late out of unfashionable ones. There is probably no worse investment strategy than following the conventional wisdom with a time lag, but that is precisely what many small investors do – often with the encouragement of their advisers.

Realism can be depressing. You may want to close the book at this point, and either continue, alone, the search for the twenty bagger, or decide that you might as well leave your money in the bank. Both decisions would be mistakes. There is no reason why you cannot do as CalPERS and other large investment institutions do, and consequently do more or less as well as these institutions. You can follow their asset allocation. And you can buy the benchmarks which they follow. I will explain in more detail in later chapters how to do this using low-cost funds which track these benchmark indices. In this way you can more or less guarantee yourself a return, which may be good or bad, but which will not be very different from that obtained by the world's largest and most sophisticated investors.

The effects of compounding

Albert Einstein is reported as saying that compound interest is the most powerful force in the universe. There is no evidence that Einstein said this, and it is unlikely that he did, but the sentiment has some truth. The reinvestment of returns over a long period has dramatic consequences.

Over forty years, €100 invested at an 8 per cent rate of return becomes €2,172. However, if fees, charges and poor investment strategy reduce that return to 3 per cent, an underperformance typical of retail investors, the sum would be only €326. Your nest egg would be 85 per cent less. The power of compound interest means that halving the return considerably more than halves the value of your accumulated savings.

Let's be optimistic. An average return of 8 per cent a year before tax and before inflation is a demanding, but not impossible, target for the intelligent investor. If inflation and tax reduce that return by 3 per cent, then a corresponding real after-tax return is around 5 per cent. An 8 per cent return will turn €100 into €215 in ten years, and even a 5 per cent real return will add over 60 per cent to the purchasing power of your savings in a decade. While 8 per cent may seem a disappointing rate of return to locker-room braggarts, viewed as a return on productive investment, rather than on financial investment, 8 per cent appears high. While businesses often target higher returns on investment than this, they rarely achieve them.*

Look at it in another way. The return on secure assets such as cash and government bonds is today between 0 and 3 per cent depending on the length of time for which you are willing to invest your cash. If you succeed in earning an 8 per cent rate of return, that means you are receiving an additional 5 to 8 per cent per annum – the risk premium – for adopting a more adventurous strategy. This is a handsome reward. Nevertheless, it is not unrealistic.

This generous level of return for investing in more volatile assets has proved achievable over very long periods – a century or more. The question of why the risk premium is so high has puzzled financial economists, who call it the 'equity premium paradox'. I'll come back to the equity premium paradox in Chapters 7 and 8. The size of the premium is a reason why most investment institutions allocate very little to cash. You should do the same. (There are stronger reasons for making allocations to indexed bonds.)

If you set yourself a target rate of return of 8 per cent, you are already differentiating yourself from many conventional and most professional investors. I have described the significance benchmarks have for professional investors. Benchmarks don't have the same relevance to you. When you become your own investment manager, the incentives and consequences are different. The money you manage is your own, and while you can blame 'the market' for disappointing returns, the exercise is pointless. Relative performance may pay the salary and bonus of a fund manager, but relative performance doesn't pay the bills of the investor. What pays bills, in the long run, is total return,

* The return on equity they say they earn is often much higher. After reading Chapter 6, you should understand why.

in absolute terms, after tax and expenses. In the next chapter I'll review the ways in which shares, bonds and property can contribute to that objective.

3

Investment Options

Sense about shares

You might buy a share in an initial public offering (IPO), when a company raises capital by selling stock to the public. It is much more likely that you will buy on a market that trades shares in established businesses. Exxon Mobil, the oil giant, and Berkshire Hathaway, the investment vehicle of the legendary Warren Buffett, are the largest companies listed on the 'big board' of the New York Stock Exchange (NYSE), the venerable institution which was founded in 1789 under the buttonwood tree at 68 Wall Street. But Alphabet (the holding company for Google) and Apple, today the most valuable companies in the world, are traded on NASDAQ, the upstart rival to the NYSE. NASDAQ was established in 1971 as an electronic alternative to the trading floor.

The stock price of these large companies varies every minute of the trading day. You can get this price from a wide variety of internet sources (possibly the price as it was fifteen or twenty minutes ago). The real-time price is considered valuable information and is typically available only to people who pay for the information or are clients of stockbrokers. As I write this in June 2016, one Berkshire Hathaway share costs $211,940 to buy and can be sold for $211,820. Berkshire Hathaway is unique in having a share price so high that one share in the company is equivalent in value to a modest house. Apple stock is at $99, while Exxon Mobil stands at $89. The difference of $120 between the buying and selling price of Berkshire stock – the spread – is only 0.05 per cent of its value, and for Apple and Exxon the spread will only be a few cents, because the volume of trade in all these companies is large. The difference between buying and selling price for a small, lightly traded stock will be many times higher. The spread, and the broker's commission, is the price you pay every time you trade.

In 2015 Exxon made a profit after tax of $3.85 per share, from which it paid dividends of $2.88. The directors of the company decide how much will be paid to shareholders in dividends and how much will be retained for investment. The company doesn't have to pay the shareholders anything. What the directors decide to pay can be, and generally is, varied in line with the performance of the business. But if the company does declare a dividend, all shareholders have an equal right to receive it. If the company is wound up, the shareholders are entitled to whatever is left – normally very little – when all the liabilities of the company have been met. Most companies are worth more than the realisable value of their assets if they remain a going concern, and the usual reason a company is wound up is that the business is failing. But the possibility that the value of the business could be distributed to the shareholders influences the value of the stock, even if such a distribution rarely happens in practice.

These entitlements are universal, but the status of shareholders depends on the company law of the country in which the firm is incorporated. People often say that shareholders 'own' the company. They don't, as you will find out if you turn up at Apple's spectacular new headquarters campus at Cupertino or Berkshire's small office suite in Omaha, Nebraska, to assert your 'ownership'. What shareholders own is their shares, and ownership of shares confers a variety of rights. The value of a share is the value of these rights.

A key right conferred by a share is the right to vote. But what you are entitled to vote on depends on the constitution of the company and local law and regulation. At annual general meetings of companies, shareholders may be able to elect directors and can pass, and sometimes propose, resolutions to determine the policy of the company. In practice, these meetings are typically agreeable but insignificant occasions attended by professional advisers and a few, mostly retired, small shareholders.* All nominations and resolutions are put forward by incumbent management and approved by overwhelming majorities. The process resembles elections in totalitarian states. In recent years, however, there have been the beginnings of shareholder dissent, mostly over excessive executive remuneration.

Most people find it surprising that shareholder rights are more extensive in the UK than in the United States, where there is a continuing battle over 'proxy access' – the ability of shareholders to put their own resolutions, including nominations of directors, to the shareholder meeting. One reason is that in the US there is competition between individual states to attract company registrations. The competition has largely been won by Delaware; the state has more incorporations than people, and 1209 North Orange Street, Wilmington, houses the registered office of around 300,000 corporations. This is not because Wilmington, Delaware, is a hub of industrial activity but because Delaware law is particularly favourable to the interests of incumbent management (which in practice makes the decision about where the company will be registered).

The 2015 financial statement of Exxon Mobil values the

* The Berkshire Hathaway AGM, at which Buffett holds court in front of 35,000 admiring shareholders in the Omaha Arena, is a conspicuous exception.

corporation's assets at $335 billion, of which $250 billion is the value attributed to the company's infrastructure – its oil wells, refineries and tankers. The balance is made up of stocks of oil, cash and other short-term assets, and investments in other companies – mainly joint ventures with smaller or local partners. At $335 billion, the book value of the company (the asset value recorded in the accounts) is similar to the $370 billion market capitalisation of the company – the value reached by multiplying the share price of $89 by the 4.2 billion shares in issue.

However, Exxon Mobil is unusual among modern companies, both in having very substantial physical assets and in having a market capitalisation in line with the book value of these assets. The accounts of Apple show a very different picture. At end-2015 the total value of Apple's physical assets – property, plant etc. – was only $22 billion, less than one-tenth of the figure for Exxon Mobil, and less than Apple's own long-term debt. Apple had an incredible $200 billion of cash on deposit, the result of the company's exceptional profitability – the $53 billion recorded in 2015 is the highest annual return any company has recorded. With 5.8 billion shares in issue, Apple's earnings per share were $9.28, out of which it paid a dividend of $1.98. (The company financed that dividend through long-term debt because its cash is largely outside the United States and there would be a tax charge on profits remitted stateside. However, its shareholders are predominantly in the United States.) At $99 per share in June 2016, the market capitalisation of Apple – the total value of its shares – is $550 billion.

Two key metrics used in share valuation are the price:earnings ratio and the dividend yield. For Exxon Mobil, with a stock price of $89, earnings per share of $3.85 and a dividend of $2.88, the price:earnings ratio is 23 ($89 ÷ $3.85) and the yield 3.2 per cent ($2.88 ÷ $89). The equivalent figures for Apple are a price:earnings ratio of 11 and a dividend yield of 2.0 per cent.

Lower price:earnings ratios and higher dividend yields are

generally treated as indication of slower growth prospects for the company (and hence slower growth of both earnings and dividends). And a year earlier, the relative price:earnings ratios of these two companies would have been more or less exactly reversed. But the collapse of oil prices in 2015 halved Exxon Mobil's profits, although its share price increased; Apple increased its already record-breaking profits by 30 per cent, yet its share price fell.

The fortunes of companies go up and down, and so do their share prices, but few companies have experienced twists and turns of fortune as extreme as those of Apple. At the time of Steve Jobs's return to the company in 1997, the company's stock was worth little more than $1. This had increased to $10 by the time the New Economy bubble burst in March 2000. But even after the iPod was successfully launched in 2002, the stock price had declined to $2 by 2004.

The stock had recovered to $20 by the time the iPhone was launched in 2007: it lost almost half that value in the global financial crisis, so that in 2009 you could have picked up Apple stock for little more than $10. But by the time of Jobs's death in 2011 the shares were worth $60. They continued to rise to over $100 in 2012. In the year that followed they halved in value, before recovering to their all-time high of $132. But then the stock price fell again to below $100, and Alphabet overtook Apple as the world's most valuable company (and Warren Buffett had taken the opportunity to acquire a stake).

Some of these wild gyrations were in response to genuine changes in the trading prospects for the company. Others – the precipitate rise in 1997–2000 and fall to 2004, and the collapse of the share price in 2008–9, reflect overall market conditions that had little or no relevance to Apple. Some fluctuations – the sharp decline in 2013 and subsequent recovery – do not appear to have any rational explanation at all. During the week I am writing these paragraphs, the difference between the highest and lowest price for Apple shares was $10 – equivalent to a difference of more than $50 billion in the overall value of the company.

People in markets offer 'explanations' for these constant price fluctuations. Sometimes these accounts relate to broad economic events – the release of new data, or a Delphic utterance from the chairman of the Federal Reserve Board. Others may be company-specific – such as rumours about new products. The idea that these events can add or subtract $50 billion to or from the value of Apple's assets and earnings makes no sense. These share price fluctuations are what natural scientists call 'noise': random interference in physical processes. Developing this analogy, financial economists describe people who trade on hunch and gossip, with little skill or knowledge of what they are doing, as 'noise traders'. Most tip sheets, and many of the books on how to trade the market, are written for noise traders.

While day-to-day share price fluctuations dominate short-term returns on investment, in the long run dividends represent an important part of total return. For example, if you had held Exxon Mobil stock for the last ten years, and reinvested the dividends as they fell due, your initial $58 investment would now be worth $114 rather than the $89 current stock price. If you had bought Apple shares for $1 or $2, of course, your experience would have been very different, and virtually all your return would have been the result of capital gain.

But a lot more people owned Exxon Mobil at $58 than Apple at $2, and you will be fortunate indeed if you are the person who bit into Apple when it appeared poisonous. If you have been a shareholder in Apple, it is difficult to have lost money in the long run – as a committed holder over a five-year period. But not impossible – if you had bought in 1999 and sold in 2004, you would have seen most of your investment wiped out. If you had followed prevailing market opinion, you might have done just that.

The value of shares in Apple, Exxon Mobil and other companies depends partly on the fundamentals of the company – its assets, earnings, cash flow and dividends, its brand, competitive position and management strengths – and partly on market sentiment towards it. Returns from shares are the result of the interacting influences of the company's fundamentals and 'the mind of the market'. These issues will be the subject of the next three chapters.

Basics of bonds

In 1888 Britain ruled the waves, and Queen Victoria was on the throne. The British government consolidated many of its debts into a security – known thereafter as Consols – which would pay 2½ per cent interest each year, for ever, on every £100 subscribed. Bonds have always been part of the conventional investor's portfolio. The signature bond today is the bund, securities with maturities of ten and thirty years issued by the Federal Republic of Germany, perhaps the most secure investment on the planet. A €100 bund from the current thirty-year issue will pay you €2.50 every year till 2046.

This return is guaranteed only if you hold the bond until 2046. The German government may not and will not pay your capital back a day earlier than the maturity date of 15 August 2046. If you need to realise your investment before then, you will have to sell it to someone else, and the price you receive will depend on the level of interest rates at the time. This is interest rate risk, and accepting it is part of any investment in bonds; the later the repayment date of the bond, the greater the interest rate risk. When interest rates in Britain reached almost 20 per cent in the 1980s, the price of Queen Victoria's 2½ per cent Consols fell to only £15.

The 2.5 per cent bund maturing in 2046 is today on sale not for its repayment value of €100 but for €147. That means that the yield is not 2.5 per cent but 1.7 per cent (€2.50 per €147 invested).

And since the German government will still only return €100 in 2046, you will have to factor into your calculations a loss of €47 over the thirty-year life of the bond. This loss, which will accumulate year by year, reduces the effective rate of return on your investment to only 0.7 per cent. This effective rate of return is known as the gross redemption yield (GRY).

Interest rates differ depending on the length of maturity of the bond. The normal shape of the yield curve is upwards, and that is its shape today. A five-year German government bond is priced at €102 and pays an interest rate of 0.25 per cent. The effective return on this investment is nothing at all.

You can do a bit better in other countries and other currencies. A thirty-year Treasury security from the US government currently (June 2016) yields 2.5 per cent (in dollars) and a thirty-year gilt from the UK yields 2.1 per cent (in sterling). An equivalent Japanese bond, however, offers only 0.3 per cent (in yen). Over five years a bond will return about 0.75 per cent per annum in the UK and 1.2 per cent in the US, but in Japan, as in Germany, you will earn nothing at all. In 2015 the Swiss federal government issued a ten-year bond with a negative yield. You do not have to pay the Swiss government on a year-by-year basis. In fact they will pay you some interest: they will just return rather less than you paid for the bond. If you wonder why anyone would invest at a negative interest rate, the answer is that while you can keep 1,000 Swiss Francs under the mattress, you cannot sleep safely or comfortably with 10 million Swiss Francs under the mattress. Entrusting it to the Swiss government is simply the most economical way of safeguarding your cash.

The differences between the interest rates available on bonds of different governments reflect expectations about what will happen to currencies rather than perceptions of the creditworthiness of the borrower. Bonds issued by the governments of major, well-managed economies, such as Britain, Germany, Japan, Switzerland and the United States, carry virtually no credit risk – risk that the states concerned will fail to repay. Government bonds usually offer the lowest interest rates available in the currencies in which they are denominated. (Governments other than the US and outside the eurozone may often borrow in dollars or euros.)

But Puerto Rico is currently failing to service bonds, Greece has effectively defaulted, and Latin American states have routinely done so. Significantly, when the US Congress was gridlocked by grandstanding Republicans attempting to derail the federal budget and debt ceiling, the rates required from the highest-quality private-sector borrowers – firms such as Exxon Mobil – fell below those available to the US Treasury. Bonds from countries with unstable governments, or from companies less asset-rich and soundly financed than Exxon Mobil, naturally carry higher interest rates to reflect their credit risk. Ford and General Motors were once among the most respected companies in the world. But by 2006 fears over these companies' obligations and their weak current trading meant their bonds were rated as junk. In 2009 GM filed for bankruptcy and its bondholders were forced to accept a writedown of the value of their holdings.

Inflation after 1888 led not only to a reduction in the price of Consols due to the associated rise in interest rates, but also to further loss of value through rising prices. While £100 in 1888 might have bought a modest house for one of Queen Victoria's subjects, in 1974 the £15 value of the investments would not have been sufficient for a replacement of the front door. Conventional bonds provide certainty of cash return. Only indexed bonds – first introduced in the 1980s – provide certainty of real return.

However, in Britain and Germany this certainty is obtained at the price of a accepting a real return that is actually negative. A five-year indexed bond in either country will erode the real value of your investment by almost 1 per cent per year. A thirty-year security also offers negative yields. United States Treasury Inflation Protected Securities (TIPS) look slightly better. While they will still lag inflation over five years, they provide a 0.8 per cent a year real return over thirty years.

Realities of real estate

If you own real estate, you own both a building and the land on which it stands. If the property is in a large city, the land may account for most of its value: my own central London house has a market value more than five times its value for insurance purposes, which is an estimate of what it would cost today to build a similar property. An office block in central London or Hong Kong may now have a life of only twenty years. Because it is the location that is valuable, rather than the building, it may often be profitable to replace the structure with one that is more attractive to the changing needs of tenants. Some London office blocks are being demolished to build flats because the land is today more valuable in residential than in commercial use.

But there are also properties which, did they not already exist, would not be built, or would not be built in a similar style. Houses in depressed regions sell for less than their replacement cost. You can buy a French château, wholly impractical for modern living, for less than the price of a modest apartment in the centre of Paris. The historic building is a liability, not an asset. An industrial warehouse on the fringes of a town is, in contrast, little different from any other item of plant and machinery. It will depreciate in use over twenty or thirty years until the structure is replaced, and the land on which it stands has little value.

If you draw up a personal balance sheet in the way a company would, you are very likely to find that your house is your most valuable asset by far. Yet your house is not quite like your other investments. You bought your house in order to occupy it, and for the rest of your life you have to live somewhere. That doesn't, however, mean you are indifferent to its value. When house prices rise substantially – as they did in many countries in the years between the turn of the century and the inception of the global financial crisis – many people discover that they are earning more each day from the appreciation of the value of their property than by working. This gives rise to a lot of confused discussion.

As a homeowner, you are both an investor in housing and a consumer of housing services. When you are young, your investment in housing is probably modest, and your prospective consumption of housing services extensive. As you age, your investment in housing is greater and the date at which the graveyard caters inexpensively for your accommodation needs draws closer. Young people want housing to be cheap; older owner-occupiers can benefit from its being expensive. People in middle age may intend to move to a smaller property when their children leave the nest. Retirees may use equity release schemes to realise some of the value in their houses.

Much of the value of an owner-occupied house will accrue to the heirs of the purchasers. Only the owners themselves can decide how they view that legacy. For all these reasons your house, and the associated mortgage, cannot be treated in the same way as the assets you own for purely investment motives. And housing and house prices are inevitably a politically charged issue because they have considerable influence on the distribution and transfer of wealth between generations.

Most people first encounter the concept of leverage when they buy a house. Suppose you borrow €150,000 of the €200,000 you need to purchase a property. If the value of the property rises to €300,000 – a 50 per cent increase – then the difference between the property value and the loan is now €150,000. Your initial investment of €50,000, often called your equity in the property, has trebled in value.

If leverage sounds too good to be true, it is, because it operates in both directions. In the years before the global financial crisis, many people thought that 'flipping properties' was an easy path to riches. Books elaborating this proposition reached the best-seller list, seminars were packed with expectant – and greedy – participants. If you borrowed 90 per cent of the cost of a new €200,000 apartment, and were able to sell it for only 10 per cent more than you had paid for it, you could double the value of a €20,000 investment in only a few months.

But if prices instead fell by 10 per cent, your savings would be wiped out. And when the housing boom stalled and the credit crunch developed, many people found that the properties they had hoped to flip quickly at a profit could not be sold at all. Folk wisdom has it that house prices always go up, at least in the long run. The truth is that experience is varied. In parts of Germany, Switzerland and Japan property values are lower today than they were twenty-five years ago. In most of the rest of the world prices have risen over time, but with substantial short-term volatility. Scandinavian house prices plunged in the early 1990s; in this century Spain, Ireland and some parts of the United States, such as Florida and Las Vegas, have experienced spectacular booms and busts. For owner-occupiers, the timing of an initial purchase and any significant subsequent 'trading up' has often been as important as career choice in determining personal and household wealth. Like share prices, property values go up and down. The history of the property market is full of stories of well-known names who have discovered to their considerable cost that leverage can work both ways. Donald Trump has been to the bankruptcy court four times: three times in failed casino ventures and once after his highly leveraged acquisition of New York's grandest old hotel, the Plaza.

'Safe as houses' is true only if you plan to live in one. The positive experience of owner-occupiers has encouraged many individuals to buy houses and flats to let. Although an invest-ment property of reasonable quality is likely to cost €100,000 or more, gearing means that such a property can be bought with a deposit of €30,000 to €40,000. While residential property is less volatile than most other asset classes, leverage multiplies the risk. Buy-to-let is a low-risk strategy only for someone rich enough to make such investment a modest part of a larger portfolio.

While individuals have recently been active in buy-to-let investment properties, there has been little new institutional investment in residential property. Insurance companies and pension funds prefer commercial property – shops, offices and industrial premises – which only rich individuals can hold directly. Small investors can access these properties through funds, and they generally should.

Ownership of property was once bound up with power and status – landed estates were associated with aristocratic titles. In the early days of industrialisation the capitalist owned the premises – the mill, the shop, the factory – where the workers laboured. Today great estates are liabilities, not assets, and businesses rarely own the premises they occupy. Financial markets have become more sophisticated, and premises have become less specialised. Once, a textile business or a steel company would build a mill or a plant to its own particular requirement. Modern companies will often rent space on an industrial estate, in a unit adaptable to many alternative uses. Much retail trade has moved to warehouses out of town. The specifics of the terms of leases, the conventions of the property market and the legal framework are vital to property investors, and vary substantially from country to country. For these reasons – and because of tax complications – it is much more difficult to buy overseas property than overseas shares. But funds allow individuals with small sums to invest in foreign property.

Owning and letting a residential investment property is an investment option for anyone with a portfolio of reasonable size. (I shall discuss what this means in Chapters 10 and 11.) While it was once true that institutions owned large amounts of residential property, this sector declined as a result of a history of rent control and the growth of owner-occupation among middle-class households. Rental property today is mostly owned by social landlords – national or local governments or not-for-profit agencies – or by private individuals. Institutional investors today generally prefer commercial property – shops, offices and industrial premises. Since these normally represent larger units, only investors with substantial assets can hold them directly, but everyone can access them through investment funds.

Facts about funds

There are two basic kinds of investment fund – open-end funds and closed-end funds. Open-ended funds are usually called mutual funds in the United States, unit trusts or OEICs in Britain, SICAVs in much of continental Europe. Each investor owns a fraction of a portfolio of the assets of an open-ended fund. The portfolio is regularly revalued, and units of the fund can be bought or sold at a price based on that regular revaluation. Open-ended funds grow or shrink as holders add to or redeem the units they have. Very occasionally an open-ended fund may close to either new money or redemption. Most of the investment funds marketed to small savers are open-ended funds.

A closed-end fund is usually a company with shares quoted on a stock exchange: in this respect, like Apple or Exxon Mobil. But instead of operating a business, the closed-end fund holds an investment portfolio. Berkshire Hathaway is a closed-end investment fund, although a rather unusual one, because of the size of its holdings in portfolio companies (100 per cent of many of them). There are some investment companies with focused portfolios similar to Berkshire Hathaway in Britain and the United States, rather more in continental Europe.

But the more common type of closed-end fund is the investment trust. Investment trusts holding portfolios of company securities were widely distributed in the early years of the twentieth century, but they lost popularity in the United States after they were at the centre of many investment scams in the years before the Wall Street crash. UK funds were more conservative, and many are still in operation, but restrictions on listed companies marketing their own shares, or paying commissions, led most sales efforts to be devoted to the marketing of open-ended funds. A new generation of US closed-end funds came into being in the 1960s, when legislation permitted real estate investment trusts (REITs), and the innovation has been copied elsewhere.

While the size of open-ended funds expands or contracts with purchases and redemption, the size of the closed-end fund is determined by the amount initially subscribed, and the subsequent investment performance of the portfolio. You can dispose of your share of the portfolio in a closed-end fund only by selling it to someone else. Traditionally, this meant a closed-end fund could be more adventurous and invest in assets that were not easily realisable, which made it an appropriate vehicle for real estate and private equity funds. A closed-end fund can also use leverage, which is generally not permitted to an open-ended fund.

The value of your share in a closed-end fund can be more or less than the value of your share of the underlying assets in the portfolio. The possibility of variability in this discount or premium to asset value compounds the investment risk. If property is currently a fashionable investment, then real estate investment trust shares may sell at a premium to their asset value – the value of the shares is greater than the value of the properties the company owns. If emerging market stocks are unfashionable, it may be possible to buy shares at a large discount in investment companies specialising in emerging market stocks. You can sometimes buy out-of-favour funds at substantial discounts. Closed-end funds involve extra risks but also extra opportunities.

Most funds, open- or closed-end, are actively managed: the

fund manager selects a portfolio of stocks and buys and sells in the hope – not often fulfilled, as I shall describe in Chapters 8 and 10 – of outperforming the market. Passive funds simply replicate the performance of an index. A computer buys and sells shares to minimise the tracking error – the difference between the index and the value of the assets the fund holds. The exchange-traded fund (ETF) is a more recent innovation. The mechanics of ETFs are more complex – a hybrid of open- and closed-end fund – but the objective is that the investor can buy or sell a share that will reproduce almost exactly the performance of an index – the FT all-share index, an index of Brazilian stocks or a basket of commodities.

In the first UK edition of this book I strongly recommended exchange-traded funds as a tool for intelligent investors. But, as so often, the greed of financial innovators messed things up. Complex ETFs, 'synthetic' funds based on derivatives and supported by collateral drawn from the dustbins of the sponsoring banks, proliferated. While many transparent and honest ETFs remain, it is more difficult for the intelligent investor confidently to separate the wheat from the chaff. I'll make some more specific suggestions in later chapters, since ETFs continue to be a useful – and globally available – vehicle for investment.

In this chapter I've described the three main asset categories available and the choice of direct or indirect investment. In the next three I will review the relationship between prices and values – the fundamental issues of intelligent investment. In Chapters 10 to 12 I'll explain how to build these different assets into an investment portfolio.

4

Efficient Markets

Efficient markets and asset values

Few of the many jokes about economists are funny. One tells of the finance professor walking down the street with his wife. 'There's a $10 bill on the pavement,' she says. 'Don't be silly,' he replies, 'if there was, someone would already have picked it up.'

The joke refers to the efficient market hypothesis (EMH), but the joke is on the teller. There are few $10 bills on the street, for the reason the professor elucidates. People rarely drop $10 bills, and when they do, the notes are quickly picked up. Most pieces of litter that look like $10 bills are, indeed, litter. The professor's theory of why there are no $10 bills on the pavement is illuminating. It will save considerable time for anyone who plans to make a living searching for bills on the streets. The theory is not, however, true. There are occasional discarded $10 bills. There are also people who make profits by picking them up. Otherwise, $10 bills in the street would be easier to find.

In a securities market the $10 bill is the difference between the price and the value of an asset. Since the efficient market hypothesis is illuminating but not true, such differences occur, but rarely, and they are hard to identify with confidence. So what determines the relationship between price and value?

An economist, another joke goes, knows the price of

everything and the value of nothing. The relationship between price and value is a subject with a long history – particularly among accountants.

There are two basic approaches:

- the value of an asset is what someone is willing to pay for it;
- the value of an asset is the cash it will generate over its life.

I'll call these the 'mark-to-market' principle and the 'funda-mental-value' principle. Almost all valuation methods are based on one or both of these principles. If you are appraising a prop-erty, you might call in a valuer. The valuer will have experience of transactions in similar properties in the area and should have a good idea of what the building will fetch. The mark-to-market principle is easy to apply in this case.

The fundamental-value principle looks instead at the cash generated over the life of the asset. Begin with the flow of quar-terly rents from a property, taking account of possible increases at future rent reviews, then deduct any expenses you might need to incur to preserve the value of the property.

Perhaps the building has a finite life, like an industrial ware-house or modern office block; you will need to consider what the property will be worth when the structure needs to be replaced. Other buildings can, with some attention, maintain a satisfac-tory flow of rental income for ever.

The fundamental value of a company is calculated in a similar way. Look at either the path of dividends or the stream of earnings. If you focus on dividends, observe the current dividend level and conjecture how rapidly the company will increase that dividend in future years. If you focus on earnings, you need to estimate their probable growth, bearing in mind the growth rate of the economy, the industry and the specific prospects of the business.

The mark-to-market principle and fundamental-value principle are certainly different, and seem incompatible. They involve different styles of thinking and lead to different approaches to investment. The mark-to-market principle is easier, and less speculative. But it is a common mistake to emphasise what you can measure at the expense of more important things that you can't. It is generally better to be approximately right than precisely wrong.

Which of these two principles, price or value, should be applied? Market prices can't be completely independent of fundamental value because opinions about fundamental value influence market prices. This is the metaphor of markets as 'voting machine'. Everyone who trades registers an opinion. The results of this survey of opinion are reported in the financial papers every day. The metaphor contains a possible reconciliation of the mark-to-market and fundamental-value principles: the market price is the result of a plebiscite on fundamental value.

The market is democratic in the sense that everyone is allowed to vote, but it is not a fair election. The weight given to your opinion depends on the amount of money you can put behind your vote. The votes of a large fund management group such as BlackRock or an investment bank such as Goldman Sachs count more than the votes of you and me. Perhaps this is as it should be. If you are really confident of your opinion, you can make that opinion count by putting a lot of money behind it. I shall describe how George Soros pulled off a spectacular coup by doing exactly that.

The concept of the market as voting machine provides a justification for my claim that every investor can access, without charge, all the expertise that the financial services industry can bring to bear. That idea leads to the efficient market hypothesis. If the market price were an average of informed estimates of fundamental value, markets would be efficient not only in the narrow technical sense that all available information is in the price but also in a broader sense – market prices provide signals that guide the efficient allocation of investment funds.

In this chapter I'll focus on the narrower interpretation of market efficiency, the one relevant to investors. But there are three sub-interpretations, because there are three variants of the efficient market hypothesis involving progressively more demanding assumptions:

- the weak form – past movements of prices convey no information about future price movements;
- the semi-strong form – all public information about securities is already reflected in their price; and
- the strong form – everything that could be known about securities is already reflected in their price.

Louis Bachelier, the little-honoured Frenchman whose PhD thesis on 'The Theory of Speculation' proved to be the foundation of finance theory, discovered that the data he compiled about stock price movements resembled the observations of natural processes, such as the movement of small particles suspended in a fluid. Physicists call this behaviour Brownian motion. Financial economists, more engagingly, employ the term 'random walk'. A random walk is directionless. Every step is independent of every previous step and just as likely to be in one direction as in another. All three versions of the efficient market hypothesis claim that securities prices will follow a random walk. The random walk is a mathematical concept inseparable from the EMH.

Most of the evidence observed by early researchers was favourable to the random walk theory. The earliest evaluations were undertaken by statisticians – until the 1950s, Wall Street and the City of London were innumerate and there was no serious finance theory in business schools. At Stanford University, Holbrook Working showed that long series of commodity prices followed a random walk. The British statistician Maurice Kendall analysed long series of stock prices and more than a hundred years of cotton price data. He concluded that 'The Stock Exchange, it would appear, has a memory lasting less than a week.' While none of the three versions of the efficient market hypothesis is true, each offers its own shafts of illumination. Markets may have no memory, but commentators on markets do, and the random walk theory suggests that most of their observations and analyses are of little use. 'Shares are 20 per cent lower than a year ago – this is a buying opportunity.' 'The market needs to pause for breath after its recent rise.' 'The dollar is experiencing a technical correction, which will continue.'

You regularly hear statements like these in popular discussion. The weak form of the efficient market hypothesis claims that no such statement can ever be justified because prices move without knowledge of their history. The probability that they will rise next year, or next month, or today, is unaffected by whether prices rose yesterday afternoon, or last week, or in the first quarter of 2011.

The weak EMH is a blow for people who rely on projections of historical trends, or identification of recurrent patterns, to make their investment decisions – most of all for chartists, whom I'll describe in the next chapter. But the weak version does nothing to discourage people from looking at fundamental values. Rather the opposite – the weak EMH encourages you to believe that you might make money at the expense of noise traders by paying close attention to fundamentals.

There is a considerable practical difference between weak and strong EMH. Strong EMH – which postulates that everything that could be known about securities is already in their price – essentially rules out any possibility of investment skill. Legendary investors such as Buffett have simply been lucky. No research or analysis can be useful, because its results will be reflected in the market. Put like this, the theory seems absurd.

Indeed, the strong version of EMH contains an inherent contradiction. If it were the case that research and analysis could never be profitable, because the result of that research and analysis would always be 'in the price', why would anyone undertake such research and analysis? If prices were always efficient, what could be the process by which they become efficient?

The semi-strong version of the efficient market hypothesis is less extreme, claiming only that information is 'in the price' if publicly available. Thus the semi-strong version does not exclude the possibility that insightful new analysis, unpublished or not yet widely circulated, might be valuable to those who possess it. It certainly permits possibilities of profit from trading on private information. The investment banker who knows of a planned takeover and the corporate executive who knows that the coming results will be worse than is generally expected can both deal advantageously on the basis of this inside information.

Such insider trading was once the daily practice of brokers and fund managers, and put small investors at a substantial disadvantage. But most countries have made it illegal for people who have inside knowledge to deal. These laws do not cover all forms of trading on private information, nor can they ever be perfectly effective, but they have probably reduced the incidence of these practices.

Outside the United States, few people are convicted of insider trading, and not many there. This is because evidence is hard to obtain, not because the activity is rare. Cases that have come to court show that criminal insiders often made little profit from their unlawful activities because their actions moved market prices against them. Martha Stewart received a five-month prison sentence and suffered incalculable reputational damage for a $45,000 profit. Information held by insiders does not have to be announced to percolate into the market-place.

That observation has important implications for intelligent investors. Be very wary of sustained individual price movements that seem to have no explanation. A falling share price may be the result of inside knowledge; a rise that cannot be accounted for may herald a possible takeover. Perhaps information the investor does not know, and may never know, is already reflected in the market. Be suspicious of advisers whose predictions are based on extrapolations from past price movements, or who claim to see patterns in data.

Illuminating but not true

The efficient market hypothesis has a sufficiently strong hold on the investment world – particularly among finance academics – for deviations still to be described as 'anomalies'. Over the last two decades evidence of anomalies has accumulated steadily. One collection of essays is provocatively titled *A Non-Random Walk down Wall Street* (Lo and MacKinlay, 1999), in deliberate contrast to Burton Malkiel's popular introduction to efficient market theory in *A Random Walk down Wall Street* (Malkiel, 1973). Robert Shiller, who achieved wide attention by publishing *Irrational Exuberance* (Shiller, 2000) at the peak of the New Economy boom, has become the intellectual leader of the sceptics. In a bizarre conjunction, the 2013 Nobel Prize in economics was shared between Eugene Fama, for his work in developing the efficient market hypothesis, and Shiller, for his work in refuting it.

There are many investment maxims, mechanical rules that promise superior returns. 'Sell in May and go away.' Benefit from 'the small company effect' – consistently higher returns on smaller companies that may be the subject of less intensive research. Buy 'the dogs of the Dow' – the worst-performing large companies of the previous year. These ideas rarely work. There are several problems. It is always possible to find some such pattern by studying the past; that doesn't mean that the same pattern will persist in future. Even if the scheme appears profitable, profits may be inadequate to offset the costs of turning over a portfolio. And the very fact of publishing these seemingly attractive investment ideas may lead others to desist from the behaviour that gave rise to the so-called anomalies. The efficient market hypothesis strikes back.

So, is the empirical claim that prices follow a random walk correct? You may still be puzzled by the equivalence of the weak EMH and the random walk theory. Why does the assumption that all information is 'in the price' imply that prices follow a random walk? Bachelier's empirical observation of the random walk, and Kendall's supporting data, long preceded a comprehensive explanation of the relationship.

The definitive account of why price movements in an efficient market would appear random came in 1953 from the Nobel Prize-winning economist Paul Samuelson, whose introductory textbook is familiar to everyone who has taken a basic economics course. Return to that metaphor of markets as voting machine. The result of every election depends on the question you put to the voters. The question that is put to the voters here is not 'What do you think the Federal Reserve should do?' It is not even 'What do you think the Federal Reserve will do?' The question is 'How do you think the bond market and the currency market will react to what the Federal Reserve will do?'

Suppose people think that the Federal Reserve Board will raise American interest rates or that Apple will announce good results. These expectations lead these people to sell American bonds and buy dollars, or to buy Apple shares. Views about the future are therefore built into the level of prices we see in the market today. If the Federal Reserve Board is expected to act, bond yields and currencies will already reflect this, and will move only if these expectations change. If Apple's business is improving, the market price will already acknowledge the improvement. The price will move only if people think that outcomes will be better still, or that these outcomes will not, after all, be as good as previously expected. Traders are not voting on what Apple's results will be, or whether Apple is a good business; they are voting on what they think will happen to Apple's share price. They vote 'up' when they buy, and 'down' when they sell. John Maynard Keynes described this process through the analogy of a newspaper beauty contest. Competitors were asked to choose the most beautiful faces, and those who selected the most popular faces, according to the majority choices of all competitors, were the competition winners. As Keynes explained, what thoughtful entrants are trying to do is not to choose the most beautiful but to decide what they think others will find most beautiful, or even what they think people will think other people will find most beautiful – and so on.

Samuelson elaborated on this idea. Everyone in the market knows that prices will change in future as sentiment changes. If more people are expecting favourable changes in opinion than unfavourable, they will buy. If they think these yet unknown market events are more likely to be adverse, they will sell. So at any time prices will be bid up or down until the expected impact of future changes is equally likely to increase values as to reduce them. That is why, Samuelson claimed, properly anticipated prices fluctuate randomly.

Market reactions to events and to changes in the trading environment are not easy to predict and may seem disproportionate to the events that trigger them. Certainly they may be larger than can possibly be explained by reference to assessments of fundamental value. The worst day in the history of modern stock markets was 19 October 1987, when the Dow Jones Industrial Average, the most widely followed US stock index, dropped 22 per cent. The Brady Commission, established by the government to investigate, concluded that the fall was triggered by a higher than expected trade deficit and a rumour of higher taxes, magnified by the use of portfolio insurance – computerised trading systems that sold large quantities of stocks when markets fell.

Perhaps. In any event, none of these factors was directly relevant to stock markets outside the United States, which fell by almost as much. Within a few days, and for no obvious reasons, market sentiment switched from sanguine optimism to unreasonable pessimism. On days like 19 October 1987 market movements can be explained only by reference to market psychology; attempts to explain them by reference to changes in fundamental value are simply false rationalisations. Prices rise or fall in the short run on ephemeral changes in sentiment, with little if any basis in fundamental value.

In some markets, such as that for Old Master paintings, concepts of fundamental value are themselves elusive. These market prices are the result of the whims of a small number of very rich men. The principle that an asset is worth what someone will pay remains dominant in this market. But it is implausible that the prices of bonds, shares or properties can forever remain unrelated to fundamental value. Prices move around fundamental value – sometimes violently so, as on 19 October 1987 or in the New Economy bubble. Constantly changing, prices are influenced, but not determined, by a fundamental value that is itself unknown and constantly changing.

From time to time the path of market prices strays far from the path of fundamental value, but these divergences are ultimately corrected. Prices display 'short-term positive serial correlation' – if you examine prices over a day, a week or a month, then upward price movements are slightly more likely to be followed by further upward price movements. Downward price movements are also more likely to lead to further downward price movements. This feature of short-term price change is called 'momentum'.

There is also evidence of 'long-term negative serial correlation'. If you look at prices over much longer periods – three or five years – upward movements are more than averagely likely to be followed by downward movements, while periods of underperformance of this length are more than averagely likely to be followed by periods of outperformance. This feature of long-term price movements is called mean reversion. Like the efficient market hypothesis with which it is closely associated, the random walk model is illuminating but not true.

Information asymmetry

Market prices measure prevailing market sentiment, incorporating all the analysis, prejudice, skills and irrationality of market players. What is general knowledge will normally be 'in the price' and of little value to investors. Information such as 'General Electric is a well-managed business', 'Warren Buffett is an investment genius' or 'Households will always need to buy electricity', though true, does not provide a reason to buy related stocks. This information is in the market.

'General knowledge' includes such knowledge as we have of the future as well as knowledge of the present and past. The term 'consensus forecast' is used to describe common expectations about economic prospects. There usually isn't a very wide spread of opinions. The canard that economists always disagree is much exaggerated. (Although there are many other, well-founded, criticisms of economists, especially of zealots who embrace the EMH with fundamentalist fervour.) You don't have to pay for the consensus forecast, or spend time reading about it – it's already 'in the market'.

The glossy descriptions of economic prospects that financial advisers, investment managers and banks circulate to clients may be illuminating (I rarely find them so), but not as a guide to investment decisions. You don't have any valuable insight into the future – and nor do they. I've sometimes asked people in business and finance, who crave accurate economic forecasts, 'If I gave you the exact figure for national income three years from now, what would you do with the information?' Useful economic knowledge is usually specific rather than general.

This central role of information, and the dependence of trade on differential information, distinguishes securities markets from other markets. Trade in modern economies is mostly the result of specialisation. I grow apples, you grow pears, and each of us gains by swapping one for the other. We call on the plumber for his specialist skills. We buy from Volkswagen because the company is organised to produce cars, and we are not. America sells computers in return for Saudi oil. All these exchanges normally benefit both parties to the trade.

Sometimes trade in financial markets has a similar character. An importer buys foreign currency because he and his customers are based in Germany, and his supplier is based in China. The commercial transaction requires a foreign exchange transaction. But most trade in securities markets – even in foreign currency markets – is not like that. Both parties to the transaction have the same need – to make as much money as possible; they just have different ideas about how to do it. Most foreign exchange trading is speculative. I think the dollar will rise in value; you think it will fall. I think Apple shares are underpriced; you think they are overvalued. In each of these trades one of us will be proved right, the other wrong.

In any market in which there is wide and irresolvable uncertainty, in any market where participants have different information and beliefs, many trades will be the result of mistakes. And in financial markets uncertainty and differential information are endemic. A brilliant exposition of the problems this would create for market efficiency – in both a narrow and a wide sense – was provided in 1970 by George Akerlof, who would receive the Nobel Prize for his analysis. Akerlof used the metaphor of the market for lemons. Some cars are 'lemons', prone to faults. The seller knows whether the car is a lemon; the buyer does not. If the price of the used car reflects the average probability that the car is a lemon, that is a good price for owners of lemons and a bad price for everyone else. Sellers will be inclined to sell lemons, but not good cars. The proportion of cars on used car lots that are lemons will be much greater than the proportion of lemons in the population as a whole. As buyers realise this, the price they will pay for any second-hand car, lemon or not, will fall. The result of this will be to reduce still further the proportion of good cars on sale. The outcome is a market characterised by mutual mistrust, low prices, low-quality products and buyer dissatisfaction.

If you fail to understand the problem of imperfect information, you may fall victim to the 'winner's curse': you think you have won, only to discover subsequently that you wish you hadn't. This problem was first identified when the US government auctioned offshore oil blocks. The bidders in all cases were the same large oil companies. Both the government and the companies quickly realised that the successful bids were higher than had been expected, or than were justified. All the companies wanted the oil and had similar access to funds. Their preferences and resources were the same, but their assessments differed. All judgements were to some degree in error, but the successful bidder was – by the nature of the auction – the one who bid highest. The most likely reason one estimate was higher than the rest was that the winning company's geologists had made a mistake.

You might think that the inevitable errors made by market participants with imperfect information would tend to cancel out. They don't. Assets will always tend to be held by people who are too optimistic about their value rather than people who are too pessimistic. This gives rise to systematic, and destabilising, asset mispricing. The growing complexity of the products that are sold in financial markets means that this problem recurs with increasing frequency. In Chapter 9 I will look at some of the consequences – and how information asymmetry has been central to the recent recurrent financial crises.

Strategic trading, moral hazard and market manipulation

In an experiment, Professor Joe Stiglitz would invite a class to bid for the money contained in his wallet. An obvious strategy would be to guess how much might be in the wallet, and offer a bit less. But that would be a mistake. In fact, to participate at all would be a mistake. If a bidder offers less than the amount in the wallet, the professor can refuse to trade. If the bid is more than that sum, it will be accepted. If the seller is willing to sell, the buyer is foolish to buy. Why do I want to buy what they want to sell? In such a market, you never do. Anyone tempted to purchase a complex financial product should ponder the lesson of the wallet auction.

Problems which have these structures give rise to a problem known as 'moral hazard'. Wherever there are imperfections of information, people with superior information can use that knowledge to sell products for more than they are worth, or to rid themselves of risks which others underestimate. As the lemon example illustrates, the result is a decline in the average quality of products and risks. Moral hazard has always been evident in insurance and credit markets (there is no divorce insurance, because only unhappy couples would pay the premium) and is widespread in financial services. The confirmation in 2008 that governments would not allow large banks to fail compounded the problem of moral hazard revealed in the banks' aggressive assumption of risk.

Sellers of securities usually have the advantage over buyers. The people who run a company know more about it than do the people who plan to invest in it. The people who issue a bond know more about the issuer than the buyer does. The people who construct a complex derivative understand its characteristics better than the people who buy these securities. Some of the derivatives and structured products of modern finance can only be valued – if at all – by the banks that devised them. This not only leaves the purchasers vulnerable but leaves the banks themselves at the mercy of the few employees who understand the models.

Once oil companies understood the winner's curse, they adjusted their bids downwards. Markets characterised by differential information are reflexive, because prices reveal information about the behaviour and the expectations of other parties. These expectations may in turn affect assessments of fundamental values by other potential buyers or sellers. If Exxon Mobil think this is an attractive block, perhaps that company knows something we at Shell don't. This interdependence of expectations may give rise to strategic behaviour. If offers to buy or sell are perceived as revealing what other people think, traders may deal with a view to influencing the expectations of others, hence creating profit opportunities in future. This strategic thinking would be refined in the algorithms devised by high-frequency traders – the businesses which use pre-programmed computers to trade with each other and which now account for much of the trading volume on London and New York stock exchanges.

In 2006 the hedge fund manager John Paulson recognised that the marketing of subprime mortgages to indigent house buyers in the United States would end in tears. He persuaded the investment bank Goldman Sachs to put together securities whose value was based on the performance of particularly egregious subprime mortgages and to find buyers for these products. The transaction had no underlying purpose other than to enable Paulson and his investors to benefit from the inevitable defaults on the mortgages. When the market did indeed collapse in 2007, the outcome for Paulson was described, with some exaggeration, as 'the greatest trade ever' (Zuckerman, 2009). Although Paulson was not sufficiently communicative to be featured in Michael Lewis's *The Big Short*, and hence escaped being played by Brad Pitt, his was almost certainly the largest of the bets against the

US housing market which that film described. Goldman Sachs would pay a fine of $550 million, without admitting legal liability, for its part in the affair.

The most entertaining form of market manipulation is 'the corner', in which a bidder attempts to dominate the whole of the available supply and force buyers (especially) to pay whatever price the bidder chooses. In 2008–9 there was a battle for control of Volkswagen within the Porsche and Piëch families (descended respectively from the son and daughter of Ferdinand Porsche). Some hedge funds believed (correctly, as it turned out) that Wolfgang Porsche and his chief executive at the eponymous luxury car maker, Wendelin Wiedeking, would not succeed in taking over the much larger VW company. These hedge funds acted as 'short sellers', vendors of shares they did not own (I'll explain this more fully in Chapter 9), in the hope of making profits when the bid failed and VW shares fell. But they misunderstood the effect of the complex shareholding structure of Volkswagen; almost all the voting stock was controlled either by Porsche or by the state of Lower Saxony. When VW shares rose in value, the short sellers discovered that there were no shares available in the market. Obliged to buy to meet their obligations to return the stock they had sold, they found themselves having to bid for VW stock at any price. The stock has typically sold for between €100 and €200; as a result of the 'corner', some shares were sold at prices around €1,000.

Investment strategies for imperfectly efficient markets

The efficient market hypothesis, although illuminating, is not true. Momentum rules in the short run mean reversion in the long run. A day is short run; five years is long run. If there were a means of telling just when the short run becomes the long run, there would be a sure-fire route to making money: ride the wave, jump off before it breaks.

This isn't possible. The two phenomena of momentum (short-run positive serial correlation) and mean reversion (long-run negative serial correlation) map into two basic investment techniques. One is understanding the vagaries of market sentiment; the other is analysing the sources of fundamental value.

The first strategy seeks to understand the mind of the market and the psychology of its participants – exploit momentum, buy into market rises, sell ahead of market falls. The alternative approach ignores these fluctuations, focuses attention on fundamental value and anticipates that, in the long run, truth will out through mean reversion. The first of these strategies can be associated with George Soros, the second with Warren Buffett. These two men are the best-known and most successful investors of recent decades. Both are now over eighty years old, having begun their public investment careers in the 1960s.

Soros left Eastern Europe as a child refugee. A devotee of Karl Popper, he would prefer to be remembered for his philosophy rather than his fortune. But Soros will go down in history as the man who broke the Bank of England in 1992. His massive bet against sterling on 'Black Wednesday' – another contender for the title of 'the greatest trade ever' – proved decisive in forcing Britain out of the European Monetary System. Soros's Open Society network has made large philanthropic contributions to the promotion of education and democracy in post-Communist Eastern Europe. His Quantum Fund – an early example of what is now known as a hedge fund – returned an average of 30 per cent per annum to its investors over the period from 1970 to 2000. The Quantum Fund traded actively, buying and selling currencies or commodities and any other assets that appealed, or failed to appeal, to Soros and his colleagues.

Berkshire Hathaway is Buffett's investment vehicle, and was a textile company when Buffett took control. Insurance is now

Berkshire's largest business. Insurance premiums are received well before claims are paid, so insurance generates a large float of investable cash. This facilitates investment, and Berkshire owns many companies – from the private jet charter business Netjets to See's Candies, famous for making the world's largest lollipop – and large stakes in businesses such as Procter & Gamble and Heinz. Buffett's investment success has taken him from modest beginnings to vying with Bill Gates (to whose foundation he is donating most of his fortune) as the world's richest man. Despite that, Buffett still lives in the bungalow in Omaha that he bought fifty years ago, and regularly enjoys a meal at a local steak house washed down with a glass of Cherry Coke (he switched brands after buying a 10 per cent stake in the Coca-Cola Corporation).

There will always be individuals who have outperformed the market – just as there will always be winners of the lottery. I'll observe in Chapter 8 how exceptional investment performance rarely persists. Most people who do well are lucky rather than clever. But Buffett and Soros not only established outstanding records; they also continued to demonstrate remarkable performance long after they had been widely recognised as the most talented managers of their generation. To win the lottery once may be evidence of either luck or skill; to win it repeatedly is evidence of skill.

You might think that the strategies of the folksy Buffett and the philosophical Soros would be the subject of intense study by students of finance and investment professionals. You would be wrong. These individuals receive a lot of journalistic attention but no academic attention. Since Buffett and Soros cannot exist, according to the strong efficient market hypothesis, they are treated as if they don't. A lot of ink has been spilt on the proposition that what plainly exists in practice can't exist in theory.

In turn, Buffett and Soros are open in their contempt for most academic work in finance. They can afford that contempt. But their contempt is not simply the practical man's disdain for the intellectual – they are both smart and well-read people. They simply believe that much of this academic work is misdirected, engaged in obsessive pursuit of narrow ideas of limited application. The distinction between the market as a mechanism for voting on events and the market as a mechanism for voting on market reactions to events was understood and expressed generations ago by Keynes and Samuelson – and by Benjamin Graham, the first intelligent investor. But the distinction is not understood by many commentators, who regard market judgements as a repository of wisdom not just about the market judgements of other market participants but about the real economy.

The distinction between the anticipation of events and the anticipation of beliefs about events is elided by most finance academics. They understand that there might be such a distinction, but have developed a group of arguments – known, in extreme form, as 'rational expectations' – to suggest that the difference does not matter. The rational expectations school is associated with the strong form of the efficient market hypothesis – all information that is capable of being known is already incorporated in prices.

But the distinction between market judgements and underlying realities, the distinction between prices and values, and the distinction between the mind of the market and economic and business fundamentals manifestly do matter. By exploiting divergences between them, Buffett and Soros have made billions of dollars. Both individuals recognise that such divergences are the basis of their success. Buffett shouts from Omaha that markets are only imperfectly efficient. Soros, quoting Keynes's metaphor of the beauty contest, writes that 'The fact that a theory is flawed does not mean that we should not invest in it as long as other people believe in it and there is a large group of people left to be convinced ... we are ahead of the game because we can limit our losses when the market also discovers what we already know' (Soros, 2003, p. 25).

The essence of Soros's investment strategy is to read, and anticipate, the changing mind of the market more successfully than other traders. The essence of Buffett's investment strategy is to emphasise fundamental values and use the volatile mind of the market as an opportunity to buy assets that are underpriced relative to their fundamental value. I'll discuss these two broad approaches in the two chapters that follow.

5

The Mind of the Market

Market psychology

People in finance use phrases such as 'The market thinks', 'The view of the market is' or even, if the person is very senior, 'We could ask the market'. Of course, the market does not think; only people can think. But the anthropomorphic view, which treats 'the market' as if it were a person, is so pervasive that the metaphor is part of everyday language. Benjamin Graham, the original intelligent investor, formulated the anthropomorphic analogy when he wrote of the moody, volatile Mr Market. Mr Market has grown in influence in subsequent decades. Mr Market features regularly in Warren Buffett's homilies.

The anthropomorphic metaphor may be contrasted with the metaphor of market as voting machine, which aggregates and weighs the different views of different players. Although there is some similarity between the two, there are also fundamental differences. The market as voting machine is democratic – the analogy supposes a diversity of views, in which all judgements are relevant (if not necessarily equal). And, as in a democratic election, the result is definitive.

The analogy of Mr Market is hierarchical – the market view can be ascertained and interpreted, but not questioned by market participants. Financiers talk of 'confidence', by which they mean the standing of an individual, organisation or opinion in the eyes of the market – in much the same way as commentators identify the confidants at the court of an autocratic politician or chief executive. Such confidence needs to be earned, and can easily be forfeited. And, as at the royal court or within the sycophantic C-suite, the autocrat can only be mocked by those outside the inner circle; the king or CEO cannot be questioned but can be outsmarted, and that is exactly how Graham and Buffett viewed Mr Market.

Of course, the person who inspires such deference, whom it is perilous to defy, has no tangible existence. There is no Mr Market. 'The mind of the market' is what people believe the mind of the market to be, and the evolution of what 'the market thinks' is a process of convergence of these common beliefs. Understanding 'the mind of the market' – a deep appreciation of the psychology of Mr Market – is a potentially rewarding investment strategy, and some people are good at it. Not, however, as many as those who think they are good at it.

Trading once took place in physical markets, where buyers and sellers would meet to exchange securities and to exchange information. Some of the information might have been true, other parts of it false; some information would be contained in what they said, some of it contained in the way they behaved. In the crudest versions of face-to-face market-making, such as the 'pit' of the Chicago Mercantile Exchange, the physical capacity of the traders to elbow aside their colleagues would contribute to their success. This short-term trading environment was a testosterone-laden world. Technology transferred trading from meeting places to screens.

The rise of financial conglomerates means that dealing rooms are now the places where the traders of Goldman Sachs or Morgan Stanley sit beside each other and make electronic contact with their competitors at other firms. The atmosphere is still frenzied – and still very masculine, even though there are

now some women traders. You will still hear frequent obsceni-
ties on trading floors; many financial firms have faced claims of
sex discrimination and harassment; and lap-dancing clubs can
be found around the fringes of areas where traders congregate.

Most traders are now employees of major investment banks.
These conglomerate institutions manage assets for investment
clients, execute deals for fund managers and provide advice to
major corporations, as well as trading on their own account.
Banks are required to maintain 'Chinese walls' in order to
prevent people in these different departments communicating
with each other. There are differing views on the effectiveness
of the Chinese walls. Within these institutions are assembled
expertise and information, unparalleled elsewhere, about all
aspects of securities markets and, indeed, about wider economic
and geopolitical events.

While most trades are made on behalf of clients, the bank
is itself acting as principal in these transactions – the intermediary is more like the used car dealer, who buys and sells
vehicles from his own stock, than the real estate broker, who
is facilitating a meeting between a buyer and a seller. When
the 'Volcker rule' limiting the scale of proprietary trading –
dealing purely on the banks' own account – was introduced
in the United States after the 2008 crash, banks claimed that
such trading constituted only a small part of their overall activities. However, trading profits account for most of the reported
revenues of investment banks such as Goldman Sachs and a
significant part of the revenues even of organisations which are
principally commercial banks.

Traders use the capital, credit and reputation of their employers. They take a significant share of the profits from their
activities, but not the losses. The penalty for making large losses
is being fired. This asymmetric structure of incentives encourages trading strategies and styles that return regular profits while
countenancing occasional exceptional losses that may, over time,

swamp the profits. These incentive structures play a central role in modern finance, and I'll come back to them in Chapter 8.

If markets are characterised by weak positive short-term serial correlation – momentum – and weak negative long-term serial correlation – mean reversion – then it ought to be possible to analyse the processes that give rise to these 'anomalies'. George Soros describes the boom-and-bust process associated with momentum and mean reversion. He illustrates how in a variety of markets, from conglomerate acquisition to real estate investment trusts, a momentum-driven boom creates the seeds of its own destruction and leads to an inevitable downturn.

But describing the cycle is not at all the same as picking accurately the turning point of the cycle. Soros did, indeed, identify correctly the broad shape of some large swings in behaviour during the 1970s and 1980s to profit both on the upswing – following the momentum-driven herd – and on the downswing – benefiting by anticipating a period of mean reversion. These judgements proved very profitable. But such success became harder to achieve.

Can mathematical techniques help with understanding past and future cycles? Many amateur speculators rely on charts or other forms of what is known as technical analysis. This approach to investment analysis involves the identification of recurrent patterns in price series. The technical analyst looks at a chart of recent prices and identifies trends, believing that it is possible to identify buy and sell signals from inspection of the chart.

Purists among chartists do not care what the chart records – whether it is the stock price of Apple, the exchange value of the dollar or the price of an index-linked bond. Chartists look for pictures in the data – the 'head and shoulders' is an especially popular image. They draw trend lines through market rises and declines and horizontal resistance levels across more stationary ones. They see recurrent cycles. The Kondratieff fifty-year cycle has been discussed since the 1920s, and there is just enough evidence of long-term fluctuation to make continued attention to it plausible. The Elliott 'long wave', the discovery of an accountant and amateur investor, is a favourite of many chartists. Among the community of finance academics in universities, technical analysis has a terrible reputation. Most textbooks simply refuse even to acknowledge that the technique exists. But chartism continues to have a cult-like following, and market prognostications based on technical analysis are regularly found in the financial press and business journals.

There are good reasons for professional disdain. Many of the statements made by chartists resemble those of astrologers. The analytic component is ascientific and the predictions sufficiently ambiguous not to be falsified by any likely events. Chartists make use of the natural human inclination to see patterns in data – the same tendency that leads us to see images in ink blots and interpret rocks as sculptures.

Technical analysts are often associated with investment gurus, more common in the United States, where there are many published investment newsletters, or tip sheets. The guru makes an outlandish prediction. Sometimes the prediction comes true, so the newsletter attracts subscriptions, the seminars are oversubscribed. The guru continues to make predictions – often the same predictions – but when these are proven to be false, the audience and reputation gradually drift away. The relatively few gurus who have a long-term track record of success – or, indeed, of employment – are generally based in large institutions with substantial resources devoted to fundamental research.

Chartists, gurus and people with proprietary and secret systems are, overwhelmingly, charlatans. But the story is not quite so simple. A central tenet of this book is that the efficient market hypothesis, although illuminating, is not true. And so it is not good enough to assert that since the EMH is true, no claim that is made by chartists, gurus or for mechanical rules or trading systems can ever be valid. At most, what can be said is that there is little evidence that any individuals or systems use these methods with sustained success.

Perhaps the difficulty of identifying patterns in historic price series is the result not of the absence of such patterns but of the absence of techniques sufficiently powerful to identify them. At some level this must be correct. No one really believes that price movements are truly random, although explanations of these price movements may be so complex and so varied that we can never do better than to describe them as a random process.

Much of this book describes the theory of finance that originated in Chicago around fifty years ago and has been developed by economists since. Today that body of analysis is subject to a pincer movement, pressured from one side by behavioural economics – the applied psychology that emphasises the ways in which the beliefs of traders influence the determination of prices – and from the other by higher-powered mathematics and the computers used by high-frequency traders which analyse 'the mind of the market' by constantly offering to buy and sell. (Most of the offers to buy and sell which these computers make do not result in trades.)

Techniques brought to bear on financial markets more recently push towards, even beyond, the frontiers of applied mathematics. These approaches use models to reproduce what the most skilled traders may be able to do instinctively. In what is superficially a paradox, soft revisions from psychology and hard revisions from mathematics turn out to be two sides of the same coin. The mathematics of complex systems may help to explain the formation of expectations and the dissemination of beliefs in markets. If it does, then the ways in which expectations are formed and beliefs disseminated will change.

In the first chapter I suggested that the intelligent investor could fend for him- or herself in a world populated by financial professionals. But in the world I have described in this chapter the intelligent but amateur investor cannot fend for him- or herself. A minority of successful traders in hedge funds and investment banks have an intuitive feel for market psychology. These few individuals have honed their skills over years of experience and are exposed to a wide range of market information every minute of the trading day.

The mathematicians who build trading systems have access to the best brains and most powerful computing resources available. Successfully riding market momentum involves frequent trading, and investment banks have much lower trading costs than retail investors. Even with all these advantages it is not at all clear that over the long run the activity is profitable for investment banks. You need to set against their reported profits the losses from supposedly unforeseeable events and allegedly unauthorised trading. We simply don't know whether over a period of years banks make money out of these market judgements (as distinct from making money out of their customers' transactions), and nor do they. Most people who are described as successful traders blow up after a long lucky run.

The David and Goliath notion that with a home computer, a proprietary software package and a book of trading rules you are likely to succeed where the best-resourced institutions in the world have largely failed is laughable. Most people who claim to trade successfully in this way are themselves on a lucky run in a rising market, or engaged in self-delusion, or both.

The intelligent investor cannot match the professionals in understanding market psychology. But he or she does have advantages when it comes to fundamental value. In the remainder of this chapter, and the next one, I'll explain why and how.

When the market loses its mind

There have been asset bubbles so long as there have been financial markets. In the Dutch tulip mania of 1636–7 a single prized bulb was supposedly valued at the price of twelve acres of land, or ten times the annual earnings of a skilled craftsman.

In the preceding chapter I described the two enduring general principles of asset valuation: an asset is worth what someone is willing to pay for it; and the value of an asset is the cash it will generate over its life. The characteristic of a bubble is that the first of these principles overwhelms the second. Assets are bought with little or no regard for their fundamental value because people believe that, whatever their fundamental value, someone else will pay more for it. That was why a tulip bulb was, briefly, equal in value to twelve acres of land.

Most bubbles have their origins in some real event – an economic, technological or geopolitical event that changes the fundamental determinants, though not the fundamental principles, of asset valuation – the spread of railways, the establishment of market economies in the developing world, the exploitation of the internet. Whenever there is such a change, there is a human tendency to enthusiasm, to exaggerate the pace and significance of that change, and that tendency is increased if the enthusiasm is profitable as well as fashionable.

So the effects spill into asset markets. And as bubbles expand, the belief that assets can always be sold at a higher price, that someone else will pay more, seems to be borne out by events. Someone else really is willing to pay more. Those who point to the absurdity of prices unrelated to fundamental value are exposed as fools who have passed up the opportunity of an easy profit. Many of them will finally join the party. That was the fate of the scientist Isaac Newton, who a century after the tulip mania was more than intelligent enough to see that the South Sea bubble was a fraud. But after watching on the side-lines, he could not resist the prospect of an easy profit, and was finally persuaded to invest. 'I can predict the motion of heavenly bodies, but not the madness of crowds,' he (allegedly) lamented as he counted his losses when the bubble burst.

When I was a student, I read J. K. Galbraith's book *The Great Crash, 1929*, about the speculative bubble of that era. The boom and then the ensuing depression had been followed by fifty years of historically exceptional stability in financial markets. How could people have been so stupid, I wondered, as I learned of the leveraged piles of junk which investment banks had put together and their customers had rushed to buy. I was soon to learn.

The first great modern bubble occurred in Japan in the 1980s. Japan's post-war economic development had transformed the country from a primitive society to a new industrial state in two generations. The growth rate this implied, projected into the future, suggested that Japan would soon dominate the economic world. Demand for Japanese assets from foreign investors and domestic speculators fuelled each other, and the share prices of Japanese companies and the value of Japanese property exploded, as did prices. At the peak it was widely claimed that the grounds of the Imperial Palace in Tokyo were worth more than the entire state of California. The Nikkei index of Japanese share prices peaked at 38,957. Twenty-five year later, it is still less than half that value.

The New Economy bubble began to inflate in 1995, with the initial public offering of Netscape, a company whose internet browser made access to the worldwide web widely available. The company, founded less than two years earlier, was valued at $3 billion, and the share price doubled on the first day. (Netscape's browser would in due course be crushed by Microsoft's Internet Explorer.) A report by Mary Meeker, 'the internet goddess', pointed to other companies that might attract similar enthusiasm.

In the five years that followed, the phenomenon of Netscape was repeated again and again. A newly established business with little revenue and no profit would be launched on the market, and its price would rise on a wave of enthusiasm. When I led Oxford's business school between 1997 and 1999, I found many students had no interest in the traditional interviews with McKinsey and Goldman Sachs because they expected to be internet millionaires within the year. Many of the increasingly ridiculous businesses that were launched had no real purpose other than the raising of funds from gullible investors. It became common to see business plans that extended only to an IPO.

Few European internet companies made it through to an IPO before fundamental values reasserted themselves. The aptly named lastminute.com came to market as the boom was subsiding. Boo.com, a fashion site and perhaps the most absurd of all internet businesses (its founders blew over £100 million on air travel, hotels and parties before the business collapsed) sold few clothes and no shares to the public. In the spring of 2000 the bubble burst.

Bubbles should be distinguished from asset mispricing. Asset mispricing occurs when market participants, faced with imperfect information and an uncertain future, get values wrong. Such mispricing occurs all the time and provides opportunities for intelligent investors. In bubbles few traders are concerned with fundamental values, and they generally hope to sell on their securities, soon, at a higher price. Intelligent investors can do nothing in bubbles.

In Chapter 9 I will describe how another bubble, in parts of the US housing market, contributed to the financial crisis of 2007–8. That bubble was promoted by brokers who encouraged borrowers to take out mortgages they could not afford in the expectation that the brokers would be able to refinance the mortgages for a higher value, and further commission, within a year or two. The structure was predicated on the assumption that house prices would rise continuously, so that even a pause would bring that structure crashing down. That pause eventually happened.

As a student, I had wondered how the markets of 1929 could have accommodated such folly. In 1999–2000 I had learned how people could indeed be so foolish; in 2007–8 I learned that such foolishness was ineradicable in modern financial services markets. The origins of these events lie not so much in innate stupidity as in the capacity of clever people, especially when blinded by the prospect of financial gain, to fall victim to the power of conventional thinking.

The power of conventional thinking

In the New Economy and credit bubbles conventional, yet magical, thinking created its own reality. It is hard to overstate the power of group thinking in business and finance. People repeat to each other the same transitorily fashionable views in mutual reinforcement. The power of conventional thinking asserts itself in the reiteration of banal opinions on fashionable issues. Today these include the excitement and paranoia over China's economic development, the obsession with climate change and the scramble for alternative assets in hedge funds and private equity.

Both truths and falsehoods spread contagiously, forming what Galbraith called 'the conventional wisdom'. These processes of contagion can lead people to believe absurd things – that Salem was besieged by witches, that the US was endangered by Communist subversion, that boo.com would dominate its market and that house prices can only go up. It is not only common but reasonable to believe what is widely believed, especially among business and political leaders, who have little time for reflection. I believe the world is round, not because I have myself verified it, but because the general belief is that the world is round. If I had lived a thousand years ago, I would have believed the earth was flat, and for the same reasons. The court of Mr Market creates and experiences its own reality.

In the complex and uncertain world of modern finance, such

behaviour takes us far away from market efficiency and fundamental value. In all market bubbles – tulips or the South Sea, the New Economy or the housing bubble – distortions are supported by commercial interests that benefit from their promotion. There was always a kernel of truth in the exaggerated propositions. Speculators in the South Sea bubble were on the verge of an industrial revolution and an explosion of world trade. Railways, electricity and modern information technology were transforming discoveries. Financial innovation did create opportunities for better risk management. The creation of the eurozone did promote economic convergence within the European Union. The people who lost money in these bubbles were not mistaken in their basic thesis, but they greatly overestimated both the pace of change and the extent to which individual companies would benefit from it.

The mind of the market became its own reality. Investors sought insight into 'the mind of the market', and that was what they received – and continued to receive. What was true was what was believed, and what was believed was true. And when the bubbles burst, what had once been believed and was therefore true was no longer believed and therefore no longer true. The dot.com shares that were once stars were now dogs; there was nothing more to be said. Practical men of the financial world, who would be appalled at the suggestion that they might be influenced by French philosophy, are the most determined of postmodernists. In financial centres across the world truth is in the eye of the observer. Jean Baudrillard notoriously remarked that 'the (first) Gulf War took place only on television'; in much the same sense, the New Economy was observed only on Wall Street.

The prevalence of short-term thinking

The misapprehensions of the conventional wisdom – true or false – affect prices and may even affect fundamental values themselves. George Soros describes this phenomenon as 'reflexivity'. Although the development of the internet was not an event of great significance for Walmart, the belief that it was a significant event had a large influence on its businesses. There was an even larger effect on the investment climate within which such companies operated. The New Economy bubble led to large overinvestment in telecommunications capacity, which itself made nemesis more likely. The massive overpayments by European telecoms companies for mobile phone licences were the result of misperceptions of reality generated by the New Economy bubble.

The senior executives of these businesses were captured by these misconceptions and could not have escaped them even if they had been more thoughtful people. Five years later the senior executives of banks were in the same position. In the distorting mirror provided by ostensibly sophisticated risk management models, they saw irresistible profit opportunities. There was a new paradigm for banks, as there had been a new paradigm for retailers and phone companies, and the winners would be the ones to pursue their fantastic vision most vigorously. The price of contradicting the mind of the market was to lose one's job.

The divergence between the interests of the investor and the interests of the businesses through which the investor's funds are transmitted runs all along that chain of intermediation. Risk for a fund manager is not volatility but underperformance relative to an index. It is, as Keynes observed, better for a career to be conventionally wrong than unconventionally right, and disastrous to be unconventionally wrong. The control of the manager's perceived risk leads to the practice of 'closet indexation'. Although the fund manager is paid for stock selection, the composition of his fund mirrors closely the composition of the index. Most fund managers receive daily reports of their overweight and underweight positions, relative to the benchmark index. As a result, many allegedly 'actively managed' funds virtually replicate an index. The successful fund manager is one who can stay close to his benchmark index but be consistently slightly ahead of it.

You might think that this could be achieved by close attention to fundamental value. If performance were measured every five years, when mean reversion would have asserted itself, such a policy might well succeed. But performance is measured not every five years but much more often – commonly every three months, often more frequently. Over such short periods momentum dominates mean reversion – this quarter's outperforming stocks are more than averagely likely to have been last quarter's outperforming stocks. Knowing the mind of the market trumps fundamental value.

If you were a professional investment manager, and you had made the – good – call that shares in 1996 were overvalued relative to property, you would almost certainly have been fired. From 1996 to 2000 shares rose steadily while property stagnated. The reversal came afterwards. If you are managing other people's money, three years is a long time – too long to be, or to appear to be, wrong.

Managers who are doing markedly worse than their peers for as long as three years will find their jobs in jeopardy. 'Where have all the geniuses gone?' *Fortune* asked in 1999. Warren Buffett 'didn't get it', and shares in Berkshire Hathaway fell by almost 50 per cent that year. George Soros failed to read the timing of boom and bust correctly, and retired from active involvement in managing other people's money, content to devote himself to the philanthropic management of his own.

Keynes reportedly said (there is no evidence that he did) that the market can be wrong for longer than you can stay solvent, warning of the risks associated with ignoring the mind of the market in favour of fundamental value. Writing today, he would say that the market can be wrong for longer than a contrarian fund manager can hold his or her job. And so it has proved.

While three years is a long time-scale for an investment manager, it isn't a long time-scale for the intelligent investor. This difference in the time-scale on which you are judged gives a big advantage to the DIY portfolio manager. Patience pays.

The malign effect on corporate performance

The emphasis by institutional investors on quarterly figures has led analysts and fund managers into a symbiotic relationship with corporate executives known as 'earnings guidance'. In pre-war days the great figures who headed large companies, such as Pierre du Pont of the chemical firm bearing his family name or Alfred Sloan of General Motors, had virtually no contact with shareholders (although they were significant shareholders themselves). The emergence of the hostile takeover was probably the most important single factor in changing this behaviour. Senior managers of large companies began to pay closer attention to the share price – their jobs depended on it. The growth of stock options as a means of payment reinforced the trend. It provided an additional reason for executives to pay close attention to the share price – their wealth depended on it.

Now, most large companies will have an investor relations department or employ a specialist firm to handle these issues. The chairman, chief executive and chief financial officer will expect to devote a substantial proportion of their time to investor relations. That means pitching the company to analysts and talking to the investment managers who are the principal shareholders. Sometimes analysts will benefit from lavish hospitality in the course of learning about the company's affairs.

The market responds not to good and bad news from

companies but to news that is better or worse than market expectations. Therefore many businesses want to manage both outcome and expectation themselves. They seek steady earnings growth just a little faster than the market is anticipating, and manage their quarterly reporting in order to achieve this. I will describe in the next chapter how much scope finance directors have for keeping their reported earnings on a steady path. Often the main criterion by which analysts judge the quality of management is whether executives do the things they say they will do. This mutually rewarding process of earnings guidance has only the loosest of connections with how the business is actually performing. Eventually, of course, fundamental value breaks through. But this process may take time. The favoured analysts of companies such as WorldCom and Enron – for example Grubman and Curt Hamner of CSFB (Credit Suisse First Boston) – continued to puff these stocks until the companies collapsed.

A major part – in many cases much the largest part – of the remuneration of senior executives is now related to movements in the company's share price. That makes it inevitable that the mind of the market takes precedence over fundamental value. In tribute to the power of Mr Market, many companies display the constantly fluctuating share price in their reception area. Some chief executives have it on their desks, and it is not unknown for them to check it several times a day. Their business plans are heavily influenced by the conventional wisdom of their peers, analysts and bankers, rather than their own judgement. Success, as measured by the market, is being able to anticipate the new fashion slightly more quickly than other people. Advance insight into the conventional wisdom is the commodity that many consultants, business gurus, journalists and investment analysts now sell.

The intelligent investor's advantage

The unproductive contact between finance directors and analysts provides an opportunity for the individual investor – the rewarding opportunity to ignore it. You aren't party to earnings guidance, but it doesn't matter, because the information such guidance provides has little to do with the substance of the business. You don't have to remain popular with company management to do your job. You don't have to worry that you will be fired if you underperform the market in one quarter, or several. Being close to the market is not necessarily an advantage. Occasionally fund managers have developed such a strong reputation with investors that they can ignore the braying of analysts and the pressures of the dysfunctional cycle of earnings management and guidance. While Buffett was criticised for refusing to participate in the New Economy bubble, he could laugh all the way to the bank, and the steak house. In Omaha, Nebraska, far away from Wall Street.

Best of all, you can emphasise absolute, rather than relative, returns. That emphasis enables the intelligent investor to focus on the analysis of fundamental value, rather than the mind of the market. For the intelligent – and therefore patient – investor, there is a simple reconciliation between the mark-to-market and fundamental-value principles: an asset is worth the higher of its fundamental value and its market price.

If the market price is above fundamental value, an intelligent investor can sell for the market price and look for something else. If the market price is below fundamental value, an intelligent investor can continue to hold and enjoy the benefit of the projected stream of cash returns.

This freedom gives the intelligent investor an immediate advantage over the majority of professional fund managers, bound by the routine of quarterly performance measurement. For the professional fund manager, the mark-to-market principle rules – an asset is worth what someone is willing to pay for it.

Being able to take a detached view of fundamental value is a big advantage. But it is not easy. Estimating fundamental value requires a view of the long-term prospects of the company. The information you need is extensive, difficult to obtain and changes constantly. The analysis of fundamental value is speculative, and different people are likely to come up with different answers. In the next chapter I'll look at what is required.

6

In Search of Fundamental Value

Accounting for earnings

Fundamental analysis of a company begins with its profits. In 2015 Exxon Mobil earned $3.85 per share, and the corporation's stock price was $89. The price:earnings ratio – the number of years of current earnings needed to earn the current stock price – was therefore 23. The price:earnings ratio is the most common single metric used in stock valuation.

Table 3 shows the price:earnings ratio of some sectors of the US stock market at January 2016.

The wide variation across industries is the result of different perceptions of growth prospects. In 2014 Exxon Mobil earned $7.60 per share, and in June 2015 the stock price was $82, equivalent to a PE ratio of 11. The market was already discounting lower profits as a result of falling oil prices. The highly rated pharmaceutical sector, however, includes many companies with considerable earnings growth potential. Profits from software are mostly in the future rather than the present. These future differences are reflected in current ratings.

The ratio between the price:earnings ratio and the growth rate of earnings (the PEG) is an indicator popular with many investors. Their reasoning is that a low PEG ratio suggests that future growth can be bought at a relatively modest price. It's

Table 3: **Current PE ratios, various US sectors, January 2016**

Banks (money centre)	17.4
Automobile	14.0
Pharmaceutical	32.1
Oil and gas (integrated)	27.0
Retail (general)	22.1
Tobacco	35.0
Utility	19.3
Software (systems and applications)	127.7

Source: Stern School, New York

not that easy: a measure such as PEG is at best a simple screen for identifying companies whose fundamentals deserve further examination.

Just as price:earnings ratios vary across companies and business sectors, so they also vary over time. The cyclically adjusted price:earnings ratio (CAPE) is a measure popularised by Robert Shiller. This measure looks at the ratio of the current market price to average earnings (adjusted for inflation) over the previous ten years.

For the US, Shiller has calculated the long-run historical average CAPE (over more than a century) for the market as a whole as 16.5. A 'normal' range has been between 10 and 25. Price:earnings ratios also vary considerably across countries. Table 4 shows how at July 2015 CAPE was low in many European markets, while for the US the figure is close to the top of its historical range.

If you measure performance over ten-year periods, the outcome is generally better if the CAPE is at the bottom end of its normal range than near the top. And on the three occasions when the US market has broken through the top end of

Table 4: **CAPE in different equity markets, July 2015**

Spain	9.4	France	15.3
Austria	9.8	Germany	18.0
Italy	11.0	Japan	24.2
UK	12.1	US	24.4

Source: Wellershoff and Partners

this range – the late 1920s, the mid-1960s and the late 1990s – the event has been followed by a major stock market decline. (The crashes of 1929 and 2000–1 are well known; there was no 'crash' in 1966, but the Dow Jones index did not regain its 1966 level until 1982.) CAPE is not a method of timing the market, but the apparent predictive value of CAPE, resulting from the power of long-run mean reversion, is nevertheless relevant to the patient investor.

But less relevant to the herd. When the price:earnings ratio rises outside its conventional range, analysts opine that historical experience is no longer applicable. When Japanese share prices soared in the 1980s, they advised that Japanese companies should be viewed differently from companies elsewhere. A decade later, many financial commentators argued that the New Economy and the economic and political environment that followed the end of the Cold War had changed the basic principles of stock valuation. In the noughties, new tools of risk management had tamed financial risk, and a 'great moderation' was in progress.

Once again, the world had not changed, only opinion. Long-term mean reversion struck, and PE ratios returned to more normal levels. There is a saying that the most expensive words in investment are 'It's different this time'. Sceptics who were reluctant to believe the rules had changed avoided the bubbles in Japan, the New Economy and the credit boom to their ultimate benefit.

For a stock such as Exxon Mobil with a price:earnings ratio of 23, the earnings attributable to each share are equal to a little over 4 per cent of the share price. This ratio, the inverse of the PE ratio, is known as the earnings yield. If a normal PE ratio is between 10 and 25, a normal earnings yield lies between 4 and 10 per cent. Since shareholders do not receive the company's earnings, the earnings yield is not directly relevant to the shareholder. However, it is indirectly relevant, since earnings determine the dividends the company can pay. The earnings yield is a guide to the long-run rate of return that it is reasonable to expect from owning shares.

Creative accounting

But the value of such a guide depends on the value of the information on which it is based. The collapse of Enron brought to the attention of a wider public what market professionals and companies have always known: companies have a lot of scope to make their reported earnings and assets what they want them to be. What is the profit of a company? It all depends on the meaning of 'is', as Bill Clinton famously explained. Creative accounting is the quantitative equivalent of the modern politician's lie – a statement that is in some narrow technical sense true but is substantively false.

The jury decided that the practices at Enron constituted fraud, and its former chief executive, Jeff Skilling, and former chief financial officer, Andy Fastow, went to jail for their part in one of America's most spectacular corporate collapses. But the methods that Skilling and Fastow employed were only aggressive versions of financial techniques used by more respectable companies.

Wall Street wanted corporations to report a steady stream of increased earnings (part of the process of managing investor expectations that I described in the previous chapter). So that is what corporations reported. How were companies able to manage, not their businesses, but their declared earnings in this way?

A prudent business that acquires another will take a careful look at the assets it has acquired. So will an imprudent one. The imprudent one writes down the value of these assets to low levels and then attributes to its own superior management skills the gains apparently made when these undervalued assets are sold or used in the business. The 'restoration' of value can be used to enhance profits for many years. This practice is called 'acquisition accounting', and is a relatively simple device. Recent innovations in creative accounting have been much more complex.

Most large businesses are, from a legal perspective, a group of companies under common ownership. Consolidated accounts add the individual accounts of all these companies and report the overall result as if the business were a single entity. Since shareholders are, indirectly, shareholders in all the companies within the group, this is the only sensible way to present the figures in a manageable, comprehensible form.

But companies often give stakes in associated businesses to outsiders. In a joint venture between two or more companies, each cooperating company will usually have a share of the legal entity that conducts the business. A firm establishing a new business venture may want to give shares to key individuals. Or a company may simply own shares in another business as a strategic investment.

The general principle – and it is a sensible one – is that if a company manages and controls a subsidiary or associate company, the consolidated accounts of the parent should include the relevant share of assets and earnings of the subsidiary or associate. If the parent doesn't manage and control the other company, then its interest should be treated as if it were an investment. The asset is the value of the shares, and the income is the dividend.

So far so good, if not so simple. But what exactly is meant by management and control? US accounting standards – known as Generally Accepted Accounting Principles (GAAP) – try to pin this down. But whenever standards try to pin down a concept, the creature flies away. Creating subsidiaries that you do, in fact, manage and control, but which you do not manage and control for the purposes of generally accepted accounting principles, has many advantages for the creative accountant. You can use transactions between the parent and subsidiary to create profits, or to make them disappear. Enron created hundreds of these subsidiaries. Fastow helpfully took stakes in some of them for himself. If you went through the detail of the company's accounting filings, you would discover all this. But to do so would involve burying yourself in thousands of pages of figures. Some analysts did work it out. I'll come back to them in Chapter 9.

Some companies of the New Economy era would simply exchange long-term contracts to supply each other with the same thing, enabling both to credit turnover and profits even though no real transaction took place – or ever would. Such manipulation doesn't work for ever; sooner or later these manoeuvres will have to be reversed. But you can make it later rather than sooner. And remember, in the long run we are all dead. Or, in some cases, in the federal penitentiary.

Another fraudster, Bernie Ebbers of WorldCom, reduced the slick presentation to bare essentials. He would arrive at meetings and simply point to a graph of the company's rising share price before inviting questions. Any more extensive account of what the company was doing might have taxed his business knowledge and financial expertise. The accountants of both Enron and WorldCom, encouraged to support that rising share price, took full advantage of opportunities provided by the complexity of modern accounting. As Fastow explained his activities at Enron to his son: 'Every way I could find ways to follow the rule technically but undermine the principle of the rule, I did it. And because I did that, it caused a lot of harm and that's why I should be in prison.'

A long-term contract or project will incur costs and accrue revenues over several years. A conservative approach recognises the profit when the books have closed and the money is banked, acknowledging only the bird in the hand. An optimistic frame of mind takes credit for the anticipated profit on the deal the moment it is signed, chalking up many birds in the bush as soon as the hunter's gun is primed. A true and fair view would strike a position somewhere in between. The right balance requires careful, and subjective, judgement. But the exercise of careful judgement was not the activity in which self-aggrandising executives, such as those of Enron and WorldCom, were engaged. Jeff Skilling notoriously celebrated permission from the Securities and Exchange Commission for Enron to mark its gas contracts to market with champagne for his colleagues. The agreement enabled the corporation to bring many years of potential profit into this year's accounts.

Advisers and accountants connived in these schemes. It is impossible to believe that sophisticated, intelligent investment bankers did not realise that Kenneth Lay, Enron's chairman, was an affable, skilful political operator with little grasp of business detail, that Jeff Skilling, the chief executive, was as corrupt as he was brilliant, or that Bernie Ebbers had none of the attributes needed to run a global telecoms company. But Enron's complex financial transactions and WorldCom's constant acquisitions generated large fees.

Accountants were once the butt of jokes – stuffy people with a rigid professional ethic. In the 1980s the large global firms that audit virtually all major corporations in Britain and the United States consolidated into what is now the big four of KPMG, PwC, EY and Deloitte. Their partners became hungry for consulting revenue as fee levels from their traditional audit business came under pressure.

Pleasing corporate clients received greater emphasis. 'Eat what you kill' was an increasingly common slogan in law and accountancy firms. Partners would take home the revenues they had personally earned rather than a share of the collective profits. The characterisation of customers as prey is revealing. Arthur Andersen, always the most commercial of the major firms, would pursue new clients, and the interests and wishes of those clients, most aggressively – and would be destroyed by its acquiescence in Enron's frauds.

The main counteracting force to the effect of competitive pressures in reducing standards is public regulation of accounting standards and the sale of securities. The most important accounting standards bodies are America's Federal Accounting Standards Board and the global International Accounting Standards Board. The latter body determines International Financial Reporting Standards, the analogue of GAAP for Europe and much of the rest of the world. All countries have financial regulators, and America's Securities and Exchange Commission is the most formidable.

These organisations have done much to rein in abuses and, as a result, formal accounting statements now contain much less rubbish than they did even a decade ago. Still, the presentation of company accounts remains confusing. Many companies highlight partial or misleading information, and commercial pressures on analysts to join in corporate self-congratulation and facilitate the process of earnings guidance remain strong.

Beware of EBITDA (Earnings Before Interest, Tax, Depreciation, Amortisation), a measure devised in the 1990s to enable technology start-ups to flatter their accounts. Interest and tax are costs. Be particularly suspicious of 'pro forma earnings' or any numbers that include or exclude supposedly non-recurring items. These figures that company executives present to the public are sometimes described as 'earnings before bad stuff'.

The issue of revenue recognition – how to account for profit from projects with a long time-scale – is fundamental to an understanding of corporate accounts. Depreciation and amortisation are costs: the terms are more or less interchangeable, although depreciation is most often used in relation to fixed assets and amortisation in relation to intangible assets. Look closely and sceptically at amortisation of intangible assets, which may often be related to acquisition accounting.

But depreciation of fixed assets is generally real enough; your car loses value as you drive it and wear it out, and loses further value every year whether you drive it or not. But this cost is not money out of your pocket in the way the fuel you buy to fill the tank is a cost. Money leaves your pocket when you have to shell out for a new car. Because expenditure on fixed assets is lumpy, your cash flow profile differs from your income and expenditure profile – I will say more about income, expenditure and the prudent spending rate in Chapter 11.

In a similar way, the contrast between the erratic pattern of capital expenditure in a business and the smoothed path of accounting depreciation means that the stream of properly calculated profits differs from the cash flow. Even Apple does not build a new $5 billion headquarters campus every year, nor Exxon Mobil open a new oilfield. A growing business will often have profitability running ahead of cash flow, while a declining one will be generating more cash than profit. 'Free cash flow' is the difference between net revenues from operations and necessary expenditure on productive investment.

But you may need to look carefully not only at cash flow and profits but also at the underlying business activities in order to determine whether a business is really investing for the future or is effectively running itself down. Managers given a target of finding 5 or 10 per cent cost savings, a frequent corporate practice, can usually deliver. Sometimes this can be done with little effect on the efficiency of the business or the quality of its product. We have all encountered people who reduce, rather than increase, the effectiveness of the organisation that employs them, and whose services can profitably be terminated. You can always spend less on maintenance, or on customer service, or press employees to work harder. These actions will have an impact on future profits, but the consequences will be some time ahead, and may prove to be more or less expensive than the initial cost savings.

Most large companies have engaged in successive rounds of these cost savings in the last decade, either to enhance measured efficiency or to produce the 'synergies' that supposedly justify their merger activity. Partly as a result, corporate earnings have grown faster than revenues or the economy as a whole. Some of these cost savings represent real efficiency gains; others enhance current profits at the expense of future profits. Often, only time will tell.

In the first edition of this book I illustrated the issue with the example of BP, the British-based oil company which had taken cost-cutting too far, especially in the US Amoco business which it had acquired. One result had been a major explosion at its Texas City refinery in 2005. But much worse was to come. A year after publication of that first edition, the Deepwater Horizon rig in the Gulf of Mexico caused the largest oil spill in the history of the industry, costing BP tens of billions of dollars in fines and compensation.

But BP is not the only case where the pursuit of short-term earnings damaged the company's performance in the longer run. Banks sold their customers payment protection insurance on which many of the policyholders stood no chance of a successful claim until regulators forced them to return billions in compensation to their customers. Pharmaceutical companies stressed marketing and cost reduction and spent their ample profits on buying each other rather than on new research, leaving their pipelines of new drugs empty and endangering the fragile implicit contract between the industry and the public.

Despite these deplorable examples, many businesses are

better and more tightly run today than two decades ago. Almost every company can reduce cost at the expense of future revenues and, if analysts project this growth of earnings into the future, the stock price gets a double bonus. The key issue in every case is to look at the sustainability of the business strategy and, above all, the sustainability of the firm's competitive advantage. Competitive advantage can be understood only by going behind the earnings statement.

One clear pointer to the problems at Enron was that the company, while supposedly very profitable, was not generating the cash that matched its reported earnings. Cash is a good reality check. A common feature of all the accounting wheezes described above – dubious transactions between the company and its subsidiaries, premature revenue recognition, inappropriate writing down of acquired assets – is that increased reported earnings have no cash counterpart. Tax is also a clue to what is really going on. Revenue authorities have many faults, but they do not often levy tax on profits that do not exist. High profits and a low tax charge may be explained by clever tax planning, or by large investment programmes that produce large deductions. Another possible explanation is that profits are not what they seem.

There are ways of piercing the fog created by earnings reports. One is to focus on the ability of a business to generate cash. Another is to look, usually in a more qualitative way, at the inherent capabilities of a company's business – its competitive advantages. I'll look at each of these approaches in turn.

Cash is king

Most thoughtful analysts look at cash flow and assets rather than reported earnings when they try to assess the fundamental value of a business. The general principles of asset valuation apply just as much to a company, and to the assets of a company, as to a security:

- an asset is worth what someone is willing to pay for it; and
- the value of an asset is the cash it will generate for its owner over its life.

Applying the second of these principles requires a process for translating a stream of cash that accrues continuously over time into a value at a particular point in time. The cash flow will come from the dividends on a share or on the earnings of a company. The standard method is called 'discounted cash flow' (DCF), the first and indispensable tool for any quantitative investment analyst.

Compound interest at 8 per cent per year means that $100 now will be worth $108 a year from now, $117 in two years' time and so on. If $100 is worth $108 a year from now, then $100 a year from now is today worth $93 ($100 ÷ 1.08). A similar calculation would make $100 two years from now worth $86 today ($100 ÷ 1.17). The method of discounted cash flow derives in this way a set of conversion factors, like exchange rates, which can be used to convert cash at any future date into an equivalent value of cash today ($100 in 2018 corresponds to $86 in 2016). A promise to pay $300 in three equal annual instalments, starting now, is worth not $300, but $100 + $93 + $86, or $279. All you need do is choose an appropriate discount rate. The choice of an appropriate discount rate is not a minor problem, as we shall see.

The method of DCF valuation can be applied either to the cash flow accruing to the shareholder – the dividends to be paid – or to the cash accruing to the business itself. I'll look in turn at each of these approaches.

Suppose a company, such as Exxon, is paying a dividend of $2.88 per share. We need to estimate the likely growth of that dividend. If dividends grow at 5 per cent, next year's dividend might be $3.02, rising to $3.17 the year after and so on. All we need to do is write down that stream of cash flows, discount it at, say, 8 per cent, and we can calculate the fundamental value.

If 5 per cent growth is the long-term average, there is a simplifying trick. Subtract 5 per cent, the growth rate, from 8 per cent, the discount rate. The difference, 3 per cent, should be the dividend yield on the share, as in this case it more or less is (3.2 per cent). It is easy to work through the mathematics, but you may prefer just to believe the result. The fundamental value that emerges from this calculation is $96, close to the current share price.

The DCF approach requires knowledge of the appropriate discount rate and of the appropriate cash flows. The usual approach is to say that future cash flows should be discounted at the rate the company has to pay to raise money – the cost of capital. In the calculation above I used an arbitrary 8 per cent – the target rate of return of Chapter 2 – as the discount rate (a common procedure), but if the technique is to have scientific value, the number requires a more principled basis.

One common practice would be to take the yield on long-dated bonds, currently 2.5 per cent for a thirty-year US Treasury bond, as a starting point. Payments of interest and principal by the US government are secure. But since the future values, profits and dividends of Exxon Mobil are speculative, it is common practice to use a much higher discount rate to reflect the greater volatility associated with investment in shares. This allowance for business risk is the 'equity risk premium'. The simplest and commonest way of measuring the equity risk premium is the average historical difference between returns on shares and the return on safe assets such as US Treasury bonds. The data in Chapter 2 might justify a figure of about 5 per cent, which is broadly consistent with an 8 per cent figure for the cost of capital, equal to the intelligent investor's target rate of return. I'll come back to the calculation of this risk element of the cost of capital in the next chapter.

The alternative approach to DCF appraisal of the cash that a corporation will return to its shareholders is to look at cash flows generated within the business itself. The 'free cash flow' approach starts from the cash generated by a company's operations – the difference between net revenues from operations and necessary productive investment, as defined above. If we had a sufficiently long series of future free cash flows, the DCF technique would enable us to calculate the fundamental value of the business. But that is a big if.

A successful business may have negative free cash flow because the company is spending more on building the business than it is currently earning. Most new companies are in this position. Only after several years will projected cash flows become positive. Many years of data are therefore required before any clear assessment of fundamental value can be made.

A further difficulty then emerges. As illustration, go back to the DCF valuation of Exxon and use the dividend growth approach. Over the next five years the DCF value generated from dividends will be around $15, less than 20 per cent of the hypothetical value of the share. Most of the projected cash flow lies in a far distant future.

Worse still, the result of the calculation is extremely sensitive to the assumptions. Suppose the dividend growth projection is 6 per cent rather than 5 per cent, and the discount rate is 7 per cent rather than 8 per cent. These small adjustments raise the projected share price to $300. Or suppose you are more pessimistic. Put dividend growth at zero and the discount rate at 10 per cent; then the shares are worth only $30.

At this point you may be inclined to give up on the use of DCF measures of fundamental value. Yet the DCF technique doesn't create the problem – it reveals it. Most of the value of today's major businesses really does lie in a future beyond the five or ten years that seem reasonably foreseeable. Small changes in assumptions, compounded far into the future, have large effects on current values. DCF calculations are illuminating, but don't make the mistake of believing that any particular DCF calculation is true.

There is a partial solution to these problems, which is to cut off the cash flow analysis after a period – five years is a common choice – and make an assumption about the value of the business at that date. This is not a very satisfactory answer. It resolves the difficult question posed initially – What is the fundamental value of the business now? – by requiring an answer to a more difficult question – What will be the fundamental value of the business five years from now? At this point the first principle of asset valuation – the value of an asset is the cash it generates for its owner – becomes confounded with the second – an asset is worth what someone is willing to pay for it.

That emphasis on asset value suggests another approach to valuing a business. Look not at the earnings but at the assets the business owns. Every company in which you might invest produces a balance sheet, an accounting statement of the value of the assets it owns. Traditional accounting practice held that the balance sheet should report the lower of the amount the company paid for an asset and the value of the cash the asset will generate over its life. While this formulation closely mirrored the general principles of asset valuation, it did so in a deliberately cautious way. This caution arose, first, from insisting that the lower of the possible answers was used, and, second, by substituting the amount the company paid for the asset for the amount someone else would be willing to pay for it.

The pioneers of securities analysis, such as Benjamin Graham and David Dodd, operated successfully by simply having the skills and energy to penetrate accounting statements. Since the assets reported in the balance sheet were generally estimated conservatively, shares whose prices were below the reported asset value were generally good buys. Some investors became rich by identifying companies where the value of the assets the company owned – shops or land – was greater than the value of the company as a trading entity.

Those days of easy returns have long gone. The techniques Graham and Dodd employed were possible because they were early to realise that business assets had become less specialised. The value of a railway or brewery was inseparable from the value of the company that ran the trains or brewed the beer. But the modern office or shop has many potential tenants; the trucks and the distribution warehouses can distribute many different products. Today most companies have stripped their own assets. When assets have a value separable from the company that uses them, companies have generally realised that value.

The important assets of modern businesses are no longer their buildings, plant and machinery but their intangible property – their reputation with customers, their relationships with suppliers. When pompous executives proclaim, 'Our people are our greatest asset', what they say is often true. Most other assets are likely to be owned by, or pledged to, the financial sector.

Financial companies directly or indirectly own much of the plant or the property occupied by other industrial and commercial businesses. For banks and insurance companies and for property and investment companies it remains important to understand the structure of their assets. There are a few sectors, such as oil and house-building, where the market position of the company will depend on its control of future reserves of petroleum or of land. But while company accounts report a figure for the net assets of the company, the asset value is usually now a poor guide to the value of its shares.

Investment analysts used to distinguish value and growth investing. Broadly speaking, value focused on companies with strong tangible assets, growth on companies with strong intangible assets. Nowadays these categories have become too blurred to be useful. Some people think that more systematic attempts should be made to include the value of intangible assets in company accounts.

Accounting theorists want to revive the balance sheet for a modern era; creative finance directors want to present the most favourable impression of the company's affairs. But the goodwill you find on corporate balance sheets is usually an accounting fiction that arises when a company pays, or overpays, in the acquisition of another business. These numbers should be disregarded. Corporate accounts reveal imperfectly, or not at all, the most important determinant of a company's fundamental value – its competitive advantage.

Competitive advantage

In the nineteenth-century businesses that Karl Marx described, the capitalist owned the factory and the plant in which workers produced the goods, and that state of affairs defined both the economic and the political relationship between them. The analytic framework of that era lingers, although the modern business environment is quite different. The bosses of large corporations have authority because of their job titles, not their wealth (though they are increasingly inclined to use the former to secure the latter). They don't own the place where they work, and nor, as a rule, does the company that employs them.

The modern company is best viewed as a collection of capabilities. It is defined by its brands and its products, through its internal systems and its relationships with customers and suppliers, by the resources to which it has access and the operating licences it holds, and by its reputation with the public, governments and prospective employees. We have capitalism without capital.

When the company's most valuable assets descend in the lift

at the end of the month, they take their pay cheques with them. The ability of the company to generate returns for shareholders depends on its ability to add value to its employees through its own capabilities. In a competitive market-place a business can add such value only if there is something distinctive about these capabilities that yields a competitive advantage.

A distinctive capability becomes valuable when it yields a sustainable competitive advantage. That is what Warren Buffett understood when he bought stakes in Coca-Cola, Gillette and the *Washington Post*. He didn't think he was buying a head office in Atlanta, a razor blade manufacturing line or a printing press. He was buying powerful brands and irreproducible market positions.

Let's look at the competitive advantages of some of the largest companies in the world. Exxon Mobil is the largest of the successor companies which were established on the break-up of John D. Rockefeller's Standard Oil in 1911. The sustainability of its competitive advantage is demonstrated by the durability of the 'seven sisters' which ruled the world industry from that break-up to the rise of OPEC in the 1970s. The seven have been reduced to four by mergers. Exxon acquired Mobil, while Chevron is the combination of Gulf Oil, SoCal and Texaco. Alongside these were the European leaders BP and Shell. Although the power of the oil majors has been somewhat reduced by the greater influence of the governments of oil-producing states and the national champions they have created, the skill base that originated in Rockefeller's day remains distinctive and indispensable.

It is hard to imagine that any firms outside that small group could replicate their integrated systems or ability to attract and develop strong teams of managers and engineers. The well-resourced national oil companies of major producing states such as Norway and Saudi Arabia have not really tried, while Russia's predatory Gazprom continues to depend on Western expertise and distribution systems. The distinctive capabilities of these businesses extend from privileged access to oil reserves through their integrated production and distribution systems to their retail brands.

HSBC has an even longer history than Exxon, although its emergence as a major international bank is recent. As the Hong Kong and Shanghai Banking Corporation, the company facilitated trade and investment in the Far East in the heyday of the British empire. In 1980, with China still emerging from the rule of Mao and the status of Hong Kong uncertain, the future of the business seemed in doubt. But the company's fortunes have since been transformed by a programme of acquisitions around the world and the emergence of China as an economic powerhouse. Well-established banks have a series of competitive advantages: a name that others trust, although they have squandered that asset in pursuit of short-term profits; a customer base of corporate and private accounts; and branch networks. The company has attempted to develop HSBC as a global retail brand, re-badging the local banks it has bought in many countries.

Novartis is the combination of the pharmaceutical businesses of three of Europe's largest established chemical companies – Ciba, Geigy and Sandoz. Although the company's headquarters is located in Switzerland, the company undertakes research, manufacturing and sales around the world. Its chief executive and the head of its pharmaceutical division are both Americans, and the US is by far the company's largest market.

Novartis's competitive advantage depends in significant part on the intellectual property it derives from drug patents. Even though these patents have a limited life, drugs continue to have brand value even in the face of the generic competition that emerges when such protection expires. As Europe's leading pharmaceutical company, Novartis enjoys a privileged position in association with the strong academic science base of Britain and Switzerland.

But original research in pharmacology is moving from large pharmaceutical businesses towards a mixture of publicly funded basic research and smaller specialist businesses financed by venture capital. The era of blockbuster drugs, which alleviate but do not cure the chronic illnesses of the well-to-do, is coming to an end. Companies like Novartis are increasingly organisations focused on marketing and the management of the complex processes of regulation.

Nestlé, also headquartered in Switzerland, is the world's largest food company. Its nineteenth-century foundations lie in the discovery of patented processes from the manufacture of condensed milk and milk chocolate. The company's brand names include not only the ubiquitous Nescafé but also Carnation, Gerber, Maggi and Purina. Even more than Novartis, Nestlé is a genuinely global company. Its current CEO is Belgian, and his predecessor, now chairman, came from Austria.

These companies illustrate common types of competitive advantage. Generally, the distinctive capabilities that create competitive advantages fall into four broad categories:

- Brands and reputation – the essence of Nestlé. Also important for Exxon Mobil, both for the retail brands that attract its customers and the reputation that encourages governments to select the firm as a partner in exploiting oil reserves. Brand and reputation are also a strength of HSBC, although the value of financial brands has been much reduced by recent misconduct and incompetence.
- Strategic assets – exclusive access to specific resources, such as the licences of HSBC and the reserves controlled by Exxon.
- Proprietary architecture – systems and structures, such as those of the oil companies and banks.
- Innovation and intellectual property – vital to Novartis.

The value of competitive advantages depends on the extent to which they are appropriable and sustainable. A competitive advantage is appropriable only if the company can defend it against suppliers and customers. An asset is not appropriable if it can go down in the lift – much of the value created by financial firms is paid out in bonuses to employees. A competitive advantage has continuing value only if it is hard to replicate.

In a slow-moving industry like food, a brand like Nescafé can be sustained, with appropriate management, indefinitely. If the market can be developed through geographic expansion – introducing Nescafé to China – or product extension – such as the creation of Nespresso – the value of this competitive advantage may continue to grow.

In a fast-moving market, such as consumer electronic goods, a brand can maintain its value only if the name can be attached to a stream of innovative products. Apple has enjoyed astonishing success in this. The company's technology is not, in itself, remarkable – the underlying electronics is available to everyone. But the company has repeatedly shown itself able to package these capabilities in products which meet consumer needs – often consumer needs which the consumers did not know they had.

Apple's first breakthrough was the graphical user interface (GUI), which allowed small computers to be used by people who understood nothing of DOS or programming. But this innovation – which had in fact been pioneered by Xerox – was soon imitated by Microsoft with Windows. The idea of a GUI could not be protected by patent or copyright, while the computer code of the Microsoft operating system did enjoy such protection. But Apple could repeat its innovative performance, more sustainably, with its music and video player, the iPod, and then with the iPad. The market leadership these products delivered proved sustainable. Although the concept of the smartphone could be imitated – and was – the operating systems, linked to Apple computers, were intellectual property. These various contrasts raise questions about the economic effectiveness of such legislation.

The value of such innovations depends critically on their timing and presentation. The tablet computer had been invented several times before – even by Apple itself. But only when the range of mobile services had reached a certain stage of development did this idea appear irresistible to customers. Innovation is not only, or primarily, about the application of advanced science. Commercial success in innovation is largely about marketing and timing. Pharmaceuticals is one of relatively few industries in which intellectual property protection is sufficiently powerful to make innovation appropriable.

Patents and other strategic assets, like those of Exxon or HSBC, are powerful and valuable capabilities. But these depend on governments, and what governments give they can also take away. The Russian government expropriated part of BP's assets in that country, while Exxon's Russian assets were much diminished in value by sanctions imposed after Russia's invasion of Ukraine. Western governments rarely expropriate but can, and do, set and alter the terms on which monopoly franchises are offered, as demonstrated in the US government response to BP's failures. Regulatory authorities can reduce the value of existing franchises by issuing more of them, as with airline liberalisation. More sustainable strategic assets are found where the monopoly is intrinsic rather than government-conferred, as with Heathrow and other London airports (owned by BAA, now a subsidiary of the Spanish company Ferrovial) or the *Financial Times* (now owned by the Japanese company Nikkei), which operates in a niche profitable for one newspaper but unlikely to be profitable for two.

Valuable competitive advantages are sustainable over time, appropriable for the firm that holds them and defensible against pressure from competitors, suppliers and customers. Is it possible to use these principles to compute, numerically, the fundamental value of a business? It is certainly possible to sketch the outlines of a calculation. Such an exercise may have value as a reality check – could these competitive advantages equal, or be much more or less than, the value implied by the current market price?

You should treat such calculations as illuminating rather than true. I'll discuss bogus quantification further in Chapter 8. The analytic framework described here, like many others, is better used as a set of questions. What are the sources of competitive advantage? Are they replicable, sustainable, defensible, appropriable? The calculations are a better guide to relative valuations than to absolute ones.

Value investing was once the purchase of tangible assets at levels below their market value. Value investing today is buying sustainable competitive advantages at a good price. Charlie Munger, Buffett's partner, has recalled how Berkshire's purchase of See's Candies in 1972 marked that transition. The opportunity to acquire such competitive advantage arises most often because the mind of the market is distracted by essentially short-term considerations: a poor economic outlook for the industry, a strategic mistake by the business, weak management or simply negative momentum.

These are the signals for the intelligent investor to make contrarian purchases. Buffett began his legendary run by purchasing a large stake in American Express when the share price was depressed by a large, but ultimately inconsequential, fraud involving salad oil.

7

Risk and Reward

Risk and uncertainty

The first share I bought was in a small shipyard called Robb Caledon. The purchase was both a rewarding investment and a rewarding lesson in investment.

You might naturally begin to establish an investment portfolio with a selection of blue chip stocks, such as Apple and Exxon Mobil. Such a strategy sounds much less risky than a stake in Robb Caledon. But when I bought Robb Caledon, I was learning about the capital asset pricing model (CAPM) – the dominant theory of modern financial economics. That theory suggests the opposite conclusion.

Fast-forward more than two decades. I am at a meeting between British government economists and senior executives from defence contractors. The largest of these firms, BAE Systems, had recently suffered huge losses from cost overruns on a major project. Its business was in turmoil, its shares depressed, and loss of confidence and aversion to risk had affected the whole sector.

The government economists, who had recently studied the CAPM at the best graduate schools, explained that the cost of capital to these companies was very low – on a par, in fact, with the government bond rate. They repeated themselves several times. They needed to – the business people reacted as they would have reacted to aliens describing life on another planet. The two sides meant completely different things when they talked about risk. In this chapter I'll explain the CAPM and illustrate the different interpretations attached to the term 'risk' by business people and financial professionals.

During the New Economy bubble, stocks carried large risk for investors. Speculators hoped for – and sometimes made – large profits, and ultimately suffered very large losses. The principal risk faced by investment managers, confronting the same opportunities, was that they would lose the support of their customers by failing to match the performance of their rivals. The risk perceived by the fund manager was different from the risk faced by the customer.

Common sense tells us that flying is risky. Travelling in a metal tube at high speed and an altitude of 10,000 metres is intrinsically dangerous. But precisely because flying is potentially dangerous, planes are scrupulously maintained, pilots are rigorously trained, and safety precautions are extensive. Fewer than 1,000 people per year die in commercial plane crashes (and in 2014 and 2015 the four most serious air accidents were all caused by criminal activity, either by aircrew or from the ground, rather than by pilot error or equipment failure). Falling down the stairs is a more common cause of death.

Worldwide, 1.2 million people die each year in road accidents. But the death rate from motor accidents in Sweden is less than one-fifth the global average, despite high levels of vehicle ownership and use. Fewer children are killed on the roads in Britain today than in the 1920s. The roads are more dangerous, but, because parents recognise this, their children are safer. The statistics do not lie, nor do our assessments of risk. The dangers that risks pose to our health – and our financial well-being – are the product both of the intrinsic riskiness of an activity and of the measures, both social and individual, that we take to counteract the dangers. The figures showing that flying is safe and the intuition that flying is risky are both correct. It all depends on what you mean by risk.

Until recently, households found security in large families. In many parts of the world they still do. Infant mortality was high, and only in a big family was it probable that some children would live to become providers and carers. Few people in rich countries now think in this way. Large families are more exposed financially and run more serious risk of grief through accident or serious illness. What is risky in one context may be prudent in a different one, and vice versa.

The government economists who thought some risks could be completely diversified used a different frame of thought from the business people who worried that a risky project might bankrupt their companies. The investor who worried about losing his shirt and the fund manager who worried about losing his job had different perceptions of risk. The nervous passenger and the student of accident statistics see flight risk differently. Some parents think it would be improvident to have a large family; others think it would be improvident not to.

The antithesis of risk is security. Much of the ambiguity in the meaning of risk results from different concepts of security. Do not confuse security with certainty. Certainty is knowing what is going to happen, but perhaps what is going to happen is not very satisfactory. The man who knows he is going to be executed tomorrow has certainty but not security. More generally, low aspirations give a degree of certainty but rarely security. People who crave certainty frequently achieve its appearance by relinquishing control over their lives, only to find that there are no certainties. People who seek careers that offer lifetime employment only to see their employers renege on the implicit promise. People who make career and retirement plans and are suddenly diagnosed with a grave illness. The lowest percentiles of the risk distribution are generally the consequence of wholly unanticipated events.

The citizens of East Germany functioned in a predictable environment at the price of a dull life and a modest standard of living. Many were willing to accept that deal, only to witness the collapse of the regime which had made the promise. To take control of one's own life or financial affairs may seem to create uncertainty, but it is a prerequisite of security in a world that is inescapably uncertain. The most attractive financial goal for most people is to have enough money not to worry about money.

Security is a high degree of confidence that one's reasonable expectations will be met. Not 100 per cent confidence, because in a real world – as distinct from a model – there can be no such thing. For the prudent investor, security means confidence that investment performance will allow the achievement of realistic goals, such as the standard of living that might be financed from a real return of 4 per cent; risk is failure to achieve such a goal. For the investment manager, security means earning a large bonus for outperforming the market or attracting new business, rather than being fired. All these perceptions are subjectively valid.

These multiple perspectives lead to confusion in the ways people describe and interpret risk, and to ambiguity in their use of the word 'risk'. When you and your investment manager talk about risk, you probably mean different things. These differences of definition mean that misunderstandings and errors are frequent. There are consequential opportunities to gain, and to lose, substantial amounts of money. Much financial services activity relies for its profitability on confusions and inconsistencies in attitudes to risk and interpretations of risk.

Subjective expected utility

Yet among academics who teach students the theory of finance – and I have been both student and teacher – there is one, and only one, correct way of thinking about risk: the way of thinking about risk I had in mind when I bought Robb Caledon.

The system that I will call the theory of 'subjective expected utility' (SEU) is so universally accepted in financial economics that any other behaviour is described as irrational. SEU is the basis of virtually all the sophisticated models and quantitative techniques used in financial markets today. These models are both normative and positive – they claim that people should think about risk in SEU ways and derive conclusions about market behaviour from the assumption that they actually do behave according to the precepts of the model.

Although this SEU approach dominates today, it was not always so. Early in the twentieth century two alternative ways of describing risk vied for supremacy. On both sides were an urbane Englishman from Cambridge and an assertive American from Chicago. The winners were Frank Ramsey and Jimmie Savage.

Ramsey was a Cambridge philosopher who made important contributions to economics in his spare time. He died at the age of twenty-six, but his brother, perhaps the less talented sibling, went on to become Archbishop of Canterbury. Savage was labelled Jimmie by a nurse since his parents, not expecting him to live, did not bother to name him. (He survived another fifty-three years.) Ramsey and Savage, the founders of SEU, proposed a means of taking the mathematical tools of probability theory far beyond their initial field of application – the gaming saloon – into the boardroom and onto the trading floor. They are the founders of modern techniques of risk management.

On the other side of the debate were John Maynard Keynes and Frank Knight. Keynes's fellowship thesis – in effect, his doctorate – was not directly to do with economics. (Keynes, one of the great polymaths of the twentieth century, had taken a degree in mathematics.) His subject was probability theory, and his thesis was eventually published in 1921, more than a decade after its submission. The First World War – and the peace conference at Versailles which followed, and about which Keynes would write so memorably – got in the way.

In the same year Frank Knight, a farmer's son from the American Midwest (who would come to loathe Keynes and all he represented), also published a book, *Risk, Uncertainty and Profit*, written in a different style but with a related argument. Keynes and Knight emphasised the uncertainty that arose from the necessarily imperfect nature of human knowledge. The future was not just unknown but unknowable.

Donald Rumsfeld expressed the difference between risk and uncertainty with uncharacteristic clarity. Rumsfeld famously distinguished 'known unknowns – the things we know we do not know' from 'unknown unknowns – the things we do not know we do not know'. This chapter will mainly be about risk – the things we know we do not know. The next chapter will deal with uncertainty – the things we do not know we do not know.

The claim made by the SEU school is that analytic tools can enable us to cut through much of this uncertainty with probabilistic reasoning and formal modelling. These approaches would provide the necessary underpinning for the growth in derivative markets after 1970 and the explosion of credit after 2000. They originated in the work of Ramsey and Savage, and received major extension in the modern portfolio theory of Markowitz and the capital asset-pricing model of Sharpe. In the remainder of this chapter I'll make the case for this approach, ahead of a critique in Chapter 8. Let's understand the claims of SEU by returning to Robb Caledon.

Think probabilities

Robb Caledon was bankrupt. The year was 1976, and a bill to nationalise British shipbuilding was going through Parliament. If the bill became law, the assets and liabilities of the yard would be assumed by the government, and the shareholders would receive around £1 per share. If the bill failed, the shares would be worthless. They were selling in the market at around 40p.

I had to be persistent to buy these shares. The brokers I called told me that the Labour government was incompetent, and that nationalising shipyards was a silly idea. They were right. They told me that the shipyard was on the point of financial collapse and yet the share price was twice what it had been two months before. They were right about that too. They told me that I risked losing everything I invested. Again, they were right.

All these observations were justified, but none seemed relevant. With youthful enthusiasm, I was applying the lessons I had been taught. Think probabilities – plan for different scenarios, think about the consequences of each and assess their likelihood. Be detached – don't be caught up in events and confuse what you want to happen with what you expect to happen. Mind your portfolio. The risk that is relevant to you is the overall risk of your whole investment portfolio, not the risk associated with the individual securities it contains.

Probabilities were central to my approach. Probabilities are essential to gamblers, though frequently ignored by them. The probability that a toss of a fair coin will show heads is one-half. This is a statement about frequency: if you toss a fair coin many times, approximately half the calls will be heads. If you can be bothered to toss the coin many times, you will verify this statement.

The ancient Greeks laid the foundations of modern mathematics. Although they gambled, they never discovered the – elementary – mathematics of probability, which was not developed until the seventeenth and eighteenth centuries. Two elements of probability theory and the methods of classical statistics based on it are particularly important in understanding the principles of investment – statistical distributions and expected values. Statistical distributions describe the probabilities of different outcomes of repeated random events. If you throw a fair coin twice, the probability that you get one head and one tail is one-half, and the probability of each of two heads or two tails is one-quarter. After many throws, approximately half the calls will be heads, and the distribution of outcomes is described by the most famous of all statistical distributions – the normal distribution – with its familiar 'bell-shaped' curve. The normal distribution is ubiquitous – it describes a wide variety of both social and natural phenomena, from the distribution of voting intentions to the heights of the voters. The assumption that the normal distribution can be applied to the distribution of daily movements in securities prices is commonly made in financial economics. It is an assumption that is illuminating, but not true.

The second key concept from probability theory is expected value. The expected value of a gamble is measured by multiplying the values of the outcomes of a gamble by their probabilities. If a coin-tossing game will pay you €1 if you win, and nothing if you lose, then its expected value is 50 cents. Despite the name, the expected value is not what you should expect. You will definitely not get 50 cents from a single toss of that coin.

But the more repeated events there are, the more likely it is that the outcome will approach its expected value. If instead of gambling to win €1 on a single toss, you were to gamble to win 50c on each of two consecutive tosses, the distribution of outcomes is less extreme. There is now a one in four chance of winning €1, from two heads, and a one in four chance of winning nothing, from two tails. Half the time, one coin will come up heads and the other tails, and you will indeed receive the expected value of 50c. If you gamble for a penny on each of 100 throws of the coin, the expected value is still 50c, and again you will probably receive something close to this figure.

Comparing distributions

In investment matters you will be concerned not just with the expected value but with the overall distribution of gains and losses. In particular, you will want to know what could go wrong. You might ask, 'What is the worst that could happen?' The worst that can happen is that you will be convicted of a grave crime of which you are entirely innocent, or that you will be murdered by a passing psychopath. But these events are extremely rare. What you really want to know about is outcomes that are bad but not completely unlikely. Contemplate, for example, the worst 1 per cent of outcomes, and then imagine the best of these conceivable outcomes. This is to take a gloomy view, but not so gloomy that you spend your life in bed. (Though note the observation above that more people die from falling down stairs than in aircraft accidents. There is no escape from risk and uncertainty.)

An outcome that will be exceeded 99 per cent of the time is called the first percentile of the frequency distribution of outcomes. It is not the worst that could happen, but the best of the worst 1 per cent of possibilities. Similarly, an outcome that will be exceeded 90 per cent of the time is the tenth percentile, and you might look at this percentile if you don't want to be quite so pessimistic. Table 5 shows the first percentile of the cumulative frequency distribution of outcomes for the coin-tossing game. On a single toss of a coin, zero is a very likely outcome. The first percentile of the distribution is zero – and indeed zero is the value of all percentiles up to the 50th. If you spread your bets across 100 tosses, however, the first percentile is 38p – on only 1 per cent of such trials will you win less than 38p, and on 99 per cent of occasions you will win more.

The value-at-risk models used by most financial institutions today seek to measure and control risks by setting values for these low percentiles of the frequency distribution of outcomes.

The bank asks 'How much could we lose on a bad (say, one in a hundred) day?' The first percentile of the distribution of daily outcomes gives the answer to that question.

Table 5: **The cumulative frequency distribution from tossing a coin**

Percentile	Winnings			
	1 toss	2 tosses	20 tosses	100 tosses
1st	0	0	26c	38c
10th	0	25c	36c	44c
49th	0	50c	49.7c	49.9c
51st	€1	50c	50.3c	50.1c
90th	€1	75c	66c	56c
Gain on each head obtained	€1	50c	5c	1c
Expected value of winnings	50c	50c	50c	50c

The same method can be used to describe the upper tail of the distribution. You will obtain the 90th percentile of a distribution at least 10 per cent of the time. So the 90th percentile on a single toss is €1. Just as every percentile below the 50th is zero, every percentile above the 50th is €1. For a gamble spread over 100 tosses, however, the 90th percentile is only 56c. You can expect to make more than 56c only 10 per cent of the time. To decide whether one distribution is preferable to another, it isn't really sufficient to make comparisons of a single percentile. The first percentile is a rather unlikely outcome. The prudent person, rather than the committed pessimist, might focus on the 10th percentile. You would have to be very gloomy to ignore altogether the good outcomes at higher percentiles, and you will want to look at the 50th percentile, the median outcome. In banks the traders tend to look only at the high percentiles, the risk managers only at the low ones. This creates tension between them which is sometimes constructive, often fatal.

The examples with a relatively small number of trials (one and two tosses) have lower pay-offs at low percentiles, and higher pay-offs at high percentiles. The worse outcomes are worse, and the better outcomes are better, in games of one or two tosses than those of games with twenty or a hundred tosses. That is what we mean by saying a strategy is riskier: low percentiles have worse outcomes, high percentiles have better ones.

In the coin-tossing game, the 50th percentile of all games – whether two tosses, twenty tosses or one thousand tosses – is the same, at 50c. (The single toss is different, because an outcome of 50c – the expected value – is impossible; the 50th percentile is either zero or €1, depending on whether you are a glass-half-empty or glass-half-full type of person). The median (the 50th percentile) is the expected value.

But this equivalence of median and expected value holds only if the probability distributions are symmetric. In coin-tossing, good and bad outcomes are equally likely. On a hundred tosses, you suffer a 10 per cent chance of falling more than 6c short of the expected value of 50c, and also a 10 per cent chance of getting more than 6c above the expected value. Many risk distributions, however, are asymmetric. The tailgating driver mostly gets to his destination a few seconds quicker, but occasionally dies in a car crash. The 10th and higher percentiles of these distributions are all good; the first percentile is terrible. The median outcome – the 50th percentile – is much better than the expected value, since the expected value must factor in the catastrophic losses that occasionally occur.

The outcomes of a lottery are also asymmetric, but in the opposite way. The lottery ticket buyer usually loses, but might, with low probability, win the jackpot. The 50th percentile, even the 80th percentile, of the outcomes of purchasing a single lottery ticket are lousy – you lose your stake – but the 99.9999th percentile makes you a millionaire. Tailgating and lottery tickets have highly asymmetric distributions.

The coin-tossing game has another important property: the most likely outcome is that you win 50c. Even on a game of two tosses, there is a 0.5 probability that you win 50c as against a one in four probability of either nothing or €1. The most likely outcome is called the mode of a distribution and many – though not all – symmetric distributions have this property.

Thus there are three different ways of measuring what statisticians call the central tendency of a distribution. The expected value is the mean of the distribution. The median is the 50th percentile: you are equally likely to do better or worse than the median. And the most likely outcome is the mode. The coin-tossing game has the property that mean, median and mode are all, at 50p, the same.

But this is true only because the coin-tossing game has a particular – though common – structure. The outcomes follow what is called a binomial distribution, which becomes the normal distribution when the number of trials is large. These distributions describe what is likely to be observed if the result of a process is the product of adding up the consequences of a large number of repeated but independent events – there is an obvious affinity between the normal distribution and the outcome of a random walk. Many real-world phenomena are like this, which is why the normal distribution is so widely encountered.

But many are not. And theorems that apply to the outcomes of repeated trials do not help us much in thinking about one-off events to which SEU asks us to apply subjective probabilities. If I had thought the subjective probability of Robb Caledon being nationalised was 0.7, then the (subjective) mode and median of the distribution of outcomes was £1 and the expected value 70p. If my subjective probability had been 0.3, the (subjective) mode and median would be zero and the expected value 30p. If your commute to work is scheduled for forty minutes, forty minutes is probably the mode. The most likely – though perhaps not very likely – outcome is that the train arrives on time. The median will be a bit more – the train arrives late more often than it arrives early. And the expected value will be greater still – the train will sometimes be very late but never very early.

Few people without some training in statistics distinguish carefully between the three measures of 'central tendency': expected value – the average of outcomes; median – the representative outcome; and mode – the most likely outcome. And one of the reasons for the popularity of assuming a normal distribution is that you don't have to, because the normal distribution has the property – unusual even among statistical distributions – that all three are the same. But failure to understand these distinctions is potentially highly misleading in financial markets, where many distributions are asymmetric and discontinuous. There is not much exaggeration in saying that such failure was a major contributor to the global financial crisis.

The method of comparing distributions by comparing different percentiles of outcomes is quite general. One distribution is riskier than another if it yields worse returns at lower percentiles, and better returns at higher percentiles. There will be a crossing point. The lower the crossing point, the more attractive is the riskier distribution. If one distribution has worse outcomes in its lowest five percentiles and better returns at all other percentiles, it is more likely to be acceptable than one for which the crossing point is at the 50th percentile.

A common technique simplifies the comparison of distributions with the aid of a mathematical trick. Many statistical distributions, including the normal distribution, are completely described by two parameters. One parameter is the mean or average, of the distribution – what is the average height of a population? The other is a measure of variability – how many people are over six feet or below five feet? If you know the average and the variability, then you know everything about the normal distribution. If two distributions have the same expected value, then a comparison of a single percentile – any percentile – will be enough to tell you which is riskier.

The usual statistical measure of variability is the variance or standard deviation. The Greek letter sigma is commonly used for the standard deviation. This term has entered popular usage, so that 'a six sigma event' is an event that is, or should be, very improbable. The Sharpe ratio, which is the ratio of expected return (relative to a benchmark) to standard deviation, is widely used by quantitative investors. If the analysts' distribution of returns were normal, or followed sufficiently closely another of the family of common statistical distributions – and if the parameters of these distributions were known – then techniques like value at risk and Sharpe ratios would be extremely valuable. The mathematics of probability, which opens the way to the application of powerful statistical tools, could be applied to the analysis of unique political and economic events, such as the failure of legislation and the future of a shipyard. To see some of the possibilities, let's once more go back to Robb Caledon.

My ship came in

The fate of Robb Caledon was a risk – a known unknown. People sometimes make probability statements about known unknowns, as when they say, 'The probability that Parliament will approve the shipbuilding nationalisation bill is one-half.' Such a statement is called an expression of personal, or subjective, probability.

When I talked about tossing a coin, I used the terms probability and frequency interchangeably. But I can't do that for one-off political events. Someone who makes that statement about the shipbuilding bill is not saying, 'If Parliament considers the bill one hundred times, the bill will be passed on fifty occasions.'

They are making a statement of personal opinion. Or perhaps, in this case, an absence of opinion. It is common to say, 'It's fifty-fifty,' meaning, 'I just don't know.' These expressions sound like statements about probabilities. But can they, should they, be interpreted in this way?

The idea that risk and uncertainty can be handled with the aid of personal probabilities is often called Bayesian, after the Revd Thomas Bayes, an eighteenth-century clergyman who made important contributions to probability theory. Bayesians believe that each of us has a mental probability distribution of likely and unlikely outcomes, which we constantly revise as new information becomes available. Bayesians further believe that the mathematical rules for calculating compound probabilities (and hence statistical distributions) are universal. These rules can be applied to personal probabilities in the same way as they can be applied to frequentist probabilities. There are some obvious difficulties in the use of rules that are based on the observation of repeated events – like tossing a coin – in the interpretation of one-off events – such as shipbuilding nationalisation.

Many people do not find it easy to think probabilistically about what interest rates will be, whether Robb Caledon will be nationalised or what they will be doing in retirement. They ask instead, 'What is going to happen?' A committed Bayesian believes that, however we express our attitudes to risk and uncertainty, personal probabilities govern our decisions. We can discover these buried probabilities by asking questions such as 'How much would you be willing to bet on interest rates being above 5 per cent in twenty years' time?'

Securities markets elicit information by constantly offering such gambles. 'How much would you be willing to pay for a share in Robb Caledon which will pay £1 if the nationalisation bill goes through?' Mr Market asks that question every day when he gives you the chance to buy, or sell, Robb Caledon shares. He asks you to bet on future interest rates every time he quotes a price on a bond.

To make this link from probabilities to market prices, we have to assume that personal probabilities can be used to calculate expected values. If my personal probability that the shipbuilding nationalisation bill would pass was 0.5, and the potential pay-out was 100p per share, my subjective expected value of a purchase was 50p. The implicit rule is to compare the expected value of 50p with the market price of 40p. Since the expected value – given my subjective probability – was above the market price, the stock was a good buy.

While the assertion that 'a fair coin falls heads with probability of one-half' seems to be an objective statement about the world, and can be verified by experiment, personal probabilities are unavoidably subjective. One day the dust will have settled, and Parliament will either have approved the nationalisation bill, or not. Even then no one can say whose subjective judgement, whose personal probability, was right and whose was wrong.

The issue went to the wire. In 2012 the vote on the bill was the dramatic highlight of 'This House', a play by James Graham at London's National Theatre. The House of Commons approved shipbuilding nationalisation by a majority of one, and I duly received the payment of £1 per share. I was pleased with myself, but that doesn't mean my personal probability was right. Nor, if the bill had failed, would that necessarily mean my prior judgement of subjective probability had been wrong. A Bayesian would say that the stockbrokers I consulted had personal probabilities different from mine and that was why they had not recommended the shares.

Does the price of 40p, against a possible pay-off of 100p, mean that 0.4 was the average of everyone's personal probability? No, it doesn't. Many people, like those stockbrokers, attached low personal probabilities to nationalisation – if they had ever thought in this Bayesian way, which is doubtful – and many more people had not considered the matter at all. The price of 40p indicates that the number of people who found the investment attractive was sufficient to hold all the available Robb Caledon shares. Since the shipyard was small, this number did not have to be large (the company never had more than a few hundred shareholders). Only a few people need have personal probabilities in excess of 0.4 to establish a price of 40p for the shares.

Similar reasoning is sometimes used to infer probabilities from market prices. On a Bloomberg screen you can find implied probabilities that the European Central Bank will change interest rates. Commentators sometimes say '"the market" is assuming a 30 per cent chance of an interest rate cut'. But such anthropomorphisation should be viewed here, as everywhere, with caution.

Still, there seems to be a profit opportunity if your subjective probability differs from that of Mr Market. That is what I was exploiting with Robb Caledon. With an expected value of 50p and a share price of 40p, there was an expected profit of 10p. But, just as you will never receive the expected value of 50p when you toss a coin once, the expected value was not what I would receive from my Robb Caledon purchase. I would either have lost 40p or gained 60p. If I had lost, I would not even have had the consolation that if I had bought the share a hundred times, I would almost certainly have made a profit. Coin-tossing is a repeated event. The proposal to nationalise Robb Caledon was unique.

Still, if you always approach one-off risks in this probabilistic manner, while you will lose some and win others, over the long run you will probably come out ahead. That's a good argument, though not a conclusive argument, for the SEU approach. You will need to be sufficiently detached to ride both the swings and the roundabouts with equanimity. But it does not make the Bayesian approach to risk assessment objective or value-free. Frequentist probabilities and subjective probabilities are different. Frequentist probabilities are facts; personal probabilities are opinions. Subjective probabilities are not objectively right or wrong, even with hindsight. The passage of the nationalisation bill did not vindicate my decision to buy. A decision that has a good outcome is not necessarily a good decision, and vice versa. When you can comfortably say to yourself, 'Buying Robb Caledon shares was the right decision even though I lost my entire investment,' you have learned to think probabilistically.

You have also learned why most people – and especially most large organisations – find probabilistic thinking difficult. But you have also learned why individuals who have learned to think probabilistically – such as Buffett and Soros – have an advantage over others whose ability to take risks is constrained because they will be judged by superiors who will certainly exploit the benefit of hindsight. I will elaborate on the benefits of that for the intelligent investor in Chapters 11 and 12.

Diminishing marginal utility

The principle that risky outcomes should be judged by their expected value was one of the earliest notions in probability. Daniel Bernoulli, an eighteenth-century mathematician, who played a major role in developing this theory, quickly identified a difficulty. Even if people who calculated subjective expected values would frequently end up better off, expected values were not what seemed to govern their attitudes to risk. Many people would prefer a 50 per cent chance of winning €1 million to a 10 per cent chance of winning €5 million, and the certainty of €500,000 in cash to either. But the expected value of all of the outcomes is €500,000. The example Bernoulli used to illustrate this problem became known as the 'St Petersburg paradox'.

In the St Petersburg game a coin is tossed repeatedly. If the first toss of the coin is a head, the player receives €1. If the first toss is a tail, the prize is doubled to €2 and the coin is tossed again. If the prize is not won, it is doubled again, and so on until a head appears and the game ends. There is therefore a 50 per cent probability that the game ends with a single throw and the player gains €1. There is a much lower probability of winning €4 on the third toss. Simple mathematics shows that the expected value of the game is infinitely large.

If you think this is not a very realistic game, you should know that two and a half centuries later investment bankers would invent 'payment-in-kind securities', loans on which payment would increase if the quality of the underlying credit deteriorated. In essence, these were St Petersburg games and, like St Petersburg games, not a good idea for either banker or player.

No one will pay more than a few pounds to play Bernoulli's St Petersburg game. Its large expected value depends on multiplying large pay-offs by their small probabilities. The game might run for forty throws, by which time you would be richer than Warren Buffett. But few people seem willing to pay much for that opportunity. The resolution of the St Petersburg paradox that is most widely accepted today was known in Bernoulli's time. Jimmie Savage would articulate the reasoning most clearly, and in a manner that would have great influence on financial economics. The St Petersburg paradox, he suggested, is the result of what economists call 'diminishing marginal utility'. The first million is a lot better than the second million, or at least that is what people think before they've got their first million. By the time you have $50 billion, as Warren does, the prospect of another million is of little consequence. So $50 billion is valued at much less than 50 million times $1,000, and the expected *utility* of the St Petersburg game is correspondingly low even if its expected *value* is high.

People who prefer a sure thing to a gamble with the same expected monetary value – people who prefer €500,000 in cash to a 50 per cent chance of €1 million and who are not impressed by the St Petersburg game – are described as risk-averse. The standard hypothesis is that most people are risk-averse when they invest. They are also risk-averse when they insure – they accept a certain loss in return for giving up the gamble that their house will burn down or that they will have to pay unexpected medical bills. The insurance premium will generally be greater than the expected value of the claims; otherwise the insurance company would be unprofitable. Expected value is relevant to the insurance company, which can use its portfolio of policies to think frequencies rather than subjective probabilities.

Diminishing marginal utility can account for risk aversion. Such risk aversion can be significant only when the amounts you gain or lose are large relative to your wealth. Think of a gamble in which you can win, or lose, €1, and suppose you already have €14,265. If you refuse the bet, you will still have €14,265, while if you accept it you will have either €14,264 or €14,266. Few people would think there was much difference between these outcomes. Fewer still would think, 'I'd much rather see my wealth increase from €14,264 to €14,265 than see it increase from €14,265 to €14,266.' If the amount you are gambling is relatively small, then you should simply assess small bets by reference to their expected value.

This conclusion has major implications for intelligent investors who follow SEU. Since most individual investments will be small relative to your overall portfolio, far less your overall wealth, expected values are usually the right way to deal with risk. That leads to another, and perhaps the most significant, implication of thinking SEU: always look at risk in the context of your portfolio as a whole, rather than its individual elements. Focus on the outcome, not the process. The 'mind your portfolio' principle is fundamental. To see its consequences I'll go back yet again to Robb Caledon.

Mind your portfolio

In 1976 the Labour government promoting the shipbuilding nationalisation bill was struggling and unpopular. Margaret

Thatcher had recently become Conservative leader, and her party was gaining support. If the shipbuilding bill had been lost, the government would have faced a 'no confidence' vote in the House of Commons and might have been forced to call an election, which the Conservatives would probably win. This happened, on a different issue, in 1979, and Thatcher then became Prime Minister.

A political development such as this was the main risk faced by holders of Robb Caledon shares, since a Conservative government would abandon plans to nationalise shipbuilding. While Labour's fall would have been bad news for Robb Caledon, it would have caused delight around the City, and the wider stock market would have risen immediately. Let's suppose that stocks would have been 5 per cent higher as a result of Labour's defeat. And suppose that you had £5,000 to invest.

Consider three possible portfolios:

- put all your money into Robb Caledon;
- put all your money into blue chip shares; or
- buy 250 Robb Caledon shares for £100 and put the rest of your money into blue chips.

Here is the value of your portfolio if the bill is passed, and if the bill fails.

Table 6: **Value of alternative portfolios depending on the fate of the shipbuilding nationalisation bill of 1976 (£)**

	Robb Caledon only	Blue chips only	Mixed portfolio
Government survives	12,500	5,000	5,150
Government falls	0	5,250	5,145

Which portfolio would have been best? With hindsight, of

course, you should have gone for the first, and dived into Robb Caledon's docks. But it is easy to be a successful investor with hindsight. If you felt sure the Labour government would fall, you should have gone for the portfolio of blue chips. The first portfolio is extremely risky, suitable only for the most hardened speculator. The paradox is that the least risky portfolio is not the second, which focuses on safe assets, but the third, which includes a small holding of Robb Caledon shares.

In this example, adding a small investment in a very risky asset reduces the overall risk of the portfolio. You are sure to end up with around £5,150. The risk associated with a portfolio is not measured by adding up the risks of each individual element. A combination of risks may be less risky in whole than in part.

I thought Robb Caledon was an interesting speculation for two reasons. My personal probability that the bill would pass was a good deal higher than Mr Market's. How much higher it would have had to be to have made the purchase worthwhile would seem to depend on how risk-averse I was. But I had also made the kind of calculation illustrated in Table 6. All three portfolios would have had the same expected value if the probability that the bill would be passed were slightly more than 0.4. The 'mind your portfolio' principle transforms the way you approach this problem. If I had bought some blue chips, then however risk-averse I was, Robb Caledon would have been worth buying because its shares would go down when other shares would go up and vice versa. An asset with this property is called a hedge, and adding a hedge to a portfolio reduces overall portfolio risk, even if the hedge is, in itself, a speculative investment – like Robb Caledon. So the shipyard was doubly attractive.

Assets don't have to be hedges to reduce risk. It is sufficient that individual risks are not perfectly correlated with each other. If you bet €1 on a single toss of a coin, you win €1 or zero: if you bet 50c on each of two different throws, you win 50c half the time: if you bet 1c on each of a hundred throws, what you will win, as Table 5 shows, will be very close to 50c. This is the power of diversification. A small share in a large number of independent risks is much more certain than the outcome of any of the risks taken separately.

Hedging is the purchase of assets whose returns are negatively related to the returns on assets you already own. Diversification spreads risks across many securities whose individual risks – like the outcome of the toss of a coin – are unrelated to each other. The risk and reward of a portfolio, and the relationship between them, are determined not just by expected values and the variability of return. The portfolio risk also depends on the extent to which returns from different assets are related to each other. A risk-averse individual can build a low-risk portfolio from a collection of risky assets if the risky assets are appropriately selected. It is impossible to overstate the importance of this idea for intelligent investment.

The variability of a statistical distribution can be measured by its variance or standard deviation. A similar measure – called 'covariance' or 'correlation' – describes the relationship between the variability of two different distributions. Similar assets – if one rises in value, the other is likely to rise in value – have a high covariance. Hedges display a negative covariance. Wholly unrelated variables have a covariance of zero. In a coin-tossing game the covariance between the outcomes of successive trials is zero because successive trials are independent. The probability that the next toss is a head is not affected by whether the last was a head or a tail, although many people, imbued with a folk wisdom they call 'the law of averages', find this hard to believe.

What does it mean to say that the returns from investments are independent of each other? Suppose one company is drilling for oil in Kazakhstan and another has entered a new drug in clinical trials. These outcomes are independent – the dry hole in Kazakhstan does not influence the drug trial in the United States. The risks that a shareholder loses because an exploration does not find oil or that a drug trial fails are called specific risks, because their outcome is determined by factors that are specific to the company itself. However, the returns to shareholders in Exxon and in Novartis are probably correlated. There is no direct connection between oil companies and pharmaceutical companies. But both businesses depend on economic prospects in the same countries, and the share prices of both companies are influenced by the same vagaries of market sentiment. These common risks, which affect all businesses, are described as 'market risk'.

The relationship between the risk on an individual share and the market risk of a portfolio that follows the market as a whole is described by the parameter *beta*. Mathematically, *beta* is computed from a regression equation that estimates the effect of market movements on the security in question. A security will have a *beta* of one if a 1 per cent market movement will change its price by 1 per cent.

A share may have a low *beta* for one or both of two distinct reasons. Shares will have low *betas* if their risks are unrelated to the overall risk of the market. The prices of shares whose returns are derived from oil wells in Kazakhstan, or whose fortunes depend on the results of clinical trials, will have little correlation with the share prices of Apple and Exxon Mobil. A share will also have a low *beta* if, although its returns are related to overall market risk, the company's activities are not very volatile.

Companies such as food retailers or utilities, whose sales will be little affected by economic recession, have low *betas*. Conversely, shares whose performance is very sensitive to the general economic cycle – producers of steel or basic chemicals – might have *betas* that are greater than one. An index, which by definition yields the average return on the market, will have a *beta* of one. For this reason, it is common to call the average return on that asset class 'the *beta*' of an asset class.

'*Alpha*' is then a measure of the extent to which a fund manager beats that average return, adjusted for the *beta* of the portfolio

– the outperformance after allowing for risk. Lovers of the Greek alphabet will find that derivatives markets extend the lexicon to *gamma*, *delta* and beyond. But *beta* is key to the capital asset pricing model, which is the most influential economic theory in modern investment. It is therefore important to understand its structure, its effect on investment thinking and practice – and its limitations.

The capital asset pricing model

Risk-averse investors will need to earn a premium over the yield on a safe benchmark such as bunds or indexed government stock if they are to buy less secure assets. The greater the risk, the greater the premium. But what is the relevant meaning of risk?

At the beginning of this chapter I described the gulf of incomprehension that emerged when economists explained to business people their approach to risk. The latter group did not recognise any operational value to the distinction between specific and market risk that the economists believed was so important. Most people, including those business people, would describe an investment like Robb Caledon as extremely risky. They would say the same of drilling for oil in Kazakhstan, or a clinical trial for a new drug or accepting a fixed-price contract to develop new defence technology. They would think of a big holding in Nestlé or Exxon Mobil, by contrast, as safe but boring.

The 'mind your portfolio' principle says that this view gets matters the wrong way round. Robb Caledon and the clinical trial are not really speculative, because the risk can be spread and diversified. So long as the risk of any of these individual stocks is only a small part of your portfolio you can employ diversification to sleep soundly at night. Conversely, shares in Nestlé and Exxon Mobil are risky because investors cannot hedge or diversify them much – the returns from these investments are likely to be broadly in line with those of the market. Suppose everyone thought this way. Suppose everyone was a 'rational' investor, motivated by the principles of SEU. Then the general opinion would be that shares with specific risks were not very risky but that shares with market risk were. That general opinion, like all general opinions, would be 'in the price'. The implication is that what appear to be risky securities – shares in Robb Caledon or oil exploration in Kazakhstan – would offer lower yields than boring blue chips because the speculative shares have specific risks while the blue chips suffer market risks. This idea is the basis of the CAPM that won the Nobel Prize for its inventor, Bill Sharpe (of the Sharpe ratio). In the CAPM, risk and reward are determined by the *beta* of a security. Robb Caledon had a *beta* around zero, because the risk was entirely specific (the company may even have had a negative *beta*, because its share price might have gone up when the market went down, and vice versa). Such an investment is almost as good as a risk-free asset and will therefore yield very little more than a risk-free asset. An asset with a *beta* of one will have the same expected return as the market as a whole, and investors will demand a higher return still for an asset with a *beta* above one. In principle, this approach can be applied to all assets, not just shares. You can calculate *betas* for different kinds of property and for other asset classes. Commercial risk measurement services offer quantitatively minded investors estimates of *beta* for the whole range of securities they might buy.

There is another customer base for these risk measurement services. The cost of equity capital to a firm is derived from the long-run expected rate of return on its shares. The expected return on equity is the combination of the *beta* of the individual firm and the equity risk premium for the market. For adherents of the CAPM this expected return is the return required by the market and, therefore, the basis of the cost of capital estimates needed for the DCF appraisal of business investment.

Companies such as Robb Caledon, or a small oil exploration company, or a pharmaceutical business whose future depends on the outcome of a current clinical trial, should have a low cost of capital because the risk of investment in them, although large, is perfectly diversifiable. Companies such as Nestlé or Exxon Mobil, with returns likely to be more in line with the overall market, should have a higher cost of capital. This is the argument that the government economists were presenting to the defence contractors, who did not believe it.

And empirical evidence is not very favourable to the economists. The CAPM follows directly from the notion that people both should, and do, follow SEU. It predicts that the returns on different securities will be determined by two factors: the overall return on the market and the *beta* appropriate to that security. There are problems with both parts of this claim. SEU explains the risk premium in terms of diminishing marginal utility. Investors do not judge risky ventures at their expected value because they value the second million of their wealth less highly than the first. But this factor doesn't seem to be nearly large enough to account for the size of the historic equity premium – the difference between the yield on shares and the yield on safe assets. Models based on risk aversion from diminishing marginal utility struggle to explain why the risks of equity investment would, in an SEU framework, justify a risk premium as high as 1 per cent.

The data in Chapter 2 suggested that over the last twenty years the difference in return between safe assets and shares has been around 5 per cent. The longer-term analyses published by Credit Suisse support figures of this magnitude with analysis from many markets over periods as long as a century. The inexplicably large difference between the predictions of SEU-based models and the observed equity premium is called the 'equity premium paradox'.

The second component of the CAPM is the use of *beta* to explain relative returns on different assets. The most exhaustive empirical study of the issue, by Eugene Fama and Kenneth French, concluded that estimates of *beta* contributed nothing to an explanation of the historic pattern of returns. These results have been disputed, but have not really been shaken.

Perhaps my business people, shaking their heads around the table, gave the answer. The CAPM describes what the world would be like if everyone behaved according to the principles of SEU. But its counterintuitive predictions suggest a world in which people don't behave that way. If the cost of capital were significantly lower for firms such as defence contractors, speculative oil drillers or small drugs companies, than for businesses with mainstream activities that followed closely the business cycle of major economies, then you might expect that people who had developed successful corporate careers would have noticed. I am sure those at that table were not dissimulating when they said that they had not. And nor had their bankers.

As SEU took hold in the 1950s, a French economist, Maurice Allais, developed a critique. Allais gave examples of common decisions that seemed to violate the principles of SEU (the Allais paradoxes). He wrote in French (no major economics journal would accept such an article today) and hinted that the whole exercise was an American plot. Although the power of his analysis created continuing nagging doubt, he failed to shake the consensus. Two decades later, two psychologists, Danny Kahneman and Amos Tversky, would undertake experiments in which they offered their subjects choices among risks – they found frequent examples of behaviour inconsistent with SEU. All these men would eventually receive the Nobel Prize for founding the subject now known as behavioural finance or behavioural economics. The motivation for behavioural finance is recognition that many people don't behave as SEU would seem to require.

Many real-life investors don't think probabilities, don't mind their portfolio and, above all, don't remain detached. They engage with the process, instead of focusing cold-bloodedly on the outcome. They look at their smartphones several times a day, fixated by screens and clients. They feel upset when shares they own go down (even if you are Warren Buffett, your shares will fall in value on almost half of all the days you own them). Some people need a premium to contemplate the risk of loss at all, even before they take specific account of what those losses might be.

SEU and CAPM suggest you need a premium much less than 5 per cent to compensate you for equity risks. The evidence suggests you will nevertheless earn that 5 per cent, because other investors, who don't think the SEU way, are wary of such investments. The CAPM says you have to pay a price for diversifying your portfolio. The empirical evidence says you probably don't.

SEU and CAPM are theories that are illuminating but, as explanations of actual behaviour in financial markets, are not true. They are illuminating, in part, because the investment strategies they suggest are more profitable if others don't adopt them. The equity premium paradox works in your favour if you think SEU and others don't. As with EMH, the intelligent investor can gain by understanding these theories, but will lose by believing them. That is why this chapter is the longest and most complicated, but also the most potentially rewarding, in this book.

8

A World of Unknowns

Unknown unknowns

There were no derivatives markets in the savannahs, where our ancestors developed modern brains. Casinos (in which the highest value counters were the blue chips) came into being only at a late stage of evolution, although an early stage of history. Hunters gambled in the evenings around the campfire and used animal bones as primitive dice. Human lives were always full of uncertainties, but pure risks – the well-defined problems found in games of chance that can be described using an approach to probabilities based on frequency of outcomes – were invented for popular amusement.

The claim made for SEU is that this calculus of probabilities derived from the gaming room can be applied to one-off events, such as the progress of shipbuilding nationalisation, as well as to repeated events, such as tossing a coin. Here is Milton Friedman, doyen of the Chicago economists who were founding the theory of finance, in 1976 (not entirely coincidentally, the year in which I bought those Robb Caledon shares):

In his seminal work, Frank Knight drew a sharp distinction between risk, as referring to events subject to a known or knowable probability distribution, and uncertainty, as referring to events for which it was not possible to specify numerical probabilities. I have not referred to this distinction because I do not believe it is valid. I follow L. J. Savage in his view of personal probability, which denies any valid distinction along these lines. We may treat people as if they assigned numerical probabilities to every conceivable event.

The fate of Robb Caledon was a risk – a known unknown. Either Robb Caledon would be nationalised or it would not. Its shares would be worth either 100p or nothing. Some issues in financial markets are of this kind. Interest rate risk and credit risk seem to be known unknowns. But there are also many uncertainties, unknown unknowns – events that cannot be described sensibly with probabilities, because we do not know what these events might be.

SEU may work well for 'known unknowns'. If all potential states of the world are known (even if the one that will materialise is not), if the outcome of a gamble will be clearly and definitely recorded, if the processes that determine that outcome can be treated as random, then SEU is a guide to action. The gamble on Robb Caledon had some of these characteristics. There seemed only two possible outcomes; the time-scale was short and defined; the consequences of each appeared clear. But this case was exceptional. I have difficulty in thinking of another in my investment lifetime in which the issues were posed so sharply.

And even then there was an important difference between the fate of Robb Caledon and the toss of a coin or throw of a dice; the result of the vote on shipbuilding nationalisation was no random event. The outcome would be the result of a political process – the complexity of that process well illustrated in Graham's play – and any assessment of the likely result was properly a matter of expert judgement.

When President Obama held the crucial meeting to determine whether to go ahead with the raid that killed Osama bin

Laden, he 'asked for confidence that bin Laden was in the Abbottabad compound'. 'The estimates ranged from 10 per cent to 95 per cent certainty.' Obama described his reaction: 'I'm accustomed to people offering me probabilities. In this situation, what you started getting was probabilities that disguised uncertainty as opposed to actually providing you with more useful information.' As discussion continued, the President interrupted. 'This is fifty-fifty. Look, guys, this is a flip of the coin. I can't base this decision on the notion that we have any greater certainty than that.'

When Obama said 'this is fifty-fifty', he did not mean that he thought the probability that bin Laden was in the compound was 0.5; still less was one of the most important decisions of his presidency based on 'a flip of the coin'. He was using these phrases, as people often do, to describe radical uncertainty. The mission was subject to known and unknown unknowns – the known unknown of whether bin Laden was or was not in the compound, the unknown unknowns which made the expedition by the SEALs so hazardous. Obama, and his advisers, simply did not know, and, as he recognised, the probabilistic statements of his advisers 'disguised uncertainty as opposed to actually providing you with more useful information'.

Obama recognised the limited value of probabilistic statements even in relation to 'known unknowns'. Keynes went further. Between completion of his work on probability and its publication the great economist had become famous for his polemical denunciation of the Versailles Treaty that ended the First World War. In a celebrated passage he described the confidence of the pre-war mood. The English upper-middle class viewed its comfortable, stable environment as a permanent condition. If that world was transformed by the war that followed, the world of the central European middle class was shattered. Wealthy families, whose lifestyle had seemed secure, lost everything in the default of Russian bonds, as a result of hyperinflation in Germany and central Europe, and from the expropriation of Jewish property. As parents waved goodbye to sons who went enthusiastically to war in 1914, they had no conception of what the future held in store. They fell victim to unknown unknowns – events that cannot be sensibly described with probabilities, because we do not know what these events might be.

The future has not become any more certain. The collapse of the Twin Towers was a major event for financial markets, as for international politics. No one, on 10 September 2001, could sensibly have framed or answered the question 'What is the probability that the World Trade Center will be destroyed tomorrow by a terrorist attack?' Keynes claimed that there could be no scientific basis for an assessment of probabilities in the face of such radical uncertainty. The right response to the question 'What will interest rates be in twenty years' time?' was and is 'We simply do not know.' A question about the level of interest rates appears one that might be answered probabilistically. But Keynes's confession of radical uncertainty even in that connection was oddly prescient. A holder of British government bonds in 1941 could not have been certain whether he would be repaid in sterling, in Reichsmarks or at all.*

Investors are vulnerable to defined, identifiable risks – interest rate risk, momentum and mean reversion in share prices. But investors are also vulnerable to fundamental uncertainty. Questions like 'What is the future of the Middle East?' 'What will be the economic consequences of China's rise?' or 'How will economic and political systems deal with climate change?' are open-ended. We cannot fully describe the range of outcomes, and decades from now there will still be disagreement over what the outcomes proved to be. And the question President Obama

---

* The description of Obama's decision-making is based on the accounts of Mark Bowden described by John A. Gans, *The Atlantic* (10 October 2012), and Mark Bowden, *The Finish* (Atlantic Books, 2012).

faced was not 'Is bin Laden in the compound?' but 'Should I order the raid, and what will the consequences be?'

We may attempt to transform these open-ended questions into more narrowly defined ones such as 'Will Bashar al-Assad still be in power in 2018?' or 'What will be China's GDP, or the average world temperature, in 2025?' But even if it were possible to make compelling, probabilistically expressed prognostications on these questions – and it is not – the numbers would not tell people what they really want to know. Imagine a time traveller from the nineteenth century asking us what the world we live in is like. They would not understand enough about that world to be able to frame sensible questions. We suffer not just from ignorance of the future but from a limited capacity to imagine what the future might be. People who are today concerned about conflict in the Middle East, China's rise or climate change would not have been worrying about these issues twenty years ago. They would have been worrying about the Cold War, Japan's economic pre-eminence and the effects of AIDS.

These earlier uncertainties have largely been resolved, and in ways that few people expected. But the key point is not that we mostly fail to anticipate the answers, but, rather, that we mostly fail to anticipate the relevant questions. No one predicted the catastrophes of the twentieth century – the stalemate of the First World War, the influenza pandemic, the murder of millions of people by deranged dictators.

The same was true of transforming political and economic developments – the rise and fall of Communism in Russia, decolonisation, the development of information technology, the changed role of women in society. Such failure of imagination is inevitable. If you could anticipate the functions and uses of the personal computer, you would already have taken the main steps towards inventing it. To describe a future political movement or economic theory or line of philosophical thought is to bring it into existence.

Many great geopolitical events are unknown unknowns – the First World War, the rise of Hitler, the attack on the Twin Towers. But unknown unknowns are also part of everyday life. Your journey home from work lends itself to description in frequentist terms. You have a rough mental probability distribution of outcomes in your mind, reflecting the schedule and reliability of trains, the variability of traffic conditions. But the outcome is also determined by events. You meet a long-lost acquaintance; you see an item in a shop window that attracts your attention; you slip on the pavement. You did not anticipate such events because you had not thought about them, and could not sensibly have attached a probability to them if you had.

More of these events will disrupt your journey than will accelerate it, which is why your estimate of journey length will be below its expected value. Most people think of risk as an adverse event rather than a distribution about a mean (this was another source of the gap of comprehension at my meeting between the business people and the economists). For good reasons, our thinking about an uncertain world is partly probabilistic, partly not.

In this light, consider again the risk appraisal tools described in Chapter 7, which looked at the outcomes associated with various percentiles of the frequency distribution of outcomes. Your routine experience of how long it takes you to get home from work is likely to be described well by a standard statistical distribution. But the same is not true of experiences that are non-routine: the occasional emergencies, the accidents, the days on which events at work make it impossible to go home at all.

These events are rare, but the extremes of the frequency distribution of outcomes are the product of these out-of-the-ordinary events. When the credit crunch began in August 2007, David Viniar, chief financial officer of Goldman Sachs, told news reporters that his firm had experienced a 25-sigma event several days in a row. A 25-sigma event is one with a probability so low that the noughts required to express the probability would occupy several lines of this page. Goldman Sachs could not expect to encounter a 25-sigma event on even one day if it had existed for the entire history of the universe. Of course, no 25-sigma outcome had happened. What had happened, and what Viniar perhaps intended to say, was that events had occurred which were not properly considered in Goldman Sachs's risk models.

If a coin comes up heads twenty times in a row, you should consider the possibility that the coin is biased before you conclude that the very low probability that this is the result of twenty tosses of a fair coin has materialised. The limits of probabilistic reasoning are set by the limitations of the models on which they are based, and any model is an abstraction from a more complex context. The actual distribution of outcomes is the product of a combination of the risks that the model describes and the uncertainties associated with the applicability of the model. That is the fundamental reason why a model can often be illuminating but will almost never be true. We use different tools in the face of uncertainty. Most often, we tell stories.

Narratives and patterns

If I ask people what they think is going to happen, they will usually respond with a story rather than a probability distribution. Thinking probabilities does not come easily to the human mind. Telling stories and constructing narratives do. The stockbrokers I called in 1976 could not separate in their minds the question of whether shipbuilding *would* be nationalised from the question of whether shipbuilding *ought to* be nationalised. They told a story about what they thought would happen, heavily influenced by what they thought should happen. They pontificated about the market and complained about the government, as old-fashioned stockbrokers were prone to do.

We weave narratives and fit events and expectations into them. There is evidence of halo effects – if we like something or someone, we interpret everything we know about them favourably – and of confirmation bias – people interpret new evidence in a manner consistent with the view they have already formed. The people who extended credit to subprime borrowers in the belief that house prices always went up, like the people who planned the Iraq war and thought it unnecessary to plan for the aftermath because troops would be greeted with garlands of flowers, were victims of halo effect and confirmation bias. Expectations had been confused with hopes and dreams.

Narratives and probabilistic thinking fit uncomfortably together because thinking probabilistically means thinking, at the same time, of two incompatible events – that Robb Caledon will go bankrupt, that Robb Caledon will be nationalised. It might have made sense to buy Robb Caledon shares even if you thought the bill was likely to fail. The issue for the probabilistic thinker was whether the expected value was above the market price. It may be appropriate to hold indexed bonds even if you do not think that inflation will rise, if you believe – and you should – that inflation *might* rise.

Many people find it hard to reason in these ways. Scott Fitzgerald wrote, 'The test of a first-rate intelligence is the ability to hold two opposing ideas in mind at the same time and still retain the ability to function.' And thinking probabilistically requires that capacity: Robb Caledon will be nationalised, Robb Caledon will not be nationalised. In fact, thinking systematically about uncertainty requires that capacity.

The most systematic way of trying to handle incompatible futures is scenario planning, a technique pioneered by Shell and widely used in business. Scenario planning demands multiple narratives. Work out two, three or four internally consistent projections of the future, and plan for what you might do in each. But my experience is that if you try to talk about the future in scenarios you will always be approached by someone who asks, 'So what do you really think is going to happen?' They fail to understand that none of these scenarios will happen – the scenario is only a template for systematising our thought. For a highly intelligent decision-maker such as President Obama, or John F. Kennedy responding to the Cuban missile crisis, working through various scenarios with his advisers was an indispensable prelude to action.

Our ability to tell stories is a valuable asset, the means by which we make sense of disconnected information. But in the financial world this narrative skill often misleads. Bachelier and Samuelson discovered that, in securities markets, purposive and directed behaviour can produce outcomes with the appearance, and mathematical properties, of randomness. But we resist randomness. The search for patterns in randomly generated data warms the heart, as it hurts the wallet.

Mirages, systems and hot hands

Our abilities in pattern detection often lead us to mirages in the desert of data. We observe systematic relationships that do not exist, or attribute statistical noise to imagined underlying causes. Such confusions help chartists stay in business. Popular discussion, based on a poor understanding of probability, tells of a 'law of averages' – if there has been a run of heads, the next toss must be a tail. But successive trials are independent, and the probability of head or tail remains at 50 per cent. There is no law of averages, but there are many random walks. Chaos and randomness are rare in nature but common in financial markets.

Hopeful investors and tipsters trail through historical series to find systems that would, in the past, have yielded substantial profits. There will always be some, but that doesn't mean that these systems will be profitable in any, far less all, future periods.

Many 'anomalies' in efficient markets disappear when they have been identified. This would be the case even if it were not also true that the very process of trading on the anomaly reduces or removes its profitability. The 'hot hand' – an outstanding series of scores by a player for whom it seems every ball ends in the net – is a well-reported phenomenon. Careful statistical analysis of sporting records suggests that there is not much evidence for 'the hot hand'. Sequences of extraordinary performance are no more frequent than would be expected from chance alone. But long sequences of brilliant scores (or mistakes) stick in the mind.

Are there investment managers with the 'hot hand'? Even if investment returns were the result of pure chance, some managers would seem to have a record of success. But if their returns are the result of chance, you cannot expect that these managers will perform any better in future than anyone else. And mostly they don't. Table 7 is a representative illustration of recent results, based on data compiled by S&P Dow Jones. If you are looking for a manager who will perform well over the next three years, any manager who has been in the top three quartiles is more or less equally likely to do well – or badly. Really badly performing funds, however, tend to remain really badly performing funds. Perhaps this consistently poor performance is the continuing effect of high charges and turnover; perhaps incompetence is more persistent than skill.

Table 7: **Percentage of US mutual funds in each performance quartile, 2009–12, which subsequently achieved above-median performance in 2012–15**

Quartile	1st	2nd	3rd	4th
	58	56	53	30

Source: S&P Dow Jones ('Persistence Scorecard', June 2015)

Be warned, however, that funds which perform in the top

quartile in one three-year period are more than averagely likely to be in the bottom quartile in the succeeding three-year period. Probably this is because closet-indexed funds, which differ little in composition from their benchmarks, are not likely to be either top or bottom performers. The funds that shoot the lights out are specialist funds in what prove to be fashionable sectors, or idiosyncratic managers who hit it lucky. Even if there were no long-run mean reversion, such funds would stand a fair chance of being laggards (as well as leaders) in any three-year period.

In assessing all data of this kind, it is necessary to beware of 'survivor bias'. High-performing funds are more likely to continue in existence than poorly performing funds, which are often wound up or merged into more successful funds, so that the funds whose historic performance we can observe are better than average. But even without taking account of this effect, it is apparent that you will improve your chance of an above-average performance very little by selecting a fund that has done well in the past.

There are a very few fund managers, like Buffett, whose record of outperformance is so persistent, and continues long after it has been widely identified, that the evidence of competence over chance seems irrefutable. But the hot hand is frequently – and mistakenly – detected when what we see is the result of picking dimes in front of a steamroller. This exercise may be more formally described as an asymmetric distribution that produces frequent small gains punctuated by occasional very large losses. I call these Taleb distributions, or tailgating strategies, after a book in which Nassim Nicholas Taleb offers many illustrations (Taleb, 2001). As noted earlier, tailgating drivers save a few seconds on most trips. Occasionally, you see their smashed cars on the side of the road. Participants dissociate the infrequent failures from the frequent successes. The early arrival is the result of skilful driving; the crash is caused by bad luck. The drivers' judgement is vindicated by their success so far.

The 'carry trade' is a Taleb process in financial markets. Interest rates vary across classes of borrower and across currencies. Riskier borrowers pay higher interest rates. If markets price credit risk correctly, then the premium from the higher interest rate will equal the expected value of the losses from default. For example, if a certain type of borrower will fail to repay with a frequency of 2 per cent per year, then a bank with a portfolio of such loans will break even if it realises interest rates 2 per cent higher than those charged to prime borrowers.

But the distribution of gains and losses is not symmetric. Most borrowers meet the principal and interest on loans as they fall due, and the lender collects, year in, year out, the 2 per cent premium. But when the loan fails, the loss is usually the full amount outstanding. As with the tailgating driver, lenders win most of the time on risky loans, but when they lose, they lose big-time. And when the credit bubble burst in 2007–8, they did just that. In Mr Viniar's (erroneous) description, they experienced 25-standard-deviation events several days in a row. In 2008 the steamroller ran over them.

Still, like the tailgating driver, people who collect these regular profits congratulate themselves on their prowess, win the admiration of their bosses and appear to justify both their own bonuses and those of their superiors. Beneficiaries of Taleb distributions leave their more cautious competitors behind, so a process of rivalry forces others to follow, and to suppress any private doubts. From time to time accidents happen. The losses are large, described as unpredictable, unanticipated, exceptional. One-time heroes are fired. The process begins again. The same financial follies are repeated.

You may wonder, as you view the world of business and finance, why many positions in large corporations are filled by people of apparently modest talent; find it inexplicable that dealers with so little knowledge or skill are applauded for their trading success; be surprised at the stupidity of drivers who take large risks for seemingly inconsequential gains. The answer to all of these paradoxes is the same: the people you see are on the upside of their Taleb distribution (and may remain there until they retire).

Perhaps survivor bias is part of the resolution of the equity premium paradox. I'm writing this book about investing in shares and real estate, not about how to invest in Chinese bonds or South American utilities, both of which were popular choices a century ago. The markets from which we draw our experience are the markets that have performed well. There were no books written in the 1920s on investment in Russia, but, if there had been, they would have had to acknowledge that recent performance did not justify an investment.

Sceptics and heretics sometimes observed that paintings of the devout who had survived tempests and floods after praying for salvation were not persuasive, because there were no paintings of the devout who had drowned after praying for salvation. Many heroes of the financial world are immortalised for similar reasons, and the many books about their successful investment strategies resemble those paintings of the devout.

As with managers, so with asset categories. Markets show short-term positive serial price correlation but long-term negative serial price correlation. So don't be tempted by advertisements displaying how much money has been made recently in housing or commodities (by other people) – that is more likely to be a signal to sell than a signal to buy. Assets that have recently done badly deserve attention – but not indiscriminate attention. The objective is always to exploit negative market sentiment to buy cheaply. Detect regression towards the mean; correct for survivor bias; beware data mining.

Models and their limits

Models are an indispensable part of modern finance, and all banks and fund managers use them. The professionalism and sophistication of models and modellers have increased steadily. Anyone equipped with school mathematics can do a discounted cash flow (DCF) calculation. The Markowitz model of portfolio selection, the basis of the CAPM, needs more complex mathematics. But even if Milton Friedman worried that Markowitz's work was outside the scope of the economics of the time, the mathematical techniques are quite simple (and today well within that scope). The Black–Scholes model of option pricing, introduced in the 1970s, is both dynamic and stochastic (it involves differential equations and probability distributions).

These newer models are not rocket science (though they are often called such) but do require university-level training in maths or a maths-based subject. Today an understanding of the frontiers of finance theory demands an advanced degree in maths or physics. Because the financial services sector is very profitable, financial institutions offer large salaries to able mathematicians, but the executives to whom they ultimately report have little knowledge of what these employees do.

You don't have to understand what is under the bonnet of a car to drive it, and similarly you can be a competent manager of a pharmaceutical company or an electronics business without deep familiarity with the underlying chemical or physical characteristics of the product. But you cannot drive a car if you don't understand what a car does, and you cannot organise the marketing, manufacture or distribution of a product if you don't understand what the product can do – and what it can't do.

Senior people in the financial sector – bank executives or fund managers – are not themselves able to build the models on which these activities depend. That is not the problem. The problem is that the techniques are so far outside their comprehension that they do not understand the limitations of the models. While professing scepticism, they take too seriously the conclusions that models generate. I'll call their attitude cynical naïveté. Executives seek 99 per cent certainties from their risk management systems without appreciating that in an uncertain world there are never 99 per cent certainties. This was Mr Viniar's error. Ninety-nine per cent probabilities are derived from models whose applicability is never 100 per cent certain (and that applicability is rarely measurable). The first percentile in the distribution of outcomes is typically generated by events that were not incorporated into the structure of the model.

The attempt in Chapter 6 to apply DCF calculations to asset valuation illustrated a recurrent problem for all models in business and finance. Not only did we not know the numbers that the model required, but the outcome was very sensitive to the assumptions made in entering these numbers. This ignorance leads all too often to bogus quantification. People make up numbers they cannot know to derive supposedly scientific answers to questions whose answers are fundamentally unknowable.

If you have a well-trained financial adviser – one with a financial planning qualification or, better still, a CFA certification – then he or she will very likely build a model of your portfolio in the Markowitz tradition, emphasising the variance and covariances of different assets. That is what financial advisers are taught to do. Risk assessment models in large financial institutions have a similar structure.

In line with the principles of SEU and CAPM these models have three critical inputs:

- What is the expected return on each asset you hold?
- What will be the volatility of that expected return?
- What will be the correlation between the volatility of the return on a particular asset and the volatility of your portfolio as a whole?

But neither you nor your adviser knows, or can know, the answer to these questions.

The difficulties fall into two main groups:

- The assumptions made about the statistical distributions that link the data to the model.
- The reliance on history for that data.

I'll take each of these issues in turn. A common assumption is that short-term movements in securities prices can be described through a normal distribution. If we look at day-to-day movements in share prices, it appears that the normal distribution fits them quite well. But there is a problem of 'fat tails' – there are many more extreme events, especially downside events, than these statistical distributions would permit. If share price movements fitted the normal distribution, it is improbable that a market fall such as that of the US market on 19 October 1987 – a 20-sigma event – would occur even once in the entire history of the universe. But when several such 'once in a blue moon' incidents happen in the course of a few years – as indeed occurred in the last decade – it is time to rethink one's model.

Fat tails are a particularly troubling problem for people who are modelling risk in financial markets, because they suggest that these models fail in precisely the extreme situations in which they are most needed. Although the commonest reaction to the problem of fat tails is to note the problem and ignore it, there are two main strategies that attempt to deal with the issue. One approach involves *ad hoc* modification to make the results of classical statistical distributions correspond better to reality. Examples are generalised autoregressive conditional heteroscedasticity (don't ask) and a technique more attractively labelled 'robust statistics'. These approaches continue to assume that there is some correct description of the world enabling the properties of its prospective behaviour to be deduced from historical information – that we can find models that are not just illuminating but true, that we deal with risks not uncertainties.

An alternative, perhaps more interesting, critique developed by the mathematician Benoit Mandelbrot, rejects the assumptions of classical statistics altogether. Mandelbrot looked at charts of security prices and saw not a random walk but a beautiful process known as 'fractals'. You encounter fractal geometry when you look at a snowflake through a microscope and discover that, whatever magnification you set, the picture you see is the same.

Distributions that follow fractal processes show altogether different properties from those of classical statistics, with fatter tails, and average outcomes in which extreme events play a much larger role. The physical analogies are not the diffuse movements of solids in solution described by Brownian motion, but earthquakes and avalanches – constant small slips, often imperceptible, punctuated by large shifts. Those analogies correspond to many people's experience of financial markets.

Whether you use the distributions of classical statistics, or the different mathematical structures of Mandelbrot's approach, the information you must use to build a model comes from data on what these returns have been, and how they varied, in the past. For good reasons – this historical record is the only objective information available. Such figures may not be a good guide to the future. Investment allocation models based on recent experience will probably suggest a high proportion in equities. That is because the returns from equities have in the immediate past been more than sufficient to compensate for their volatility. You may also be encouraged by asset allocation advisers to invest more in alternative assets. Alternative assets have similarly yielded high returns that were not strongly correlated, on a year-by-year basis, with other investment classes. But the model tells you these things only because someone has already told these things to the model.

No model can tell you what expected future returns on different asset classes, or the future correlation between these returns, will be. Robb Caledon was a hedge, whose price would move in the opposite direction to the main UK indices. But you would not have learned that by studying past covariances. Indeed, you would have found the opposite. Stocks subject to political risk tended to have high *betas*, moving with the general market by often violent amounts.

Only the peculiar circumstances of 1976, in which the government proposed to nationalise the company for more than it was worth, gave that share its particular risk profile. If broad economic conditions had improved, lifting the price of most stocks, there would probably have been little impact, in either direction, on the share price of the shipyard. Neither in the past nor in the present was there any stable correlation, positive or negative, between Robb Caledon and the general market.

Such observations illustrate why historic measures of *beta* have little value. Students of statistics are introduced to the alleged correlation between the stork population and the birth rate. The example illustrates that correlation does not imply causation. Births are a function of population, and dense populations attract storks. But almost all correlations between security prices have the property that gives rise to the stork fallacy. The correlation is the result of some common underlying factor that influences both variables rather than the product of a direct causal relationship between them. Since correlation and causation are not the same, only understanding the underlying causal mechanism can make it possible to know whether a correlation will, or will not, persist in any particular time period. The correlation of stork population and birth rate would continue to hold if new families moved into the neighbourhood, but would not hold if illness or a predator struck the storks. One relationship between Robb Caledon's share price and general market movements held under a Conservative government, and a different one held under a Labour government. Only information outside statistical analysis can tell us that.

The antidote to errors of data interpretation is general knowledge, what many people call common sense: the disparate facts about the world that we apprehend but do not articulate systematically, and which inform every decision we make. Keynes was a successful investor, as well as a man who achieved success in many other fields, in part because he brought to all his activities a range of experience and knowledge of both ideas and affairs probably unparalleled in the twentieth century.

The requirement for general knowledge drawn from outside the model does not make the model useless. A model that makes assumptions about correlations between variables – even arbitrary ones – can illustrate ways in which careful diversification can improve the relationship between risk and return. But the quantitative precision claimed for the results of these exercises is generally spurious. I am a better investor for having learned, and built, models of portfolio selection. I am a better investor partly because these models are illuminating. I understand the relationship between risk and return better as a result. But I am also a better investor because I understand the mistakes made by people who think these models are true.

Forecasts and their limits

If financial experts have limited ability to analyse the past, what of their ability to foresee the future? The commentators you hear on CNBC and other financial news channels make projections of general trends – the rise and fall of companies, industries and countries – and forecasts of specific economic variables – inflation, economic growth rate, exchange rates.

The record of the market pundits in anticipating events is poor. But this does not diminish the demand for their services. The power of conventional thinking strikes again. What is valued is not genuine knowledge of the future – to the very limited extent that such knowledge exists – but insight into the mind of the market. Keynes's analogy of the beauty contest is again relevant. The objective is not to predict what will happen, but to predict what others will themselves shortly predict.

The world in the 1990s experienced an unprecedented era of political and economic stability under American hegemony, following the end of the Cold War. The unthinking but contagious optimism of the era fuelled the conventional thinking of the New Economy bubble. Books and blogs proclaimed that the Dow Jones index, then around 6,000 would go to 36,000, or even 100,000, on the back of ever-soaring earnings and the disappearance of the risk premium. (It is currently around 18,000.) The beliefs were strikingly similar to those Keynes described for Britain exactly 100 years earlier. And in the noughties politicians announced the 'great moderation' until they were hit by the most serious financial crisis in eighty years.

Since we are ill equipped to handle inevitable uncertainty, the future is seen through the terms of the near present. The opening of Russia and Eastern Europe, China and India to the market economy is genuinely momentous. But the main beneficiaries of this opening will be the populations of the countries concerned. While it is certain that much money will be made in China, that does not necessarily imply that there is much money to be made there by you and me. And the rise of China and India has not exactly passed unnoticed.

The China effect is 'in the price'

People who pronounce on geopolitical developments are mostly talking not about tomorrow but about today. They tend to project current trends to an exaggerated extent and with exaggerated speed. As a result, they overestimate change in the short term while underestimating change in the long term. They treat current events as more momentous than they really are – hence 'It's different this time' or the frequency of portentous talk of 'new paradigms'. Simultaneously, such commentators fail to anticipate the transformational effect of events that have not yet happened and of which they can know nothing – the unknown unknowns that shape our lives. The safe course is to talk about current preoccupations, and that is what successful pundits mostly do. We can all then agree in being astonished by the pace of change.

Economic forecasts of recession or recovery, of interest rates and exchange rates, are part of every investment conversation. Every fund manager delivers an assessment of general economic prospects to clients. The EMH should make you suspicious when people who profess special insight into the future reveal that insight to large audiences – the value of such information would surely depend on its not being widely available. Professional forecasters have little, or nothing, to add to public information – information that is printed every day in the newspapers, which can be ascertained every hour of the day on the internet and which is available for free.

The economists who make such forecasts are valued, and rewarded by their employers, for their television manner rather than the accuracy of their predictions. It is a common perception that economists always disagree – two economists, three opinions. The facts are quite otherwise, at least as far as economic forecasters are concerned. There is typically far less divergence between different forecasts than there is between all forecasts and outcomes.

For economic forecasters, as for other financial pundits, it is better to be conventionally wrong than unconventionally right. To see correctly what others have failed to see, or chosen to ignore, damages careers more often than it enhances them.

Such prescience undermines the claim – so important to those who disclaim responsibility for what went wrong on their watch – that what happened could not have been foreseen. Ask the people who tried to warn their superiors before 9/11 (or the credit crunch). The weaknesses of forecasting are compounded by the difficulty of specifying how exactly changes in GDP, or interest rate changes, will translate into market prices. Politicians, people in business and finance, and the public at large display cynical naïveté in their attitudes to economic forecasts, as in their attitudes to models – the same mixture of scepticism and credulousness. They express disdain for economic forecasts as they lap them up. Most professional economists regard this forecasting activity as embarrassing and ridiculous, but it continues because the demand is insatiable. Because so many people want answers to questions that cannot be answered, they refuse to accept the limits of knowledge in the face of uncertainty. They justifiably deride those who profess knowledge of the future they do not have. 'Economic forecasters are always wrong.' Less justifiably, they also deride those who disclaim such knowledge, and emphasise that the future can be described only through many divergent, yet plausible, scenarios – 'Give me a one-handed economist.'

The economic environment is like the weather. We cannot forecast it accurately, but we know quite a lot about its broad properties – it won't snow in England in July, and it might rain on any day of the year. General knowledge of this latter kind is already 'in the price', and people who claim more specific knowledge of the future are mostly charlatans.

The common mistake is to believe that the uncertainty described by Keynes and Knight can, through diligent research or analytic sophistication, be transformed into the well-defined, quantifiable risk that responds to the techniques developed by the successors of Ramsey and Savage. Keynes correctly observed that the only justified answer to many questions about the future is 'We simply do not know', but no one is rewarded for saying that. Many people in the financial services sector profess knowledge of the future they do not have, and cannot have. In contrast, legendary investors such as Buffett and Soros stand out for their readiness to acknowledge the limitations of their – and all – knowledge.

Here is Soros:

> My financial success stands in stark contrast with my ability to forecast events ... With regard to events in the real world, my record is downright dismal. The outstanding feature of my predictions is that I keep on expecting developments that do not materialise.
>
> (Soros, 2003)

And here Buffett:

> In many industries, of course, Charlie [Munger] and I can't determine whether we are dealing with a 'pet rock' or a 'Barbie'. We wouldn't solve this problem, moreover, even if we were to spend years intensely studying these industries ... Did we foresee thirty years ago what would transpire in the television manufacturing or computer industries? Of course not. (Nor did most of the investors and corporate managers who enthusiastically entered these industries.)
>
> (Buffett and Cunningham, 2002, p. 85)

Recall Keynes's 'There is no scientific basis on which to form any calculable probability whatever. We simply do not know.' The intelligent investor knows that he or she does not know and (like Buffett, Keynes and Soros) can enjoy the luxury of acknowledging that ignorance. Professional investment experts mostly cannot acknowledge such ignorance – they are hired to provide answers to unanswerable questions. Never mind, they are well paid for it. But not, if you are an intelligent investor, by you.

Approaches to risk

In this and the previous chapters I've described both the dominant SEU theory and the more eclectic and pragmatic approaches to risk and uncertainty favoured by Keynes and Knight. It is time to pull together the strands and spell out their implications for intelligent investors. In SEU theory, the term 'subjective' has a double significance. The probabilities are subjective, and so are the valuations of outcomes.

In that SEU world, probabilities and valuations differ between people but, once established for any individual, are held consistently. If the risks are the same, you use the same probabilities whatever the pay-offs; if the pay-offs are the same, you attach the same valuations, whatever the probabilities. There is a powerful underlying logic to this approach. The reasons the SEU school is today dominant in risk analysis in financial markets can be traced, directly and indirectly, to a clever argument constructed by Ramsey. If you don't adopt the SEU approach, people can devise schemes that will make money at your expense. The process is called a 'Dutch book'. (Offended residents of the Netherlands have attempted, without success, to track down the origins of the phrase.) In a Dutch book you make a series of choices, each of which you believe is to your advantage, whose net effect leaves you worse off. The only sure means of preventing inconsistency in your choices is to follow the precepts of subjective expected utility. The Allais paradoxes described compellingly attractive Dutch books.

While SEU may appear a good way of thinking about risk, it is certainly not the only way of thinking about risk. Ramsey's argument was never as decisive as it appeared. In the uncertain, constantly changing world that Keynes and Knight correctly perceived, it is impossible to be sure whether behaviour is consistent or simply stubborn. You are steadfast. I am pragmatic. There can be no objective basis for the claim that two similar situations are indeed identical.

The findings of behavioural economists are often interpreted as evidence of irrational behaviour. This interpretation is simplistic. The demonstration of supposedly irrational behaviour in the principal Allais paradox rests on the human tendency to value certainties much more highly than extremely probable events. There are good reasons for this trait. There is no such thing in everyday life as an event with a calculable 99 per cent probability. The first percentile of a distribution is generally encountered as a result of uncertainties outside the model. A common feature of these behavioural experiments is that the subject applies a rule that makes sense in everyday life – which is full of uncertainty – in an abstract experimental situation in which problems can be reduced to risks that are precisely defined and described.

There are choices in which rigorous application of the principles of SEU seems to make sense – Robb Caledon – but mostly calculations have to be tempered with the more qualitative judgement that enables us to handle uncertainty. It is not easy to draw a clear line between situations for which SEU is relevant and situations for which it is not. There is tension between people who are wired to 'think SEU' and those who are not. That was the situation President Obama faced in deciding whether to go ahead with the raid in Pakistan.

These conflicts are as old as history. Throwing dice is one of the oldest forms of gambling – bones shaped like cubes were used for this purpose thousands of years ago. Games of dice and other forms of gambling were invented precisely because the results emerge from a random process. Although those players millennia ago did not know it, they had created exactly the conditions in which a probability-based SEU approach is valuable.

The modern casino similarly allows people who 'think SEU' – the operators – to make money at the expense of people who do not think SEU – the punters. The casino, like the insurance company, is concerned with expected values. The motivations of the customers of both groups of institution are more complex.

The ability to 'think probabilities', to apply the premises of SEU, is one that will save you from costly mistakes at the casino. But in an uncertain world in which risks cannot be clearly identified, we don't approach all questions probabilistically, because the probabilistic approach often isn't useful. If people turn out not to have consistent personal probabilities, the reason may be that a scheme of personal probabilities is incapable of fully describing the way they think about the First World War, the Twin Towers or even their daily journey home from work.

Detachment means that you focus single-mindedly on the outcome of a risky activity, and ignore those aspects of the process that you cannot control. This is also difficult. We worry more about risks we cannot control than about those we can, and with reason. This may be why so many people are nervous about flying, but far fewer are nervous about driving, even though it is more dangerous.

Sometimes involvement gives pleasure, as when we cheer the horses we have backed at the races. Some people experience a rush of adrenalin as lights flash on the fruit machine or as the roulette wheel spins. Sometimes involvement in events we cannot influence causes anxiety, as when I turned on the news to hear the progress of the shipbuilding nationalisation bill through Parliament.

Whether pleasurable or painful, the experience of engagement is costly. The thrill of the race and the excitement of the casino are paid for by the majority of punters who lose. Sleepless nights worrying about which way Members of Parliament will vote bring no benefit – this attention is not going to affect the outcome. But the fear of those sleepless nights dissuades most people from undertaking investments, like buying shares in Robb Caledon, even if the odds are attractive. If you are detached, you will pay no special attention to the prices of shares you have sold or decided not to buy. But you will!

In a world of unknowns, engagement is part of the process of managing uncertainty. To be detached about mountain-climbing or buying a lottery ticket is to miss the point of these activities. Regret for our mistakes is part of the process by which we learn from them. Compartmentalising our decisions and the information relevant to them – a process known as mental accounting – is the only way we can cope with a complex world.

But training yourself to think in line with the principles of SEU will give you a technique that will serve you well in investment decisions – so long as you do not make the mistake of thinking that this is the only way that you should think about risk and uncertainty, or the equally dangerous mistake of thinking that others behave according to its principles. We don't naturally or easily think probabilistically, achieve detachment, or always make decisions in the light of the totality of our circumstances. But if you want to make money in financial markets, there are substantial rewards to training yourself to think in that way. That is why this chapter and the preceding one, which are the most difficult in the book, may also be the most profitable.

If you don't practise SEU, you will be Dutch-booked – sold products that will be financially rewarding for the promoter but not for you. For years I taught that people would behave in line with SEU precepts since others would make money at their expense if they didn't. The logic was correct, but the conclusion was wrong. People often don't behave in line with SEU precepts, and others do make money at their expense, and that is a large part of what financial markets are about. Conversely, if you can learn to 'think SEU', then you will often make money at the expense of people who don't.

It isn't always a mistake to be Dutch-booked. The enjoyment

of the daydream some people feel as the national lottery draw approaches, the excitement of watching the roulette wheel spin, the worry that is removed by buying an insurance policy – these feelings are real. But they are also expensive, and the other side of the Dutch book is the profits of the lottery and of insurance companies. If you can successfully suppress emotions of excitement and regret, you will be financially better off. You may prefer to enjoy these experiences, and I'm certainly not going to label you irrational in consequence. But this is a book about how to be a successful financial adviser to yourself. And one of the best pieces of financial advice you can give yourself is to familiarise yourself with the principles of SEU.

But people who think SEU are not necessarily more successful in life than people who do not think SEU, only more successful in not losing money at the casino. In casinos, the house wins and the punters lose. But perhaps the punters have the money to stake, and the attractive women on their arms, precisely because they are over-confident. They tend to view life in terms of lively stories and vivid narratives rather than the abstract world of Bayes's theorem inhabited by nerdy economists.

So the evolutionary argument, popular with these economists, that SEU will drive out other methods of thinking, is wrong. Around the campfires of those savannahs, *bon viveurs* and entertainers brought together groups that contained many different personality types – the enthusiastic, energetic hunters who killed the game and the more analytic tribesmen who focused on dividing it out. All these groups cooperated and prospered, as they do in modern financial markets. The world accommodates different approaches to risk and uncertainty, and so must you.

9

Modern Developments in Financial Markets

Derivatives

In September 2000 Jim Chanos read the notes to the accounts of Enron. Enron's filings with the Securities and Exchange Commission ran to thousands of pages, including many notes printed in small type. The notes were ignored by the many Wall Street analysts who promoted Enron shares and didn't know, or didn't care, about the detail of the accounts. (The only Wall Street analyst to have been consistently critical of Enron, John Olson, left Merrill Lynch in 1998. His departure followed a complaint by Merrill's investment bankers, who feared being excluded from Enron transactions.) The notes described the complex relationships between Enron and associated companies. Chanos was not impressed by what he read.

If you like a security and you own it, you are 'long' of that security. If you don't like a security and you own it, you can sell it; if you don't own it, you can refrain from buying it. But Chanos and the fund he managed, Kynikos, took such a negative view of Enron that they wanted to sell it even though they didn't own it. Selling a share you don't own is called 'establishing a short position', and the market for derivatives enables such trades to be made. Derivatives are securities whose value is derived from the value of other securities. However complex the contract, almost all derivatives are based on shares, bonds, property, commodities or currencies.

Someone who is long of a security profits when its value rises. A short seller profits when the shares fall. When Enron shares plummeted, Chanos and other short sellers made substantial profits. The usual method of short selling today is to take out a 'contract for difference' (CFD). Suppose the share price today is $100. A contract for difference is an agreement that can be terminated at any time either to pay or to receive the difference between $100 and the market price. The value of the contract for difference varies from day to day in line with the market price. Such contracts are a means of speculating on price movements. Not much upfront cash is required. When Enron's market price fell to zero, the holder of a suitable contract for difference could close the transaction and receive what the market price of Enron shares had been on the day he made the agreement.

A contract for difference, like all derivatives contracts, is made with a counterparty – typically an investment bank. The bank may, but need not, hedge its side of the contract by itself buying, selling or 'borrowing' the shares. That decision will be part of the bank's management of its own portfolio of risks. In some countries a retail investor can engage in spread betting as an alternative to a contract for difference. This is a gambling contract in which you 'win' an amount for every upward movement of the price and lose a similar amount on every downward move (or vice versa).

Another common derivative contract is a 'swap'. Swaps were first widely used when exchange control made it difficult to buy foreign currency. You would 'swap' your domestic currency for an initially equivalent amount in the currency you wanted to hold, and agree to repay an increased or diminished amount depending on what happened to the exchange rate.

This market for currency swaps vanished when exchange controls did, but the underlying idea caught on, and today you can swap almost anything. Interest rate swaps are the most common. You exchange an interest rate that varies from day to day for an interest rate that is fixed for a period of years. Mortgage lenders use swaps to offer retail investors a choice of fixed and variable rate products. People who take out mortgages often trade in derivative markets even though they don't know it. When retail investors buy the structured products I describe below, they are often, even if they do not know or understand it, buying derivatives.

A futures contract is an agreement to buy or sell something in the future at a price that is fixed today. Futures have a long history. A merchant might have to wait three months till a ship reached port, and would be vulnerable to price changes while his cargo was at sea. A farmer might wish to establish, now, how much he will get for his crop. The earliest futures contracts brought such producers together with users concerned about how much they might have to pay for the raw materials they would need in future. Such contracts enabled both parties to satisfy their needs with greater certainty – to hedge. But you can buy a futures contract without any need, or intention, to hedge. You can buy it to speculate on what is going to happen to the price, and that is what most purchasers of futures contracts do.

The cost of buying a future is governed by the present price of the asset. If a commodity does not deteriorate physically, its anticipated price three months from now can't be more than the price today, plus the cost of storing it for three months. But if there is an immediate physical shortage, the current price could be higher than the futures price.

Storage costs influence the relationship between futures prices and current prices. There is a financing cost. Money that has been borrowed, or which could otherwise be invested, is tied up in the purchase. A physical commodity needs to be warehoused and insured. For securities there is only the financing cost, and this cost will be reduced if there is a dividend on the share, or interest on a bond. Interest rates differ in different currencies – generally there will be one interest rate at which banks borrow and lend dollars, and different interest rates at which they borrow and lend euros or pounds. The cost of owning a currency is the difference between the interest rate on that currency and the interest rate in your home country.

A futures contract is a firm agreement to buy and sell at a pre-agreed price at a future date. An option confers the right, but not the obligation, to buy or sell at a specified price, known as the 'strike price'. Some options have a fixed exercise date, others can be exercised at any time until they expire, but since you usually won't want to exercise an option before expiry the difference isn't great. Since the option confers right but not obligation, an option seems preferable to a futures contract, which entails both right and expectation. If the option were free, it would be preferable. But while you can usually buy a futures contract in a commodity or a security for something close to the current price, you have to pay a premium for an option. The right to buy is known as a 'call option', while the right to sell is called a 'put'. What are these options worth?

Two influences on value are obvious. The longer the life of an option, the greater its value. The value of a call option diminishes, and the value of a put option increases, the higher is the strike price relative to the current price. There is another, less obvious, principle of option pricing. The value of an option increases with the volatility of the underlying asset. The riskier a security, the more valuable are options to buy or sell it. This may seem paradoxical, but note that the riskier the asset, the more likely it is that you will be glad you own an option rather than the security itself.

Until the 1970s, assessments of option value were guesses. Then the Black–Scholes model provided an analysis of the relationship between an option price and the value of the underlying security. That apparently scientific basis for appraising derivatives was essential to the subsequent explosion of derivatives markets. The value of the option depends on its exercise price, its expiry date and the volatility of the price of the underlying security. Given these parameters, the standard model calculates an option value on the basis that successive price changes are independent of each other (follow a random walk) and observe the normal distribution. That is fine if these assumptions of independence and normality hold. But there are strong reasons for querying both.

Deviations from a random walk arise from momentum or positive short-term serial correlation. The 'fat tail problem' – extreme events happen more often than the normal distribution allows – is especially troubling. These valuation models seem to work well in relatively placid times, but it's not so clear that they work well when markets are unsettled. That's a major problem, because it is in unsettled markets that options are most useful, most profitable and most dangerous, and the need for measures of what they are worth is most urgent.

'Mind your portfolio' – look at your investment portfolio as a whole. Most derivatives are, in themselves, risky investments – the return on an individual transaction is very uncertain. But adding derivatives to an existing portfolio can reduce the risk, or improve the expected return on the portfolio without additional risk. A futures contract can hedge a portfolio against a market fall; a put option will limit the maximum loss. Derivatives can lock in profits or anticipate future needs, or allow you to benefit from a market rise while limiting risks. But hedging and insurance aren't the main reasons why people buy derivatives and related products based on them. They buy them because they think they are a good bet.

The normal experience of gamblers is that only the house makes money in the long run. This is as true of speculation in derivative markets as it is elsewhere. Valuing derivatives is complex, and there are no correct answers. But the financial institutions that sell derivative products have access to sophisticated computer programs, extensive databases, Black–Scholes and other models, and roomfuls of maths and physics PhDs. They are better at derivative valuation than the fund managers and treasurers of big companies and public authorities who buy them. Buying derivatives because you think they are cheap, rather than as hedges in a programme of portfolio diversification, is almost certainly a mug's game. The risks are in the price, and if you think the risks are not in the price, the most likely reason is that you are wrong. Why do I want to buy what they want to sell?

Trade in derivative markets has grown steadily, and the products have become more opaque. Some people – notably Alan Greenspan, former chairman of the Federal Reserve Board – explained this growth in trade in terms of an ever more sophisticated risk allocation. Perhaps the German regional banks that invested in asset-backed securities related to the value of subprime mortgages in American inner cities did so because they were particularly knowledgeable about these loans, or believed they hedged or diversified other assets in their portfolios. More likely, victims of information asymmetry, they did not understand what they were doing.

When assets are difficult to value, they will be owned by people who overestimate that value. Most derivatives are bought by people who are making a mistake, and the proliferation of ever more complex financial instruments, hard to assess even with sophisticated models, encourages these mistakes.

There is a history of spectacular crises in derivatives markets. Sometimes credulous individuals in public agencies or large corporations fall for a sales pitch. In the 1990s many embarked on programmes of trading in derivatives or structured products whose nature they at best dimly understood. The municipality of Orange County went bust after trades made by the appropriately named Robert Citron came unstuck. The London borough of Hammersmith and Fulham was spared similar embarrassment when the courts ruled that the council had no authority to gamble with local residents' money and the banks could get lost.

But the most spectacular of the many failures of that decade was certainly not the product of naïveté – or not that kind of naïveté; the demise of Long-Term Capital Management in 1998. This collapse received particular attention – and caused particular joy in some quarters – because of the personalities involved. Founded by John Meriwether, a legendary Salomon trader, the management team included two Nobel Prize-winners, Bob Merton and Myron Scholes (of the Black–Scholes model). LTCM relied on arbitrage trades based on fundamental value – reversion to the mean in relationships between similar but different securities. But momentum may drive prices sufficiently far away from fundamental value for sufficiently long to exhaust the patience, and the resources, of investors – 'markets can be wrong for longer than you can be solvent'. Apparently unrelated bets proved to be correlated in the widespread panic that followed the Asian financial crisis and Russian debt repudiation of 1997–8. The scale of LTCM's borrowings – the magic of leverage meant that this relatively small fund had liabilities of trillions of dollars – was such that the Federal Reserve orchestrated a rescue operation.

Many derivatives in modern securities markets are complex. However elaborate, they are mostly based on combinations of the four basic mechanisms I have described above: shorts, swaps, futures and options. Most private investors will not trade in derivatives directly. But they may do so through hedge funds and structured products, or through funds that invest in hedge funds or structured products.

When bonds were no longer boring

Bonds had traditionally been boring. Nick Carraway, the colourless narrator of Scott Fitzgerald's 1925 novel *The Great Gatsby*, was a bond trader. But in the 1970s and 1980s several distinct innovations turned the bond market into an exciting place. The introduction of an interest rate futures contract on the Chicago Mercantile Exchange, almost simultaneous with the work of Fischer Black and Myron Scholes at the neighbouring university, was the beginning of the development of derivative contracts related to bond markets.

The 'junk bond' was invented by Michael Milken, whose graduate school thesis demonstrated that the premium rate attached to risky bonds was more than sufficient to affect the default rate. Most of the bonds Milken studied were once sound securities whose issuers had fallen on hard times. Milken's innovation was to issue bonds that were obviously highly risky from inception.

Banks created asset-backed securities, bundling together packages of loans and dividing them into safer and riskier tranches. 'Mortgages are math,' declared Lew Ranieri, who ran fixed interest at Salomon Brothers and promoted the mortgage-backed security. Ranieri would be a central figure in Michael Lewis's coruscating 1989 account of the trading floor at Salomon. Two years earlier Tom Wolfe had described the New York of the era in his novel *The Bonfire of the Vanities*. His central figure, Sherman McCoy, Master of the Universe, was, like Nick Carraway, a bond salesman. But in a very different environment.

These innovations did not end well. The first era of junk bond issues ended with the collapse of Milken's firm, Drexel Burnham Lambert, which had more or less monopolised their issue. The 'big short' – the bet on the collapse of US house prices – was undertaken through the medium of a credit default swap based on collateralised debt obligations – a many times repackaged bundle of subprime mortgages. The failure of many of these supposedly asset-backed securities was central to the 2008 global financial crisis.

The fundamental mistake was to believe that by bundling risky loans it was possible to create relatively safe securities. The 'mind your portfolio' principle tells us that this belief is not as implausible as it may sound, but relative safety depends on the underlying risks being uncorrelated with each other. The risks of mortgage defaults were not uncorrelated. If you seek guarantees, you will have to be content with the bonds of the governments of countries such as Germany and Switzerland – and the paltry returns that go with true guarantees.

Structured products

Few retail investors will trade directly in derivative markets, and few should. But you may be offered opportunities to do so indirectly, through structured products or hedge funds. A collateralised debt obligation, the instrument at the heart of the global financial crisis, is a structured product, a security whose risk and return characteristics have been created by financial engineering. Such engineering can take the form of packaging one security with others: splitting the risk and return from an asset into several components; combining a security with a derivative based on the same or another security; or, frequently, a combination of all these methods. A synthetic investment resembles a fund, but the issuer does not hold the underlying assets to which its value is related; the risks may be (but need not be) hedged through derivatives.

Financial engineering sounds complicated, and the legal and economic structure of these instruments is indeed complicated. But good financial engineering is like watchmaking. Its objective is to create products whose properties appear simple, even if the underlying mechanisms are not. Much financial engineering, however, is more like the skills of the illusionist: what the audience sees is not the reality.

The aim of financial engineering is either to increase the yield on bonds with little addition to risk or to reduce the risk in equity investment with little loss of return. Avoid these offers. The issuer of these bonds writes a complex derivative contract with an investment bank. The bank makes a payment but is entitled to receive a much larger sum if the complex combination of events described in the small print materialises (the 'punt'). The premium pays for the higher interest rate you are guaranteed (and for the marketing expenses of the bond, which will be substantial).

The investment bank has done its own modelling and considers that the punt is a good deal. But if the punt is a good deal for the bank, it is a bad deal for you. It is very unlikely that you would buy this kind of complex gamble with negative expected value as a stand-alone product. Once again, you can apply the 'mind your portfolio' principle to the structured product by analysing its components. You will get to the same answer quickly and simply through two other principles: 'Why do I want to buy what they want to sell?' and 'Keep it simple'. Both these maxims are good guides in the world of structured products, and they tell you not to go there.

If you adhere to the 'mind your portfolio' principle, you will not want to buy structured products. The structured product alters the risk/return characteristics of individual investments. What matters to you is the risk/return characteristics of your overall portfolio. You can and should achieve the overall objectives – the balance of risk and return – by balancing your overall mix of investments. Mind your portfolio! You do not need funds or companies to gear or diversify on your behalf, because you can do these things yourself. The best and cheapest way of limiting the risk in shares is to hold a lower proportion of your assets in shares.

But rigorous application of the 'mind your portfolio' principle is hard. Many intelligent investors will feel better if they limit the risk on the individual components of their portfolio as well as on the aggregate. Others like the risk and return combination offered by particular structured products. One of the very first structured products, and still the one with most appeal to retail investors, is an enhanced bond from the British government. The premium bond was introduced in 1956 with a showman's style by the future Prime Minister Harold Macmillan. The bond offers no income, only the chance to participate in a monthly prize draw. The premium bond is a combination of a deposit account and a lottery, and since the deposit rate is competitive and the lottery is fair, the combination is an attractive proposition for people who are interested in both holding bonds and entering lotteries.

This method of analysing a structured product unravels the financial engineering of the product's designers. The technique can also be applied to any structured product, and should be applied by anyone who adheres to the 'mind your portfolio' principle. Split the package into its component parts, and ask whether each component is something you would want to add to your profits.

A bond issued by a large company will offer a higher return than a government stock, but at a higher risk. There is a greater possibility (though still not a very large one) that the company will default. Deutsche Telekom's 2023 bond has a gross redemption yield of around 0.6 per cent, as against around zero for the equivalent German government bond. Neither looks an attractive opportunity. If you buy the Telekom bond, you are in effect insuring the – admittedly small – credit risk associated with Deutsche Telekom in return for a very modest premium.

You do not have the information needed to assess the risk on these policies. There are companies that sell credit insurance (in 2008 they were rapidly disappearing). Credit insurance is an activity whose returns are strongly correlated with your overall portfolio (a situation in which Deutsche Telekom defaults on its bonds is likely to be one in which there is mayhem in other financial markets). The additional risk and return that the corporate bond implies relative to the government bond is probably not a risk you would add to your portfolio if it were offered on a stand-alone basis.

Many markets offer bundled products. Buy one, get the second half-price. Television programmes are sold as packages of channels. Buy coffee and croissant together. Eat a *prix fixe* menu. The cost of the menu is typically less than the cost of the separate components. Not so in financial markets, where the cost of the structured product is generally higher than the cost of the components, and the premium is the source of the financial engineer's profit. No one would buy a *table d'hôte* menu at a price higher than the sum of the items on the *à la carte* menu. The premium also indicates that structured products are often bought (in my view, mostly bought) by people who misunderstand them. The analogy of the illusionist is more relevant than the analogy of the watchmaker.

The market for structured products illustrates all the issues of information asymmetry. Asking 'Would I choose to buy each of the separate components of this package?' is an important discipline in both the restaurant and in financial markets, but especially in financial markets. Because structured products are often bought by people who are making mistakes, they are usually better bought second-hand. If you are going to hold bonds, hold bonds. Complex financial engineering is expensive, and the expense is likely to be yours.

Hedge funds

Keynes was an active speculator, famously trading from bed in the mornings, managing his own money and that of King's

College, Cambridge, shorting securities and dealing in a wide range of assets. He seems to have been successful in the long run, though not extraordinarily so. He died in 1946 with assets of around £½ million, a wealthy man by the standards of the time but not rich on the scale of Soros or Buffett. Benjamin Graham, the legendary value investor, would establish short positions in businesses he did not like as well as having long positions in those he did.

These styles of investing were the precursors of the modern hedge fund. The first investor to attract that label seems to have been Alfred Jones, who traded aggressively through the 1950s. Hedge funds attracted wide popular attention with the famous bet against sterling by the Quantum Fund of George Soros in 1991 and came into the spotlight again with the failure of Long-Term Capital Management in 1998.

Until 2000 hedge funds were used only by rich individuals and a few sophisticated institutions. Academic endowments, notably those of Harvard and Yale, were early and successful supporters. After the end of the New Economy bubble, investors searched for new ways of generating the high returns that had seemed to come so easily in the 1990s. They turned to hedge funds. Exceptional individuals such as Soros had been able to command high fee levels for their services, and newer funds set their charges at the same level. The prospect of such fees proved irresistible to many people in investment banks. As newcomers rushed through the door, Soros made for the exit. So did another legend, Julian Robertson. While the long-term performance of his Tiger Fund rivalled that of Soros, Robertson may have lost more money in his last year than he had made throughout his career.

Different hedge funds pursue different strategies. A long/short fund, like Graham's, will deploy the stock-picking skills of its managers to select losers as well as winners. Jim Chanos, who helped expose Enron, specialised in taking short positions.

A market-neutral fund will hedge its exposure to general market movements. It will focus on *alpha* and eliminate *beta*. A macro-economic event fund in the style of Keynes or Soros aspires to predict major financial and political developments in the world economy – such as Britain's EMS failure – and trades on the basis of these forecasts.

Arbitrage strategies, such as those deployed at LTCM, rely on stable relationships between the prices of related, but different, securities. Such pairs might be currencies within a region, or the debt and equity of the same company, or the shares of an acquiring company and its potential target. As at LTCM, arbitrage strategies are often based on complex modelling. Relying on history in this way is dangerous, as it proved for the LTCM partners. Distressed debt funds buy bonds of businesses or countries in financial difficulty. These funds may hope to profit from buying below fundamental value or to increase that fundamental value through litigation or the threat to block proposals for financial reconstruction.

Although most hedge funds are based in London or the United States, for legal and regulatory purposes they are normally registered offshore. While the City of London (and its increasingly important annexe at Canary Wharf) remains the centre of London's financial services business, hedge fund managers emphasise differentiation and exclusivity by clustering in St James's. Charging typical fees of 2 per cent of funds under management and 20 per cent of profits, the managers can afford West End rents. US hedge funds have similarly chosen to distance themselves from Wall Street, and Greenwich, Connecticut, is now generally regarded as the centre of the hedge fund world.

The fee structure, in effect, shares profits but not losses. Investors look for reliable month-by-month appreciation in the value of their funds, and hedge fund managers are closely monitored month by month. Both these incentives and this supervision encourage the adoption of strategies with Taleb characteristics

– frequent small profits, occasional large losses. Hedge funds make extensive use of the 'carry trade', which relies on interest rate differentials between good and bad credits, or strong and weak currencies.

Retail investors cannot easily access major hedge funds, because of regulatory restrictions and high minimum investments; moreover, many of the most highly regarded funds are closed to new investors. Retail investors have the opportunity to invest in more conventionally open- or closed-ended funds which themselves invest in hedge funds. Since many hedge fund managers reveal only limited information about what they do, intermediaries may be helpful. These funds of funds can diversify across funds with different strategies. The returns on, say, a long/short fund should not be correlated with the returns on, say, a distressed debt fund. Historical analysis supports this claim.

But do not count on the stability of historical correlations in times of extreme financial strain. Funds learnt this lesson in 2007–8. The shift from mainstream to alternative investments also favoured private equity. Private equity is a means by which investment institutions, either directly or through managed funds, invest in unquoted businesses. Before the late 1990s private equity used to be more or less synonymous with venture capital – the provision of funds for start-up and early-stage businesses.

Not all private equity deals were of this kind. As large corporations restructured, unwanted 'non-core' divisions were often sold to consortia led by their managers and funded by private equity. The newly established business was often refinanced or the subject of a fresh IPO within a few years. Many individual managers became very rich through these transactions, a development that helped to raise the pay aspirations of all executives.

The development of junk bond financing in the 1980s made it possible to use debt to buy even very large companies. That boom ended with the relatively unsuccessful outcome of the massive takeover of RJR Nabisco by private equity house KKR and the failure of a number of other transactions, such as the hopeless acquisition of many of America's leading department stores by the ambitious Canadian Robert Campeau. Still, the search for new investment avenues after 2000 led to explosive growth in the funds available for private equity, and the scale of the typical transaction grew rapidly. Private equity funds would buy an established business from the existing owners. These owners might be other companies, family and founding shareholders or, increasingly, the shareholders of public companies quoted on the stock exchange.

The RJR Nabisco transaction is still the largest (inflation-adjusted) private equity deal in history, though in nominal terms it has been overtaken by the $45 billion acquisition of TXU by a consortium of KKR, Goldman Sachs and a third private equity group, Texas Pacific – a transaction that ended in the bankruptcy of the largest power company in Texas. In these transactions private equity has come a long way from its roots in the provision of funds to small growing businesses. Private equity investment became an indirect and expensive method of buying shares in medium and large companies similar to those in the main index. The returns from this kind of investment will therefore be correlated with the returns from other equity investments, but, given the leverage involved, the *beta* associated with such equity is well above one.

The concentrated share ownership of private equity deals allows more effective monitoring of company management. Such concentrated ownership has been common for many years in continental Europe. Public companies find their ability to focus on fundamental value inhibited by the management of quarterly earnings forecasts and reports. Some patient private equity investors are willing to hold their financial investments for many years, encouraging more long-term strategic thinking and productive investment. But the major private equity firms, and the investors who back them, are generally in search of a rapid exit. The objective is normally to sell the company or float it on the stock market within three to five years, returning the money obtained to the investors in that particular fund.

I described in Chapter 6 the numerous ways in which businesses can enhance earnings in the short term. Private equity, and the threat of takeover by private equity, has increased pressure to use these strategies. During a recent stay in a hotel, looking at the frayed carpet and overpriced extras, I thought, 'This hotel has been bought out in a private equity transaction.' It had been. It is easy to enhance the earnings of most businesses if your time horizon is three years.

Both the citizen and the investor should be concerned about the difficulty modern management confronts in taking a long-term view of the growth and development of the business. The public company encounters the blight of quarterly earnings reporting; the private equity owned business must accommodate the time-scale of investors seeking a quick profit. This short-termism is reinforced by the incentive schemes offered to managers – even, or perhaps especially, the so-called long-term incentive schemes that now constitute a large part of executive pay. Even if you are concerned with the fundamental value of the business in which you own shares, the managers may not be.

It is difficult for the investor to judge the overall historic success of private equity, far less its prospective future returns. Some private equity houses may have been able to supervise management teams more effectively than public markets. Some may possess skills that add value through financial engineering. Private equity houses have recently (but no longer) had access to debt financing whose pricing did not reflect the risk involved. The reporting of historical performance is confounded by survivor bias – it is the more successful investors who are raising new funds – and by the capacity of leverage to produce very high returns to equity investors in a period of rising share prices (with the opposite effect when share prices are falling).

Against these potential advantages must be set the certainty of charges. 'Two and twenty' is a common charging basis for both hedge funds and private equity investments. The private equity house takes a management fee of 2 per cent of the fund per year, and 20 per cent of the profits, known in private equity as the 'carried interest'. Like other investment managers, they may also arrange for many of their own costs to be directly or indirectly charged to their funds. When these percentages are applied to large transactions – such as those of TXU – the numbers become eye-watering. Many hedge funds and private equity managers have become very rich very quickly. But what of the customers' yachts? 'Two and twenty' reduces a 10 per cent underlying return to 6 per cent. A retail investor will normally make an investment in a hedge fund or private equity fund through a fund of funds or a feeder fund, for which a charge of 1.5 per cent of assets for management and 10 per cent of profit is common. The addition of these charges means that a 10 per cent return on the under-lying investment might be no more than 3.5 per cent in the hands of the investors. Even if the fund secured a 20 per cent yield, the net return to the investor might be only half of that, with 6 per cent going to the underlying fund and 3 per cent to the fund of funds. Tax and inflation take a further bite of the return.

Such figures make no sense. Returns on financial investment are ultimately governed by returns on productive investment. While some investors in hedge funds and private equity will make excellent returns from a mixture of skill and luck on the part of their managers, most stand no chance of earning profits commensurate with the risks.

Other alternative assets

Hedge funds and private equity are not the only alternative assets. Other options include commodities such as oil, gold and other metals; undeveloped land such as farms, forests and building plots; and collectables such as wine, art, jewels and furniture.

Commodity exchanges, large and active, meet the needs of people who produce or use the physical commodities. Commodities have always been a fertile field for speculation by those who believe they can anticipate 'the mind of the market'. If this is you, then good luck and good fortune; you will need good luck to preserve good fortune. If you simply want to invest, there are funds whose value is linked to commodity prices, which I will describe in the next chapter. The growth of such funds has fuelled the remarkable instability of commodity prices over the last decade, an instability that is disrupting the supply of such commodities.

But over the long run commodity investment has not been very profitable. Despite continuing worries about forthcoming resource scarcity, new technology and new discoveries have more than offset the exploitation of existing reserves. It is cheaper to own commodities in the ground than in a warehouse, and mining companies are generally better investments than the commodities themselves, and are good portfolio diversifiers. The aphorism that a small minerals company is a hole in the ground with a crook at the top is, however, often true.

Other alternative assets are marketed to private investors either as hot tips or as additions to a diversified portfolio. The general rule is to avoid these areas unless you have specialist knowledge. Buy wine, art, jewels or furniture if you like wine, art, jewels or furniture. While it is certainly possible to make money in these investments, the differences between buying and selling prices are wide, and there is none of the regulatory apparatus that protects small investors in securities markets. If you are expert, and even more if you are not, buy only collectable items that you like.

10

The Conventional Investor

Establish your portfolio

Every financial adviser is trained to begin by asking you to define your investment objectives and your attitude to risk. As your own financial adviser, you need to pose these questions to yourself. The professional adviser must tick boxes to complete the 'fact find' so he can get on and sell you products. You really want to know the answers because they will determine your investment strategy.

Are you a net saver or a net spender? Are you building up assets or managing existing assets to support your standard of living? Most people before retirement are, or should be, net savers. Many people, after retirement, will be net spenders. People before retirement need to consider how much saving they should do. People after retirement need to consider how much they can afford to spend.

If you gathered nuts for twenty-five years, and planned to retire for twenty-five years, you would need to set aside half your nuts for your old age. If you can earn a return on your investment, you can reduce significantly the amount you need to set aside. Table 8 shows how great a reduction you can make. If you meet the 8 per cent target rate of return, 12.5 per cent of income will grow to a cache large enough to meet your needs. You can now eat almost 90 per cent of the nuts you collect.

Table 8: **Save now, spend later**

Percentage of income needed to maintain the same spending power in retirement with a saving/spending period each of 25 years						
Realised rate of return (p.a.)	10%	8%	6%	4%	2%	0
% of income required to save	8.5	12.7	19.0	27.3	37.9	50.0
% of income available to spend	91.5	87.3	81.0	72.7	62.1	50.0

Every 2 per cent that you gain or lose in investment return will make a big difference. You can sacrifice more than 2 per cent through poor investment performance, bad timing of sales and purchases or unsuitable allocation across investment categories. You might lose 2 per cent in tax, and another 2 per cent by paying more than you need in fees and charges. And you can lose 2 per cent, or more, by making large allocations to assets that advisers describe as low-risk investments which offer lower but more predictable returns.

In this and the following chapters I will describe how you can minimise the leakage of return under each of these headings. I'll suggest how to turn the timing of investments to your advantage, and how to approach asset allocation and stock selection. I'll stress the importance of keeping down costs and charges, and explain how to do it. And I will offer practical guidance on how to think about risk and uncertainty based on the principles outlined in Chapters 7 and 8. The lesson of that discussion is that you don't necessarily have to accept low returns to achieve low risk.

Chapter 2 described the essential preliminaries – listing assets and liabilities, reviewing your banking arrangements and your mortgage. Now you need a stockbroker. Most people still have an image of the stockbroker derived from the days before players replaced gentlemen: grand but seedy; with good social skills and connections; streetwise but not clever; well off but not hard-working. These people still exist but are a dying breed. They will levy annual management charges, or substantial commissions on purchases and sales, or both. They are expensive. So are the wealth management services of banks, which offer more modern versions of these services.

If you still lack confidence to build even a conventional invest-ment portfolio yourself, the robo-adviser offers an inexpensive substitute, replacing by a computer the personalised service of the individual broker, private banker or wealth manager. These online services began in the United States and have now spread to several other countries. Betterment, the US market leader, charges a maximum fee of 0.35 per cent and requires no minimum account balance. However, this chapter will explain how you can do it yourself more effectively, more cheaply – and almost as easily.

Your stockbroker should be an online share-dealing service. You need an execution-only service, in which you make deci-sions and give instructions yourself. These services are very cheap, because computers do most of the work – so cheap, in fact, that price should not be a major factor in your choice.

While many brokers will allow you to trade foreign stocks, you will need to be careful about additional charges and poor foreign exchange rates. It is often best to buy securities from a broker in the country where those securities are listed. This is not an issue if you buy ETFs, which almost all brokers will allow you to do. If you are an EU resident, and often even if you are not, you can use a broker in any EU member state. You can use a single account for all eurozone securities. (Luxembourg may be a good choice.)

When you set up this account, you will want to take advantage of the tax concessions available to retail investors. Almost all countries offer substantial tax concessions for pension savings, and there are often other schemes to favour saving, although you may find that much or all of the benefit is absorbed by intermediaries. The price of accessing the relief, through explicit charges, trading costs and management fees within funds, and inflexibility and poor-quality asset management, may exceed the tax.

While securities will be the main component of your investment portfolio, the 'mind your portfolio' principle implies that you should consider insurance at the same time as you contemplate investment. You should think probabilities when you take out insurance. But so does the insurance company, and the company knows probabilities well. That is its business.

You should be detached. While it is vexing to have your television stolen, or to lose your bag on holiday, insurance will not bring back either your television or your bag. The financial loss from a stolen television or lost bag is probably less than you will incur on a bad day on the stock market. Much of the premium on policies that insure against these minor contingencies goes not to pay policyholders but in the administrative costs of small claims.

So anyone who is truly minding their portfolio, and recognises that the insurance company has calculated the expected value of their policy, will insure only things they cannot afford to lose. You need insurance against your house burning down, but not for replacing the bedroom carpet; you need insurance against being hospitalised in the United States, but not for the cost of an extra night's hotel accommodation because your plane is delayed.

Many people find this advice difficult to accept. Insurers observe that their customers have little appetite for policies that rarely pay out, even though low-probability risks are precisely those that are appropriate for insurance. Policyholders like the reassurance of occasional small cheques even if these cheques add up to much less than their premiums. Regret is a powerful human emotion, even if often an unproductive one.

You will be financially better off if you can be objective and learn to control these emotions, but it is difficult, even for people educated in intelligent investment, to exercise such control. If, when an uninsured television set is stolen, you can't refrain from kicking yourself, or your spouse can't refrain from kicking you, then you should take out the policy. This strategy is, however, likely to cost you money – even after taking account of the insurance companies' cheques.

Pay less

Over the fifty years that Warren Buffett has been in charge of Berkshire Hathaway, the company has earned an average compound rate of return of 20 per cent per year. For Buffett himself. But also for his investors. The lucky people who have been his fellow shareholders through all that time have enjoyed just the same rate of return as he has. The fortune he has accumulated is the result of the rise in the value of his share of the collective fund.

Suppose that Buffett had deducted from the returns on his own investment – his own, not that of his fellow shareholders – a notional investment management fee, based on the standard 2 per cent annual charge and 20 per cent of gains formula of the hedge fund and private equity business. There would then be two pots: one created by reinvestment of the fees Buffett was charging himself, and one created by the growth in the value of Buffett's own original investment. Call the first pot the wealth of Buffett Investment Management, the second pot the wealth of the Buffett Foundation.

How much of Buffett's $70 billion would be the property of Buffett Investment Management and how much the property of the Buffett Foundation? The – completely astonishing – answer is that Buffett Investment Management would have $64 billion and the Buffett Foundation $6 billion. The cumulative effect of 'two and twenty' over fifty years is so large that the earnings of the investment manager completely overshadow the earnings of the investor. That sum tells you why it was the giants of the financial services industry, not the customers, who owned the yachts.

The least risky way to increase the returns from your financial investments is to minimise agency costs – to ensure that the return on the underlying investments goes into your own pocket rather than someone else's. The effect of charges on investments is so large that it is as important to understand the structure of charges as it is to understand the principles of investment analysis. The first charge that hits you when you invest is the spread between the buying price and the selling price. For government bonds and for blue chip shares, such as Exxon Mobil, this spread will be extremely small, and you can deal at any time in any quantity you like. The only other dealing costs are commission (you should expect to pay less than €20 for an internet deal) and any government or exchange levies on transactions.

Small companies are different. The spread between buying and selling prices may be 3 or 4 per cent. Even a purchase of €10,000 may require a telephone call rather than a mouse click, and telephone orders will usually incur higher commission. The difference between what it will cost you to buy and what you will get if you sell could be as much as 5 per cent.

The effect of these costs on returns depends on the frequency with which you deal. Online trading is so inexpensive and easy that you may be tempted to trade often. Only one thing eats up investment returns faster than fees and commissions, and that is frequent trading. Do not succumb. The total costs of running your own portfolio should be well under 1 per cent per year.

Investing in actively managed funds will cost you more. The choice of funds available, both open- and closed-ended, is unbelievably wide. There are more funds investing in shares than there are shares to invest in. This situation doesn't make sense, and is both cause and effect of the high charges. Costs need to be high to recover the expenses of running so many different, mainly small, funds which all do much the same thing. At the same time the high level of charges encourages financial services companies to set up even more funds.

The proliferation of funds means that choosing a fund may be no easier than choosing individual investments. You can hire an adviser to recommend funds. There are also many advisers. The problem seems to multiply itself, as do the fees. The fees attract more advisers, and so on. The underlying problem is one of information asymmetry. The marketing of financial services emphasises quality, not price, and for good reasons. It would be worth paying more – a lot more – to get a good fund manager. But since it is hard to identify a good fund manager, good and bad managers all charge high fees, with the consequences described above. It is hard to escape the dilemma posed by this market inefficiency.

If you own an actively managed equity fund for five years, it is possible that the direct and indirect costs and charges you incur in buying, holding and selling that investment will total 3 per cent a year. Other investment funds may cost you more. The total charges on a fund of hedge funds are such that it might yield less than a government bond even if the underlying investments returned more than 10 per cent per year.

Costs and charges for funds fall into three broad categories:

- annual costs of managing and administering the investment;
- costs and charges incurred in buying and selling the investment, which include initial fees, commission charges and any difference between the quoted buying and selling price (the effect of these charges on your annual return depends on the length of time for which you hold the investment);

- costs incurred by the fund manager and charged against the value of the fund (e.g. commission on transactions and the difference between the buying and selling prices of the underlying securities).

Annual management charges range from 0.1 or 0.2 per cent for some indexed funds to 2 per cent or more for an insurance-linked fund or a hedge fund. Other administrative costs will usually be between 0.2 and 0.4 per cent. If you buy a fund of funds that invests in other funds, you may have to pay more than one level of these charges. Some funds also charge a performance fee, which gives the managers a share of any profit, or of outperformance relative to a benchmark. If you buy one of the funds recommended to neophyte investors, you will probably end up in an open-ended fund linked to a selection of mainstream shares.

Most such funds are closet-indexed – although they are actively managed, their composition is very close to the make-up of the index against which they are benchmarked. That minimises the risk – to the manager – that the fund will significantly underperform the market. If the largest holdings are the largest companies in the country, the fund is closet-indexed. You can achieve a similar result much more cheaply yourself, and you should.

Today most of the largest providers of retail funds globally are specialist asset managers such as Vanguard, BlackRock and Fidelity. These businesses do not suffer the conflicts of interest inherent in the cross-selling of retail products or the provision of investment banking services to companies in which the funds invest. In the United States, Vanguard Group, a not-for-profit company with a messianic founder, John Bogle, pioneered low-cost index funds for retail investors, and competitors have followed suit. In many other countries banks and life assurance companies still have a large share of the market, typically with high management fees. However, the worst US fund managers are greedier, and probably more corrupt, than their counterparts elsewhere. And, as Table 7 showed, their performance is dismal.

However Vanguard, Fidelity and BlackRock all now operate internationally. All provide open-ended index funds with very low charges. However, you may find that you have to use a 'platform' – an agent – to access these open-ended funds, and with some platforms charging 0.5 per cent or more per annum this can dramatically increase the cost of these options. You may be able to find a platform with a low fee, or one that charges a flat fee which will be almost irrelevant if your portfolio is large enough. The best option available for an open-ended fund varies from time to time and country to country. Although I would recommend an open-ended tracker if you can access it cheaply, an ETF – both BlackRock and Vanguard offer ETFs – will always be available cheaply through an execution-only stockbroker.

The conventional investor's portfolio

Where to begin? Many people will sensibly start the job of being their own investment manager as conventional investors. The conventional investor is hesitant to trust his or her own judgement and prefers to rely on the consensus of professional opinion. The conventional investor is probably hesitant to 'think SEU' and is still not quite convinced that a share such as Robb Caledon is part of a low-risk investment strategy. I shall describe a strategy for the conventional investor and then suggest how that strategy might be developed by those who are more ready to use their own judgement.

Even twenty or thirty years ago the commonest form of long-term saving was through the investment funds of life insurance companies, which managed a complete range of investments – shares, bonds and property. In this way the conventional investor could hand over investment allocation decisions to a fund manager. But recent returns on with-profits policies have been poor and the bases on which returns are determined opaque, and these are no longer attractive investments (except to those who sell them). Even conventional investors must now make their own asset allocation decisions.

Large institutions that are conventional investors get advice on asset allocation from consultants, such as Mercer or Towers Watson. Most of these firms originated as actuarial practices (actuaries measure the liabilities of insurance companies or pension funds) and have broadened their business activities. Consultants will usually base their advice on portfolio models and on their knowledge of what other similarly placed investors are doing. The activities of consultants are a means of disseminating conventional thinking.

The conventional investor can, simply and cheaply, replicate the portfolio of these institutions with a sum as small as €20,000. Let us begin by matching the average asset allocation of the three giant investors discussed in Chapter 2 – the Norwegian Oil Fund, the principal Dutch pension fund, and CalPERS. We will put €10,000 into global equities, €7,000 into bonds, €1,500 into real estate and keep €1,500 in cash – or for fun, in other investments that take our fancy.

You can invest €10,000 in the Vanguard Total World Stock ETF. You now own a share of Apple, Exxon Mobil and Microsoft. The largest non-US companies you hold are Nestlé and another Swiss-headquartered company, the pharmaceutical business Novartis. You also own some Sony, and BMW, and Apple, and HSBC. You are invested in over 7,000 companies overall, about the same number as the Norwegian fund. With only €10,000! And for an annual charge of 0.17 per cent.

Seven thousand euros is earmarked for bonds. We'll give €5,000 to the BlackRock Global Index Bond Fund. About 40 per cent of this is lent to the US Treasury, and 16 per cent to the government of Japan. Only about 6 per cent is in Germany, because the prudent Germans don't have much debt. Your investment is roughly equally divided across short- and long-dated securities. I am going to put €2,000 of your €7,000 bond allocation in inflation-linked securities – again either BlackRock or Vanguard will let me do this for you through a fund diversified across the countries (principally the US and UK) which have issued such bonds.

You may have a choice of leaving the currency of your ETF unhedged or hedging these funds into your own or another currency. For a long-run investor I don't think the choice matters much. Microsoft is an American company and Nestlé a Swiss one, but they sell to customers around the world in local currency, not in US dollars or Swiss francs. And while your future liabilities will be in your own currency, you give yourself a degree of protection by holding assets whose value is determined by the global economy rather than your own.

Finally, there is €1,500 for property. You are not going to buy a property of your own for €1,500, so your choice is between funds. The best option – which is sometimes available – is to buy a closed-end property fund with modest gearing at a discount to its asset value.

And that is it. With four clicks of a mouse you have a diversified portfolio similar to that adopted by a well-advised large investment fund with long-term aspirations to total return. And you have constructed it at low initial and ongoing cost. You can safely forget about this portfolio for a long time – years if you like. Your investments may or may not do well, but their performance will most likely be similar to, but better than, the balanced portfolio a consultant or adviser would construct on your behalf. Similar to, because it reproduces the balanced portfolio of the conventional institutional investor; better than, because you have greatly reduced the costs of establishment and management.

You should have aspirations to do better still. The conventional investor should consider separating a part of his or her portfolio in order to test his or her own judgement. As experience and confidence grow, the plan is to devote more and more funds to intelligent investment.

11

The Intelligent Investor's Strategy

Developing a strategy

Conventional investors – often tacitly, sometimes knowingly – employ a conventional approach to risk, based on SEU. In that approach, risk has the same meaning for everyone: i.e. short-term volatility. The well-advised conventional investor finds a balance between risk and return by selecting a point on the 'efficient frontier' described by Harry Markowitz. The appropriate choice of the point on the frontier depends on your 'risk appetite' or 'risk tolerance'. Risk has a market price, determined by the average risk appetite of all investors. A financial adviser will quiz you to establish your 'risk tolerance'; this interrogation is an essential part of the 'know your client' exercise which all financial advisers and investment consultants must undertake.

Actually, most conventional investors do not really think this way: they mostly follow conventional wisdom and do what other people in loosely similar situations do. When Markowitz was asked how he had invested his own retirement savings, he replied:

I should have compared the historical advantages of the asset classes and drawn an efficient frontier. Instead, I visualised my grief if the stock market went way up and I wasn't in it, or if it went down and I was completely in it. My intention was to minimise my future regret. So I split my contributions 50/50 between bonds and equities.*

For the intelligent investor, risk is *not* short-term volatility of asset prices. Risk is failure to meet realistic aspirations. So the intelligent investor needs to begin by defining his or her investment goals. Every individual has different objectives, but the purposes of investment generally fall into a few broad categories. Most people need to save for retirement. You may want to save for some other specific purpose – to make a deposit on a house, or to buy a secondary property, or to fund your children through college or help them buy their own apartment. You may have a lump sum to invest, perhaps from inheritance or from the sale of a property or business. A cautious person will not want to splurge it right away but hope to earn returns in order to enjoy a more comfortable standard of living in future. Or you may have no very clear objective in mind – you are saving for a rainy day, or perhaps for a sunny one.

Whatever his or her objectives, the intelligent investor thinks total return. In Chapter 2 I suggested that 8 per cent was an appropriate target for that total return – a figure that includes both income and capital gains, but is measured before allowing for tax and inflation. But the intelligent investor should plan around another, lower, rate of return figure – the prudent spending rate. How much can you draw from your investments without impairing their long-term capacity to allow you to maintain or increase the level of expenditure to which you have become accustomed?

The prudent spending rate is a key concept for the trustees

---

* Interview reported by Jason Zweig, 2008.

of endowments: the managers of the Norwegian oil fund, the overseers of the Harvard endowment, the trustees of the Gates Foundation. Because sophisticated investors like these think total return, they are no longer bound, either legally or in their own planning, by the traditional convention that you should match your spending to the income you receive – the total of the dividends, interest, rents etc., arising year by year. But faced with considerable volatility of total return as a result of gyrations in market prices, they have to make decisions as to how much it is provident to spend. And so will you. If you have built up a fund for retirement, or benefited from a windfall, you will need to construct a portfolio of assets and decide how much you can safely withdraw each year.

The definition of income given by the economist John Hicks provides the starting point. Hicks defined 'a man's income as the maximum value which he can consume during a week, and still expect to be as well off at the end of the period as he was at the beginning' (Hicks, 1939, p. 172) (The sexism is remarkable since Hicks's formidable wife was a much better practical manager than her husband.) So if you plan for an 8 per cent total return, and achieve it, you could spend 8 per cent of the value of your portfolio each year and still meet Hicks's test.

Well, not quite. First, 8 per cent is a target, not money in the bank. Prudence suggests you should plan on the basis of a lower return, and therefore spend less. Second, taxes will eat into your total return. I've suggested you might allow 2 per cent for that, giving a realistic target return of 6 per cent. Third, inflation will erode the value of your assets. Even if prices rise at only 2 per cent per annum, you will need to earn a 2 per cent total return simply to stand still. Taking these factors of prudence, tax and inflation together, you might conclude that spending 3 to 4 per cent of assets each year would be consistent with Hicks's test. This is the sort of prudent spending rate widely used by sophisticated charitable funds such as university endowments. US foundations are required to spend 5 per cent of the value of their assets each year. This is to prevent the establishment of trusts such as the Netherlands foundation of Ingvar Kamprad, the fabulously wealthy Swedish founder of IKEA, which spends very little and grows indefinitely in value. The prudent spending rate should be a little less than your target rate, converted into a real post-tax rate of return, and should be revised from time to time in line with experience.

As an individual, you might choose a prudent spending rate a little higher than 3 to 4 per cent. Trustees must be more conservative than individuals. You, however, are mortal. Ben Franklin famously remarked that only two things were inevitable: death and taxes. For individuals, both are inevitable; for charitable institutions, neither applies. In setting a target rate of return, you might plausibly conclude that one roughly offsets the other. You can spend more than a fund with an indefinite time horizon, because you are mortal and there is no point in being the richest person in the graveyard: but you are probably subject to heavier taxation than the endowment. Older people, therefore, might be a little less conservative than younger ones – conventional wisdom tends to have it the other way round. Enjoy those round-the-world cruises!

Buying an annuity was a traditional method of providing for security in old age by converting a lump sum into a fixed lifetime income. In the modern world these investments are not attractive. Annuity rates are poor, because of high charges and investment strategies that focus on individually low-risk assets. There is also the problem of moral hazard created by information asymmetry. Annuities are bought by people in good health, not people with low life expectancies. Purchasers of annuities are more long-lived than the population as a whole. So a man aged sixty-five can expect to live another seventeen years, but an annuity for him will today yield, before tax, less than 6 per cent and, if linked to inflation, less than 4 per cent. These are rates available in dollars or sterling; an annuity in euros may offer 1 per cent less. All these figures are well below a realistic target rate of return.

Reviewing your goals

Turn now to these various categories of investment purpose: relevant planning, saving for a specific goal, prudent management of a lump sum and 'rainy day' saving.

Retirement planning is critical for almost every household, and even young ones must give it thought. At the beginning of the last chapter I offered an illustrative calculation of what you might need to save. You might want to make a similar calculation based on your own circumstances. You will want to tweak the figures in many ways. You will probably need less in retirement than in your working lifetime. You are likely to spend less, you will pay less tax and you will have some other sources of pension income.

Readers of this book are, on average, healthier than average, so your plan should cover at least twenty-five years of retirement.* But – if you can – you should also plan to save for more than twenty-five years before retirement, to benefit from the extraordinary power of compounding returns. Your capacity to save may increase over time, along with your income. You may already have some assets which can be invested more effectively. Your calculation needs to be tailored to your particular circumstances.

This is the sort of problem that a model helps to solve. Remember that no such calculation will be true; like any model, it gives you the 'right' answer to the arithmetic problem, but not necessarily to the substantive problem – there are too many unknown

---

* Seriously. Life-expectancy increases with education and income level.

unknowns. But the exercise can be illuminating and will help to illustrate whether your hopes and plans are feasible. You may want to use one of many useful programs on the internet. But with simple arithmetic you – or your children or grandchildren – should be able to construct a spreadsheet to calculate what you should aim to save for your retirement.

If your investment goal is a specific purchase, the lowest-risk method of achieving that objective may be to buy it now, even if you have to borrow. If you accept that risk is failure to achieve your realistic investment objectives, then both the financial difficulty that may follow excessive ambition and the inability to achieve your financial goals that may result from overly modest aspirations are risks. You will have to balance the risk that servicing the borrowing will prove difficult against the risk that you will not be able to afford to make the purchase in future. We are taught to regard the former, but not the latter, as a risk – to shun failure, but to accept disappointment. But both are sources of unhappiness and regret. The 'mind your portfolio' principle tells you that leverage is not always risky.

If you cannot, or do not want to, achieve your goal immediately, then you may be able to hedge it in whole or part. Buying a property – a secondary residence for yourself or an apartment for your children – is a common investment objective. The clearer you are about the characteristics of such a property, the better placed you are to hedge. Buy-to-let property may be relevant. If you are determined to buy a house in France, then you can bias your portfolio towards property and assets denominated in euros. Another common specific investment objective is to fund the education of your family. There are many schemes to help you do this. Take advantage of any tax breaks offered, but do not pay initial commissions or high ongoing charges to access these schemes. DIY will often be the best route.

The cautious investor of a lump sum will build a diversified portfolio of the kind I will describe below, but should not aim to do so immediately. Gradual investment, drip-feeding your funds into your portfolio, will allow you to benefit from 'dollar cost averaging', a potent 'get rich slow' scheme which I will also describe below.

For the lump sum investor looking to supplement earnings from investment income, determination of the prudent spending rate is critical. Of course, you may not want to spread the benefit over the whole of your life, but the calculation of a prudent spending rate provides a key benchmark. You may well find that annual interest and dividends are less than your prudent spending rate. If so, you will need to sell assets from time to time if your expenditure is in line with your prudent spending rate.

You may find this hard. The notion that a cautious person spends no more than his or her income is firmly ingrained in our culture, and for good reasons. A wise farmer would divide the crop into the amount that should feed his family and provide for their clothes and education – the income – and the amount – the capital – that should be planted for next year's crop. But principles that worked well on the land do not necessarily serve us well in a world of swaps and derivatives. Habits honed by evolution can be costly. It requires discipline to resist mental accounting. One mechanism for challenging this mental accounting is to set up an automatic transfer from your broker's account to your bank.

And then there is the 'rainy day' saver. The most attractive financial goal for most people is to know that no likely contingency will cause financial embarrassment. While your own circumstances will be particular to you, the meaning of financial security for most readers of this book is confidence about their future standard of living. There are several threats to the achievement of such security through an investment portfolio. The portfolio may decline in monetary value through market risk or credit risk. The monetary value of the portfolio may lose its purchasing power through inflation risk. I will discuss below how to control these risks through diversification, emphasis on long time horizons and a focus on real assets.

But beyond these known unknowns, the world is also uncertain. There are many historical instances of people who thought they had secured their financial future but who were proved wrong. Wealthy central Europeans, who had never expected to work for a living, discovered in the economic turbulence of the 1920s that they had lost all they had, because banks failed or because hyperinflation made their savings worthless. Prosperous Jews thought that owning their own houses gave them security but discovered that they would have been better off with assets overseas when Nazi persecution made it impossible for them to enjoy their German property.

Many people pay a high price for the appearance of certainty – docile citizens of East Germany, or the people who accepted dull jobs in large corporations in the belief that their jobs were for life. Both groups discovered that the certainty they craved was illusory. To take control of one's own life or financial affairs may seem to create uncertainty, but taking control is a prerequisite of security in a world that is inescapably uncertain.

It is impossible to eliminate financial worries altogether, as those twentieth-century European households discovered. More recently, Mikhail Khodorkovsky and Boris Berezovsky became billionaires in the 1990s as oligarchs prospered from the collapse of the Soviet state. But both these individuals fell out with the Putin regime. Khodorkovsky spent ten years in prison. Berezovsky, who had fled to London, was engaged for years in ruinous litigation with another oligarch, Roman Abramovich, until, bankrupt, Berezovsky was found hanged in unexplained circumstances in 2013. Such vicissitudes of fortune have been the experience of many oligarchs throughout history.

A few investment gurus, harbingers of the apocalypse, recommend gold bars, or the equivalent, which can be cashed in the event of financial collapse. Barton Biggs, Morgan Stanley's long-term naysayer, urged everyone to have 'a farm or a ranch somewhat far off the beaten track but which you can get to quickly and easily'. This is not a realistic recommendation for most people. But there are episodes in history in which coins or jewellery have literally been lifesavers.

Diversification is the key to managing risk

The conventional investor believes that there is a trade-off between risk and return. This is another aphorism that is sometimes illuminating, but often untrue. The assumption of trade-off gives insufficient attention to the 'mind your portfolio' principle. Even if high risk and high expected returns were indissolubly associated at the level of the individual security, it does not follow that the same relationship holds in a portfolio. You cannot measure the risk of a portfolio by simply aggregating the risks of individual investments.

A portfolio that consists of a collection of idiosyncratic but individually risky investments, such as Robb Caledon, can be a low-risk portfolio. Such a portfolio may carry a lower risk, in fact, than a collection of blue chips – stocks that are individually safe, but whose returns are likely to be strongly correlated with each other. For the intelligent investor, risk is a characteristic of a portfolio, rather than of the individual security. This is the illuminating insight of the capital asset pricing model, and that insight remains valid independently of reservations about the truth of the CAPM.

In fact, the insight is profitable for investors precisely because the capital asset pricing model is not true. The pattern of returns on different assets reflects other people's views of risk, uncertainty and security. The risk premium they offer is the product of the average of other people's attitudes to risk. But other people's attitudes to risk are different from yours. They avoid mistakes for which they might be criticised. They are wedded to benchmarks. They focus on the riskiness of individual assets, rather than the risk of their overall portfolio. Their mistakes, or at least their different approaches to risk, provide your opportunities.

Conventional investors regard risk as short-term volatility of return, but the intelligent investor has a different conception of risk. *Your risk is your failure to meet your realistic aspirations.* Your strategy is the product of your long-term investment goals, and the longer your time horizon, the better the opportunities for you to achieve satisfying combinations of risk and return.

Suppose the premium that volatile assets command over what are conventionally described as risk-free assets is 4 per cent, a common assumption for the size of the equity premium. The magnitude of this figure reflects these conventional investors' fear of short-term fluctuations in the value of their assets. Suppose also the standard deviation of annual equity returns is 15 per cent (approximately the historical average). Then over the next week the expected return on an equity investment is less than 0.1 per cent more than the risk-free asset.

And the spread of outcomes is much wider; that follows from the way risk has been defined. Even Warren Buffett and George Soros lose money most days. If the distribution of returns is normal – a reasonable assumption over one week – then there is almost a 50 per cent chance that the 'risk-free' asset will do better. Over a year, however, the expected value of the additional return from volatile assets is 4 per cent, and the probability that there will be *some* additional return to compensate for not, has risen to around 60 per cent.*

Stretch the time horizon to twenty-five years, and the

---

* This calculation assumes that the distribution of returns is normal and that successive period returns are independent. As I have explained, there are good reasons for scepticism about both these assumptions. These illustrative figures should be treated as illuminating rather than accurate.

divergence becomes much greater. The expected value of the 'risky' portfolio is 167 per cent higher. If the distribution of returns is normal, this 167 per cent advantage is also the median and the modal outcome. Only the very lowest percentiles of the distribution of volatile returns will fall short of the returns on the 'safe' asset. In fact, you will do better in the risky asset on almost 99 per cent of occasions. And the longer the time horizon, the more certain it is that volatile assets will outperform (on the assumptions above about risk premium and volatility). The notion that cash and short-dated bonds are less risky than more volatile assets is the product of the confusion between certainty and security identified in Chapter 7.

Moreover, we have seen that there is no such thing as a risk-free asset. Extreme percentiles of the distribution of outcomes are typically generated not by risks but from uncertainties. These extreme events are sometimes the result of very low-probability risks incorporated in models: the risk that a fair coin comes up heads twenty times in a row. But disastrous outcomes are most often a consequence of the large-scale breakdown of social, political and economic institutions; the Russian Revolution, the hyperinflation of the Weimar republic and the lawlessness of the Nazi regime which followed and, as I am writing this, the break-down of the Venezuelan state. It is events such as these, rather than runs of bad luck, which are most likely to destroy the value of an investment portfolio.

Even in Britain such institutional breakdown was within sight on three occasions in the last century: in 1931, when the Great Depression threatened political stability; in 1940, when Britain faced the real prospect of hostile invasion; and in 1974, when securities markets collapsed as a weak government presided over inflation and labour unrest that seemed out of control. The United States weathered the political and economic crisis that had closed the nation's banks as Franklin Roosevelt was inaugurated President in 1933; but the survival of the US market economy was no foregone conclusion. In these latter cases break-down was averted. But in none was the margin so wide as to suggest that collapse was inconceivable.

Since distributions of investment outcomes have fat tails, especially at the lower ends of the distribution, even the most conventional portfolio can suffer from events that fall far short of these apocalyptic outcomes. The financial failures with which we are more recently familiar – the 1987 crash, the credit crisis of 2007–8, defaults of Greek debt – represent bad, but not extreme, percentiles of potentially predictable risk distribu-tions (although, as Mr Viniar revealed, even these events were not within the range of possibilities contemplated by Goldman Sachs's risk models*). Big upsets come from even milder crises – the Asian collapse of 1997–8 or the bursting of the New Economy bubble. All these events, however, are sufficiently abnormal to have fallen outside the scope of conventional modelling.

You do not know what investments will pay off in these extreme circumstances, and nor does anyone else. You can build an investment portfolio for a rainy day, but what of a monsoon? The only certainty you can have is that a well-diversified portfo-lio gives you the best chance that at least some assets will return their value – as it did for those refugees who fled with their jewellery.

The illusory security of cash and bonds

Over the years since 1980, intelligent investors have been able to make a lot of money in bonds. As worldwide inflation sub-sided, interest rates steadily fell from the peaks they achieved in

---

* Perhaps significantly, Goldman had done more than its competitors to protect itself against the events of 2007–8, suggesting that its qualitative analysis was more reliable than its modelling.

the 1970s. These declines in short- and long-term interest rates provided capital gains to bondholders. Even Queen Victoria's Consols proved a highly rewarding investment.

But even after inflation had more or less ended in developed economies, bond yields continued to fall and their prices to rise. The policy known as 'quantitative easing' was adopted in response to the 2008 global financial crisis. Central banks – initially those of Japan, the UK and US, and more recently the European Central Bank – have bought bonds in enormous quantities. The Federal Reserve Board holds US Treasury securities worth trillions of dollars. The resulting distortion of the bond market has made the sector unattractive to intelligent investors.

Safe bonds from stable countries with interest rates that are around zero or even negative do not sound like attractive investments, and they are not. If you were thinking of buying the 2046 bund described in Chapter 3, with its 1 per cent redemption yield, you might instead consider an apartment in Berlin or Frankfurt. That investment will yield between 3 and 5 per cent. Even if the rent never rose and the property was worthless, by 2046 you would have earned more from the property than from the bund. Instead of the thirty-year US Treasury bond, you might consider the stock of Johnson & Johnson, the diversified healthcare company. These shares yield 3 per cent, more than the 2.6 per cent GRY on the US Treasury bond. But while the Treasury will make a fixed pay-out till 2046, Johnson & Johnson has increased its dividend every year for the last fifty years, and that dividend today is well covered by the company's earnings.

Since safe government bonds today are so unlikely to pay more than reasonable alternative investments over the long run, who holds them, and why? As a result of quantitative easing, governments themselves are, through their central banks, by far the largest owners of their own securities. But even now, most government bonds are in private hands. Some long-dated bonds are held speculatively, by people who hope to sell at a profit next week and have no interest in what happens in 2046. Others are held by institutions which are only interested in what happens in 2046. These are typically pension funds and insurance companies, which have fixed monetary liabilities stretching far into the future, and which are under regulatory or other pressure to find assets that more or less exactly match these liabilities.

But you do not fall into either category. You are not trying to anticipate the changing 'mind of the market', nor attempting to meet a fixed money claim falling due in 2046. With bonds so unattractive that you do not want to hold them directly, you also do not want to hold them indirectly, by participating in insurance or pension funds which hold them in significant quantity.

Cash and short-dated bonds are often described as low-risk investments. But they are not low-risk investments for those who want to protect their future real living standards. Many people find that statement difficult. Part of the problem is confusion between the minimisation of risk and the search for certainty. With cash and short-dated bonds you know – in a sense – what is going to happen; it is highly probable that you will get back the cash you put in. But if security is confidence in your long-term standard of living – the ability to be relaxed about retirement, the confidence that you can provide for your children or one day buy the property you have dreamed about – then cash does not provide that security.

Few if any of your long-term future liabilities are fixed in money terms. Your plans for the future are defined in real terms – the cash needed to fulfil your objectives is dependent on the purchasing power of the money of that future time. The inflation protection provided by index-linked bonds potentially offers greater certainty. Even then it is difficult to match the bonds exactly to your personal objectives. You are exposed to interest rate risk unless the pattern of payments on the bond precisely corresponds to the time path of your planned expenditures. You are also exposed to personal inflation risk – the price of the goods and services you buy is not the same as the representative basket chosen by official statisticians. And the return is extremely low; currently most maturities of index-linked bonds offer a negligible or even negative real yield.

Even in more normal circumstances cash and bonds have little to offer the intelligent investor. The greater certainty that cash appears to provide is perhaps only the certainty that you will not do well, since nothing can provide certainty that exceptionally unfavourable outcomes are unlikely. Even in a relatively stable political and economic environment, a portfolio of bonds offers little security. Investors in British Consols lost more or less their entire wealth in the course of the twentieth century. A portfolio of indexed bonds would perform better, although this is a modern asset category that has never been tested in extreme conditions. Risks can never be eliminated, and uncertainties are inescapable. The key issue for the intelligent investor is to understand that achieving security lies not in avoiding all risk – which is impossible – but in diversification. Do not be too vulnerable to any particular contingency, however improbable. Hold as many options as possible against a necessarily unpredictable future.

The relevance of bonds to an investment portfolio is not that they are risk-free, but that they may do well in circumstances in which other investments will not. British government bonds served their holders well in the Great Depression of the early 1930s, and were the only major asset category to do so. In Britain the oil crisis of 1973–4 became a political crisis leading to rapid inflation and a collapse of shares and property values. If indexed bonds had been available, they would have performed strongly, and would almost certainly have been the only asset class to do so.

I don't think cash or conventional fixed interest bonds normally have a role in an intelligent investor's portfolio. You will want to keep enough cash on hand for impulse and emergency purchases. Many, probably most, of the investments in the intelligent investor's portfolio are as good as cash for these purposes.

You can turn an investment in a blue chip share into money in the bank within a week. But we employ mental accounting. We don't think of our liquid securities as cash. Like me, you will probably keep more money in a deposit account than you need. You relinquish return, and gain only superficial security, from these habits.

These conclusions represent a very different approach to risk from that of the conventional investor. Most financial advisers will recommend a mix of safe and risky assets, assuming that the meaning of safety is both obvious and universal, and that investors need to be paid a premium to relinquish that safety. The robo-adviser, constrained by regulation to follow the conventional wisdom, will make similar proposals. But the most rewarding strategy for the intelligent investor is to construct a low-risk portfolio from a collection of assets that the conventional investor perceives as risky.

Contrary thinking

The conventional investor avoids judgements wherever possible. The intelligent investor is willing to make judgements. But most retail investors show bad judgement. The average investor does much worse than the market average mutual fund. The US investment research house Dalbar has for many years measured the average return earned by investors in mutual funds. Over twenty years the annual return to mutual fund savers who invested in stocks has been 5.2 per cent. Not too bad, you may think – until you are told that the total return on the S & P 500 index, the principal US stock market index, has been 9.9 per cent. The average return to holders of bond funds has been a miserable 0.8 per cent, against 6.2 per cent for the equivalent bond index. This underperformance – averaging 5 per cent per year – has persisted, year in year out, in the Dalbar analysis.

Why? The average mutual fund investor, with encouragement

from the financial services industry, gets timing badly wrong. Momentum effects are picked up most quickly by proprietary traders, next by professional fund managers, and finally by the marketing departments of financial services businesses. Their sales people, naturally, promote the funds that have recently done best. So money floods into fashionable sectors. Retail investors bought technology in 1999–2000 and were encouraged to buy bond funds after equity markets had collapsed. Subsequently, property funds were strongly promoted. In each case, investors bought at the top and quickly incurred losses. Doubtless they will have the same experience in bonds when interest rates return to more normal levels.

Retail investors, towards the back of the crowd, tend to suffer from mean reversion rather than to benefit from momentum. They enter the market when short-term positive serial correlation turns into long-term negative serial correlation. Jaded investors later sell the funds that promised much but delivered little. They get it wrong both when they buy and when they sell. I suspect that more than a few readers of this book recognise their own experience.

Timing peaks and troughs in the market is as hopeless as looking for hot tips. Professional doomsters continually predict market crashes and are, like stopped clocks, occasionally right. Chartists detect patterns or investment indicators that provide buy and sell signals in randomly generated data. There is little evidence of anyone, amateur or professional, generating superior returns from systematic identification of the tops and bottoms of market cycles. George Soros and Warren Buffett understood well that the 1999–2000 New Economy bubble would burst and that markets would crash. But they didn't know the date, and so they didn't profit. Even if you know that long-term mean reversion will eventually lead prices back towards fundamental values, you can't tell when. If Soros and Buffett can't – and no longer try – nor can you.

Once you have accepted that you can't time the market, there is a great deal you can still do. The dismal record of mutual fund investors suggests a place to start. Watch what these people do, and do the opposite. Their underperformance will be your out-performance. Look at the sectors promoted in advertisements. These are the sectors to avoid. When the promotions favour technology and emerging markets, think infrastructure and property. When they show photographs of roads and offices, think technology and emerging markets. Be contrarian. Your aim is to avoid following in the rear of the crowd, and to be travelling in a different – even the opposite – direction.

Modern financial markets are dominated by the power of conventional thinking. People in the financial sector share superficial views with each other and project current trends too far and too fast. Social and commercial pressures, reinforced by ubiquitous benchmarking, encourage professional fund managers to act on these widely shared opinions regardless of private reservations.

There is, almost always, an underlying element of truth in conventional thinking. The internet was an important commercial and social development. The economic progress of China and India does have a major impact on the global economy. This information is 'in the price'. More than that – the herd behaviour of professional investors means that these conventional opinions are more than fully in the price. That is part of the reason why prices display positive serial correlation in the short run and negative serial correlation in the long run. In the short run, momentum drives prices as fashion spreads; in the long run, mean reversion drives prices as fashion fades.

There are two possible ways of exploiting this behaviour. One is to ride momentum. But this is like riding a tiger. The experience will certainly be stressful and exciting, and it may be rewarding for a time, but the difficulty of timing accurately when you get on and when you get off is so great that, sooner or later, it is probable that you will be mauled (as happened to Julian Robertson). There is not much evidence that anyone can do it successfully over a long period. If anyone can do it successfully, it will almost certainly be someone very close to the market, who can detect shifts in sentiment in that brief interval when it is still possible to act but before these shifts are incorporated in prices. It is very unlikely that you will be that person.

In the second strategy – defying the fashion – the retail investor potentially has an advantage over the professional. Not being close to the market means that you are not subject to the pressures the professionals experience. You don't have to talk to trustees or clients who want to act on the news they have read in the newspaper that morning (and which everyone else has also read) – that China is growing rapidly or that the housing market is dull.

The converse of the power of conventional thinking is the power of contrarian investment. There is something paradoxical in the idea that the best way to use the expertise of the financial services industry is to do the opposite of what it recommends. This is not because that expertise is no good. It is because that expertise is 'in the price' and characteristically more 'in the price' than is objectively justified.

Some of the biggest mistakes in my own investment history have been following the crowd when the crowd was going in the right direction – for example, buying European property in 2006, when the mind of the market identified it as an undervalued asset class. Even if the crowd is right about fundamental value (and in that case I think it was), the fashion is 'in the price'. When the fashion fades, so will some of the money you have paid (and within two years, it had).

Being contrarian should not be interpreted as perversity, or counter-suggestibility. Begin by limiting your contrarian strategy to broad asset categories and to funds. Be much more hesitant about taking a contrarian view of individual shares.

There is a real likelihood that a share price has fallen because someone knows something you don't. It is a common mistake to believe that if a share once sold for €50 it will reach that value again. A stock that has fallen by 95 per cent from its high has halved in value since the date at which it had fallen from its high by 90 per cent.

A contrarian investor will, however, see cases where a stock has fallen for a specific reason but by an amount far larger than that specific reason would justify, as Buffett did at American Express. The scandal was soon forgotten by both customer and market, and the stock price rose steadily. If, however, the fall had affected all house-builders, or most Japanese stocks, then it is more likely that the explanation of the price fall is to be found in general knowledge exaggerated in conventional thinking than that it is the result of inside knowledge not yet available to the markets.

Contrarianism is equally relevant to your purchase of funds. Buy the funds that aren't promoted rather than the ones that are. Closed-end funds move to large discounts to asset value when the sector in which they specialise falls out of favour, and this is an opportunity to buy.

Market timing

Here is a scheme for beating the market that really works. Imagine a volatile share that sells for 50c in odd years and €1 in even years. If you invest €100 every year in this share, over a ten-year period you will have accumulated 1,500 shares at an average price of 66.7c, well below the average market price, which is 75c.

This system will, on average, outperform the market, and the more volatile the markets, the greater the gains. The method is known as dollar cost averaging. It works through its built-in mechanism for buying more when prices are relatively low and less when prices are relatively high. No judgement is required by the investor that prices are relatively low or relatively high.

Many individuals do, and more should, make regular savings to build up an investment portfolio. Some investment managers use the benefits of dollar cost averaging and extol the benefits of a regular savings scheme in their marketing literature. On this occasion, believe them. The benefits are real. But keep an eye, as usual, on their charges. Regular saving is a practice you can organise for yourself through an execution-only stockbroker. You do not need to pay someone a commission to take direct debits from your account.

The effectiveness of dollar cost averaging illustrates how low share prices are an opportunity rather than a problem for the intelligent investor. Conventional investors are usually excited when they hear that the market is going up, disappointed when they learn that it has fallen. As Buffett has occasionally pointed out, this is odd. We are pleased when we hear that a favourite shop has a sale, or car dealers have reduced their prices. We want high prices when we are sellers, but low prices when we are buyers. We are usually only buyers of clothes or durable goods. However, for shares – as perhaps for cars and houses – we may be both buyers and sellers at different times.

When should the intelligent investor sell? The simple answer is 'not very often'. Frequent trading endangers returns. But sometimes the mind of the market will take a security to a price well in excess of any reasonable estimate of its fundamental value. Money is a means to an end, not an end in itself, and you will sometimes sell investments in order to spend, especially if most of your total return is capital gains. In recent years the rate at which small companies have been acquired has ensured that portfolios have a regular inflow of cash from acquisitions. This will not be true if you invest mainly in funds rather than individual securities. But if you invest in well-chosen funds, you have even less reason to wish to trade.

Dollar cost averaging makes sense for both conventional and intelligent investors. Conventional investors can feel relieved that their approach yields profits without requiring judgement. Intelligent investors know that market timing is unlikely to make money and can feel happy with an approach that is inherently contrarian. The reasoning that makes dollar cost averaging attractive applies to decisions about asset classes as well as to decisions about market timing. Let's see how.

Asset allocation

Investment consultants and managed funds follow each other closely. Trustees or managers are required to set benchmarks for asset allocations, and deviations from the norm – the average of what others do – require considered justification. The best way for them to minimise risk is to do much the same as everyone else. This is, of course, not a course of action that minimises risk for their beneficiaries.

When an asset category rises in value, the proportion of that asset class in the benchmark increases. Individual investors may choose to follow the market allocation; institutional investors feel obliged to follow it. Such benchmarking has led to a steady increase in the share of equities, the best-performing asset class, in conventional portfolios.

The consequences can be perverse. At the peak of the Japanese stock market bubble of the 1980s, Japanese shares accounted for almost half of the value of all shares – American, European, Brazilian, Australian – in the world. American and European investors, who had thought they were brave if 10 per cent of their assets were in Japan, felt under pressure to acquire more securities in Japan. Fifteen years later, Japanese share prices had fallen, while those in other countries had risen. Today Japan accounts for less than 10 per cent of the market value of world indices.

Common sense suggests that an allocation of half your portfolio to Japan in the late 1980s was far too much, given that Japan never accounted for more than 10 per cent of world output. Most investors did, at least intuitively, understand this. While few people fell comprehensively into this Japanese trap, many investors have been victims of milder versions of the error, buying technology shares, bonds, infrastructure and property at the wrong times. Looking at market weightings when deciding asset allocation leads institutions and fund managers to buy high and sell low. This strategy leads them to purchase overpriced assets in order to achieve desired portfolio weightings.

The search for 'fundamental indices' is an attempt to resist these perverse behaviours. The idea behind a fundamental index is that asset-class weightings should be based not on market value but on some underlying measure of economic contribution. This insight leads intelligent investors to look behind financial assets and judge the value of the productive assets that underpin them. A benchmark for allocation to Japan might, therefore, be Japanese national income as a percentage of world national income, implying a range of 5–10 per cent that would remain unchanged by the vagaries of the Japanese stock markets.

From this perspective the model pension fund portfolio contains a heavy concentration of oil companies, pharmaceutical businesses and banks relative to the economic importance of these activities. The investor who has thought in terms of fundamental indices is bound to wonder why a conventional institutional portfolio allocates ten times as much to stocks as to property. Very large economic sectors, such as agriculture, education and healthcare, and legal and accounting services, are not represented at all in the model pension fund portfolio, or only in very limited ways.

You can change that. There are few quoted securities in agriculture, education or health, but there are some. There are (as yet) only a few stock market prices for law firms or accountancy practices (the first and largest quoted law firm in the UK was called Quindell, and many people pronounced its name with emphasis on the first syllable). There are other businesses, such as recruitment agencies and public relations firms, whose fortunes are closely related. The conventional investor's assets are much less diversified than they might be.

The numbers that emerge from analysis based on fundamental indices may be illuminating but not true – certainly no one should regard them as more than qualitative guides. The illuminating insight is that investors should be wary of allowing fluctuations in market prices to influence their target allocations to different asset classes. If the price of property rises relative to the price of your other assets, consider reducing the proportion of your assets you hold in property, and vice versa. Many people find this paradoxical. Should we really sell securities just because they have done well? In a world characterised by momentum and mean reversion, you should. That way you can realise the benefits of dollar cost averaging in asset allocation as well as market timing.

But what is the right asset allocation? How should an intelligent investor's portfolio be divided between shares, bonds and property? I'm not sure that this is the right way to pose the asset allocation question. To do so supposes that all shares are much more like each other than they are like any of the assets in the other categories, such as property and bonds, and that the same is true in turn of these asset categories.

For the assets that institutional funds typically hold, it may well be true that all the securities within a given asset class are much the same. Their share portfolio will mainly contain large, global companies, whose prices tend to go up and down together; the bonds will mainly be medium- and long-dated government securities; the properties will mainly be well-located city centre office blocks with similar prospective growth in both rental levels and capital values. These funds will have followed the conventional investor's strategy of minimising the risks on individual investments rather than the intelligent investor's strategy of looking at the risk of their portfolio as a whole. So when they buy property, they buy whichever category of property their advisers currently tout as the best mixture of return and reward, and they buy several such properties. Following this conventional strategy, they fail to diversify effectively.

The 'mind your portfolio' principle implies that you should look at the expected return from individual assets and their correlation with your overall portfolio. Your objective is that every single investment you buy should significantly diversify your portfolio. You don't need, and probably shouldn't have, an intermediate process of asset allocation. Asset allocation percentages will be the result, not the preliminary, of diversifying investment decisions about individual securities. In the next chapter I'll discuss how these securities should be selected.

12

Intelligent Investment Choices

Diversify

Diversification within an investment portfolio is the key to risk management. The conventional investor's portfolio is unnecessarily risky even by reference to its own measure of risk – short-term volatility. Between 2007 and 2009 the conventional investor's portfolio would have fallen in value by around 30 per cent. Many pension funds, insurance companies and charities suffered badly during that period. Nor was that fall unprecedented. There was a similar setback in 2000–2. The loss in 1973–4 would have been greater, and there would also have been other significant dips in value.

But in practice short-term volatility is not the only risk that concerns many conventional investors. They interpret low risk as meaning avoidance of investments that involve the possibility of significant loss, and aim to ensure that each individual stock in their portfolio is, in this sense, low risk. There is evidence that the distress people experience from losses is significantly greater than the joy they experience from gains of similar magnitude. If they react in this way to losses on individual securities as well as those on their portfolio as a whole, the discomfort they will experience on reviewing a pool of assets with any price volatility at all is likely to be considerable. Of course, they can minimise their regret by 'minding their portfolio' and refraining from looking constantly at the value of their assets; but that requires mental discipline.

And from the perspective of the pension fund trustees and their investment managers such aversion to loss is understandable. As I have emphasised, the major risk a financial adviser runs is not the risk that his clients do badly but the risk that his clients do worse than other people. Every committee and large organisation is crowded with people who will say 'I told you so' when things go wrong. The conventional institutional investor will be reluctant ever to hold an asset that the institution, or the responsible manager, can be criticised for having bought. I can take more individual stock risks with my personal investment portfolio because I don't have to justify decisions, before or after the event. I can do that even though my personal style is to maintain a low-risk portfolio. I am free to 'mind my portfolio', and so are you. The typical institutional investor is not. Robb Caledon would be a risky purchase for anyone managing someone else's funds, because there is a substantial probability of total loss.

Conventional investors focus on large, widely held stocks. There was for many years a maxim that 'no one ever got fired for buying IBM', and that held for IBM stock as well as IBM computers. Conventional investors then claim to diversify by including many of these popular stocks with big market capitalisations in their portfolio. But holding many stocks is not the same as diversification. Look behind the index and the broad allocations to asset categories and see the disposition of the conventional investor's investment in a global index. There are large holdings in the oil majors – Exxon, Shell and BP, and in General Electric, Pfizer and Nestlé, Apple and Microsoft. The portfolio will, even after the recent collapse of the banking sector, have a large exposure to finance. All these companies sell mainly to the advanced economies of the United States and Western Europe. Their fortunes wax and wane with the world economy, and so does market sentiment towards them. Returns from all these stocks are strongly correlated with each other. Neither the market indices nor the conventional investor's portfolio are well diversified.

So how should the intelligent investor approach diversification? You do not need to hold many different securities if the returns from those you do hold are uncorrelated with each other. Recall how the volatility of outcomes of the coin-tossing game diminished rapidly as the number of tosses of the coin increased. Understanding correlation is the key to successful diversification.

In the last decade many conventional investors who emphasise asset allocation between broad categories – quoted equities, real estate, private equity etc. – have been concerned that all these asset classes appear strongly correlated with each other. During the global financial crisis all these real assets performed badly, and even companies whose business was little affected by the financial crisis experienced stock price falls as conventional investors, struggling for liquidity, sold whatever could be sold. Then the loose monetary policies of low interest rates and quantitative easing pushed up all asset prices almost indiscriminately.

But while short-term correlations are governed by the mind of the market, long-term correlations are the product of fundamental value. An apartment in Berlin, a field of land with development potential within reach of London and an office block in Hong Kong are all classed as real estate; the stock of Apple, shares in a supermarket chain in Taiwan and a Silicon Valley start-up are all categorised as global equities. And in the short run, market liquidity and herd behaviour have similar effects on them all. But over twenty years the factors that determine the success of each of these investments are not only different but specific to each individual property or stock.

While the covariance matrices that investment consultants use help to focus attention on diversification, they are of little use to intelligent investors. The asset categories they use are insufficiently granular – domestic equities, real estate – and the historical data used to compile them are often too short-term and are always likely to be undermined by technological or institutional change. The only way of understanding the correlation between Robb Caledon shares and the wider market in 1976 was to have knowledge of the peculiar politics of that time – knowledge that could never be expressed in a covariance matrix.

Almost everyone thinking about investment opportunities begins by asking the question 'What is likely to go up?' But general knowledge about companies, industries and countries is knowledge that you share with everyone else; it is already 'in the price'. The record of most investment professionals in correctly identifying what will go up is poor. You don't know what is going to go up. That is why you may have been tempted to take advice. But those who offer to advise you have little or no more valuable knowledge than you, and they have different interests from yours.

The intelligent investor gives as much attention to correlation as to expected return and looks at both by reference to fundamental value. There are two groups of question to ask in considering any particular proposed investment. First, is the potential return on this investment consistent with my overall investment objective? Can I reasonably anticipate that this holding might meet my target total return of 8 per cent per annum over a five-year period? And second, what are the factors specific to this asset that will determine its success or failure over that five-year period, or longer? Are the characteristics of this investment significantly different from those of other securities I already own?

This approach means rejecting investments for which there is a plausible case because the returns from these investments are correlated with investments you already have. This will happen often, since the reasons that made the earlier purchase seem attractive may also apply to the new one. An indexed portfolio is more diversified than a portfolio in which you keep using similar arguments to buy more assets of the same kind.

An indexed portfolio is neither diversified nor contrarian, because the weights in the index are driven by the power of conventional thinking. A more diversified portfolio should offer you expected returns similar to those of an indexed portfolio with lower volatility. (I need to enter again the health warning that if you accept the conclusions of the CAPM, as most finance academics – though few practical people – do, then the diversified strategy will be so popular that it will force down the average return from adopting it. Perhaps that proposition should be true, but I don't think it is.)

Increasing diversification means less in pharmaceuticals and oil companies, and more in sectors whose performance is less strongly correlated with the investments you already hold. General insurance companies, for example, experience cycles of their own that are not necessarily in sync with the general economic cycle.

The performance of gold mines or other commodity producers is likely to be very different from that of the general stock market. Diversify internationally. But there is no point in reducing your holding in Glaxo in order to increase your holding in Pfizer – these companies have very similar businesses. A small pharmaceutical company – whatever its nationality – whose fortunes will probably rise or fall with the success of individual drugs rather than the sector as a whole will offer returns with lower correlation. Look to Japan, or Russia or Taiwan, but real diversification from these investments will come from companies oriented to their domestic economies, rather than businesses with which you are more familiar. Sony, Gazprom and Lenovo sell to the same people as Microsoft, Shell and Apple.

Fund selection

Most investors will, and should, begin with funds rather than individual stocks. Funds may be distinguished by investment style or by sectoral or geographic specialisation. Choose funds whose returns are not strongly correlated with each other – be diversified. Choose funds which are out of favour rather than fashionable – be contrarian.

A web site such as Morningstar will give you a wide – far too wide – selection. In every category there are many similar funds doing similar things. I am not going to recommend specific funds, but the criteria I will describe will narrow the range very considerably.

You might consider exchange-traded funds here, since the range of simple index funds is limited, and this sector offers a variety of country options. You can invest not just in the indices of the major developed markets but also in Chile or Taiwan and other small and emerging economies. In the larger markets you can choose to focus on smaller or larger companies, or on a particular sector, such as utilities or real estate. Plan to build up a diversified portfolio of such funds, emphasising sectors that are unfashionable.

Then consider an allocation to actively managed funds. Pick two or three funds with widely different styles and approaches. This gives a better balance of risk and return. But keep a close eye on charges. A company that charges 1 per cent or more for a closet index fund is ripping you off. Buying a closed-end fund with low charges and a large discount to asset value gives you a chance of earning the return generated by the underlying productive investments. Most closed-end funds go to a discount of 15 per cent or more from time to time if you are content to wait. The widening of the discount is a good contrarian signal when it is the result of the unfashionability of the sector rather than the poor performance of the fund. If management costs are not substantially less than 1 per cent, the fund must justify these charges by the proven success of its distinctive style (including low correlation with market indices).

How to distinguish proven success from the 'hot hand'? Favour funds that are strongly identified with an individual. Good fund managers are people rather than corporations, although on occasion good processes are the creation of innovative founders. Idiosyncratic funds with a strong record are typically provided by boutiques, but there are exceptions – legendary fund managers Anthony Bolton and Peter Lynch ran funds for Fidelity.

Buy funds that have a history of good performance, but look for a long history and, above all, ensure that the track record was good both before and after the fund manager became famous. Many good track records are the product of lucky streaks, and are then aggressively marketed, only to disappear. There is some evidence of investment skill, but it is rare.

Property

While most equity funds are open-ended, most property funds are closed-end. Many countries, including the US and UK, have established a special real estate investment trust (REIT) tax status, under which shareholders are taxed broadly as if they owned a share of the properties of the fund. There are also closed-end property funds that do not qualify as REITs, typically those with large development programmes and extensive borrowings.

Closed-end property funds generally have substantial leverage – much more so than closed-end funds that invest in shares. You need to be careful about this leverage. Your €1,000 investment in a fund might correspond to €3,000 of property and €2,000 of borrowings. If you hold leveraged assets, you should remember the 'mind your portfolio' principle, and understand that the leverage of the fund is also your leverage. Your €1,000 in the fund corresponds to a €3,000 commitment to real estate.

Open-ended property funds mostly do not use leverage. Some

invest directly in property, and sell and redeem units at a price that reflects the value of the underlying assets. When the property market fell in 2007, some open-ended funds suspended redemption. Other open-ended property funds hold REITs and other property shares. While some property funds cover a wide spectrum of properties, most have a bias towards particular geographical areas or sectors. As in other areas of investment, closed-end funds are attractive when you can buy them at significant discounts to their asset value; again, do not buy closed-end funds at a premium. You should expect to pay higher management charges for a property fund than for an equity fund, because the costs of looking after buildings are greater than the costs of looking after paper.

With such a range of possibilities it is easy with two or three purchases to construct a portfolio of property assets diversified across different kinds of property – offices, shops, industrial, residential – and across geographical locations.

Stock picking

As your experience of intelligent investment grows, you will wish to consider individual stocks. Even if you have a large, diversified portfolio, you will probably not own more than 1 per cent of the stocks you could potentially buy. That means you can, and should, be extremely selective. It is as though you were speed-dating thousands of potential partners. You are fortunate in being spoilt for choice, and one good reason for rejection is enough.

The basic principles of stock picking follow from Chapters 5 to 8. You are concerned with fundamental value, not momentum in the share price – with the characteristics of the company, not the stock price history. Conventional investors are unduly averse to specific risk which affects one company alone and which can and should be diversified. You do not mind that an individual stock is risky, so long as it does not add greatly to the risk of your portfolio as a whole. That proposition implies, of course, that you can understand what these risks are.

If conventional investors are sometimes too prone to avoid risk – the known unknowns – they are also too prone to accept uncertainties – the unknown unknowns. Use probabilities to assess risk, be detached and minimise uncertainties by knowing when you don't know.

Everywhere and always in financial markets, you are vulnerable to information asymmetry. The company and its executives know more – or are at least capable of knowing more – than you do. The greater the information asymmetry, the more likely it is that you are being offered a lemon. If you don't understand something, or the affairs of the company or the strategy or construction of the fund appear unnecessarily difficult to understand, do not buy. If the share price is falling for inexplicable reasons, do not buy.

Institutional investors will have access to the research on companies that banks circulate to their clients. You will find it difficult to obtain much of this, although you can see similar material in newsletters (tip sheets) or even on bulletin boards. Research reports are more useful for the information they contain than for their recommendations (though you probably will have readier access to the latter). You should understand a little of what financial analysts do, not in order to reproduce their conclusions but because their approach and conclusions are 'in the price'.

An analyst will provide 'coverage' of a group of companies with similar activities. If these businesses are very large, the analyst will be responsible for only a very few companies, though an analyst of smaller companies may cover twenty or more stocks. The bank that employs the analyst frequently hopes to obtain corporate finance business from the companies on which it undertakes (or has already undertaken) research; for small companies, the bank that managed the IPO will often provide the only coverage. This limits objectivity.

An analyst is rewarded for 'good calls'. (ThomsonReutersExtel ratings, based on opinion polls of institutions, have a major influence on the reputation and remuneration of analysts.) A good call is a successful prediction of a sharp upward or downward movement in a share price. But the time-scale on which the call is judged will rarely exceed six months. Although many research reports appear to be concerned with fundamental value, a good call will often anticipate a news announcement relevant to the company (generally either merger and acquisition activity or a substantial revision to earnings expectations). Or, in the manner of Keynes's beauty contest, an analyst may make good calls by being quick to ascertain the changing mood of other analysts.

The favoured analyst will be close to the companies he follows, able to infer from nudges and winks whether announcements will be behind, or ahead of, market expectations. The less favoured analyst – one whose reporting has a critical tone – will be shut out. Analysts who take a negative view of a company frequently receive abuse from chief executives, and the senior management of banks that employ critical analysts frequently receive complaints from the offended companies.

As I described in Chapter 5, the effect of the rise of financial conglomerates was to transform analysts into a sales force for investment banks. Following the New Economy bubble, the damage to the reputations of the financial conglomerates concerned, and pressure from regulators, forced investment bankers to concede greater independence to analysts. Recommendations still have a strongly positive bias, but experienced investors know this and are able, at least in part, to discount this bias. Analysts' research is focused on short-term earnings announcements and projections.

Most analysts simply project current earnings in a mechanical fashion. Even if they are trying to assess fundamental value, they typically do the calculation by making estimates of earnings and translating them into a DCF model. These analysts' valuations are what is 'in the price'. Estimates of fundamental value play a relatively minor role.

Stock selection

A basic checklist for any company you consider investing in should contain the following points: the company should be clear and transparent in the presentation of its affairs and accounts; and the background and remuneration of its senior executives should suggest that they are experienced in and interested in the business, rather than that they are people whose primary concerns are self-aggrandisement or self-enrichment. These are necessary precautions against information asymmetry, and necessary preliminaries to judging risks. If you wouldn't buy a used car from the directors, then you shouldn't buy a share in the company, for essentially the same reasons.

There should also be a clear, comprehensible business model, based on a distinctive capability that has the potential to create sustainable and appropriable competitive advantage. The only sources of fundamental value are tangible assets and competitive advantage. If you cannot identify tangible assets from the accounts that support the valuation (i.e. the market capitalisation) or don't understand the source of the competitive advantage of the business, then you cannot judge either its fundamental value or the risks associated with it. Avoid unnecessary uncertainty.

You will normally look for companies that are soundly financed. Borrowings should be less than the value of readily realisable assets, and the business should generate cash. Operational risk in a company is inescapable. But when an established business compounds operational risk with financial risk, and becomes dependent on the indulgence of its bank or the vagaries of interest rates, and vulnerable to modest economic or business setbacks, it adds uncertainty to risk. Usually this vulnerability in profit and loss accounts or balance sheets is the product of debt-financed acquisitions or of financial engineering. Both large-scale acquisition and financial engineering generally send negative signals about the preoccupations of the company's management.

Where the weak balance sheet is the result of recent poor trading, the position may be more interesting. Most players in financial markets tell stories rather than think probabilities. They believe that the company is going bust, or that it is not – they rarely express the view that there is a probability of 0.4 that it might, or might not, go bust. Analysts, brokers and fund managers are not often detached. They may still be in love with the purchase they made at a much higher price, or worried by the criticism they might receive from bosses or trustees who possess the benefit of hindsight. As at Robb Caledon, the market price of a risky investment may be a poor guide to the expected value.

Be wary of companies with growing profits and negative cash flow. A new, rapidly expanding business or a firm with a large investment programme may have transparent reasons for these. But the difficulty of explaining the discrepancy between profits and cash should have steered intelligent investors away from Enron.

You can reduce uncertainties by focusing on stable businesses. There are fewer uncertainties in the markets for water – a monopoly whose basic technology was developed millennia ago – than in more competitive and exciting activities such as computers or biotechnology. Even companies in relatively stable markets can create uncertainty by programmes of acquisitions and disposals. Most of the fundamental value of any company derives from the cash it will generate five and more years into the future. If you don't know what the company will be doing five years from now, how can you assess its value? Such strategic uncertainty is unnecessary and avoidable.

Look for clarity and transparency in the company's account of its affairs: a simple business model based on distinctive capability that offers sustainable competitive advantage, and a strong balance sheet with cash flow generation and a stable business. A stock that meets all of these criteria is unlikely to be a ten or twenty bagger, but you are looking for a reliable 8 per cent annual target return, not ten or twenty baggers.

Most companies will fail to meet at least one of these criteria. But there are many more fish in the sea. Your aim is to buy good companies on a contrarian basis, probably when their sector is out of fashion. If investors generally applied these criteria in selecting stocks, their decisions would transform the behaviour of corporations. And overwhelmingly for the better. There would be less financial engineering, fewer acquisitions, simpler and more modest executive remuneration. And, above all, less emphasis on investor relations activities to influence the mind of the market and more emphasis on the creation of fundamental value through the identification and development of competitive advantage in operating businesses.

The preoccupations of most professionals lie elsewhere. They are focused on earnings guidance and their quarterly performance figures. They are fixated on 'corporate activity' – a term that is often simply a euphemism for mergers and acquisitions, and more generally means an announcement that may have a material effect on share prices. Such activity is the basis of market gossip and keeps market turnover high.

The intelligent investor isn't, and doesn't want to be, party to that market gossip. The intelligent investor isn't seeking votes in the ThomsonReutersExtel survey. Your reward comes from good investment returns, not from the bonuses you receive for the business you attract.

13

The Customers' Yachts

'Why do I want to buy what they want to sell?' This question is fundamental to investment. Both buyers and sellers own securities in the hope of income and capital gains. But the returns the buyer will obtain are exactly the returns the seller could have obtained. Why should you buy what they want to sell?

In any market in which there is wide and unresolvable uncertainty, in any market where participants have different information and beliefs, many trades will be the result of mistakes. In financial markets, uncertainty and differential information are endemic. When you trade, you need to be confident that it is not you who is making the mistake. Bear in mind the old gambler's maxim: if you don't know who is the patsy in the room, it is probably you.

Keep it simple. If you don't understand a financial product, don't buy it. We purchase cars and computers and many other things without understanding how they work – it is enough to understand their purpose. We rely on the reputation of Mercedes or Microsoft for our belief that their products will actually deliver what they promise. Many people dislike thinking about money, and would like to hand over their financial affairs to someone they can trust. Unfortunately, though, simply placing your trust in financial services businesses is likely to be a mistake and isn't enough to deal with product complexity in modern financial markets. The nature of trade in financial services and the ethics and behaviour of financial services businesses are different from those that pertain in other sectors. In the financial services sector, good reputations seem to survive bad behaviour. Many of the suckers who were ripped off in the New Economy bubble came back to be victims of the credit bubble.

The robo-adviser now offers a possible route if you simply want to hand over all responsibility to someone else and are willing to let it be a computer. But if you have reached this point in this book, I hope you have enough information and enthusiasm to do it better yourself.

Scepticism is appropriate. If it sounds too good to be true, it usually is. In most markets, you tend to get what you pay for. But that is not true of the investment world. The greater the extent of differential information, the less likely it is that costs and charges represent value. The most certain way of increasing returns on your investments is to pay less in fees and commissions. You are on your own, but today the internet gives cheap and easy access to financial products for everyone, and immediate access to information that once required diligent and time-consuming research. Innovations in financial markets – such as the growth of exchange-traded funds and property vehicles – have transformed the opportunities available to retail investors to build for themselves a portfolio that achieves low risk through wide diversification. The intelligent investor today is in greater danger of trading too much because it is easy, than of being deprived of opportunities because access is too difficult.

The notion that market prices are the result of a plebiscite on competing estimates of fundamental value is far removed from the reality of frenzied trading in modern financial markets. Most participants are preoccupied not with long-term economic trends and the competitive advantage of companies but with evolving market opinion and the ephemeral news that passes across the Bloomberg screen.

In an efficient market what is 'in the price' is an average of divergent views. Yet often what is in the price is the manifestation of a common view, generally held within the financial community, but not necessarily well founded. The New Economy bubble was an extreme instance of widely held perceptions that were also widely at variance with reality. Prices that are going up tend to continue going up – markets are characterised in the short term by short-term serial price correlation, or momentum. In the long run, prices that have gone up by a lot tend to go down – there is mean reversion to fundamental value. If only we knew when the short run becomes the long! The efficient market hypothesis is illuminating but not true. There are investment lessons and profit opportunities both in what is illuminating and in what is not true. Across the market as a whole, the profits on financial investment must ultimately depend on the profits on productive investment. For all the intricacies of modern finance, the yield of securities depends on the ability of trading businesses to find profitable ways of serving their customers, on the willingness of tenants to pay rents on shops, offices, houses and factories, and on the ability of companies, consumers and governments to service and repay loans that finance their recent investment or current consumption.

The value of companies depends on their ability to establish competitive advantages over their rivals; sustainable competitive advantage is the only enduring source of superior returns. The value of a property depends on the rents derived from it. The value of a bond depends on the interest it yields and the principal it repays. These determinants of fundamental value necessarily drive securities prices in the long run.

It is possible, though unusual, to make money out of observing and anticipating market momentum. Some people, though not many, are close to the market and have an intuitive feel for, or perhaps an analytic understanding of, its determinants. Whatever the books on trading will tell you, the chances are very small that the person who makes money out of observing and antici-pating these fluctuations will be you, the retail investor.

The only basis on which the intelligent investor can hope to keep up with, far less beat, the market, is by attention to fun-damental value. Through attention to fundamental value, the intelligent investor gains a big advantage over investment profes-sionals who are judged on their performance quarterly, or even more frequently. There is no way in which an investor, amateur or professional, who is focused on fundamental value can reli-ably outperform the market on a monthly or quarterly basis – the noise is far too loud. But, over the long run, mean reversion works in your favour.

Not being part of the conventional wisdom of investment professionals gives you an opportunity to be contrarian. Contrar-ianism requires scepticism but is not perversity. The opportunity for contrarianism arises when the question 'Why do I want to buy what they want to sell?' can attract the answer 'Because they have bad reasons for wanting to sell it.' The investment commu-nity cannot afford to ignore the noise, but you can. Patience pays. Assets are worth more to a long-term investor than to a trader.

The principal risk investment professionals run is the risk of underperformance relative to their peers. Most investment insti-tutions benchmark their performance against their competitors and market averages. There are good reasons for this practice, but also malign consequences. In any event, what interests the intelligent investor is how much money he makes, not how much money he makes relative to other people. Relative performance doesn't pay the bills.

Relative performance has no spending power, but money has equal spending power whether it comes as income or capital gain. Think 'total return'. Treat both income and capital gain as part of the yield on your investment. Set a prudent spending rate by reference to your expected total return over a period of years. If your underlying investment objective is capital growth, then reinvestment of dividends will contribute substantially to capital appreciation in the long run. If your underlying investment objective is to obtain a steady income from investments, then an 'income' can be generated, if necessary, through occasional sales from a growing portfolio. A 'think total return' strategy is equally relevant to investors who are accumulating wealth and to investors who are using their assets to support their standard of living.

The return on productive investments provides the basis for realistic expectations of what an investment portfolio can yield. If you earn higher returns than the yield on productive investments, these returns can only be obtained at the expense of other people who are obtaining lower returns than the yield on productive investment. The intelligent investor can do this through a better understanding of risk and a long-term perspective which emphasises fundamental value.

Your objectives colour your strategy. One justification for the substantial fees charged by the financial services industry is that retail investors need individually tailored advice. While there are some honest and conscientious independent financial advisers, the majority of people who make contact with small savers lack the capacity or knowledge to give competent, individually tailored advice, even if they have the inclination and the financial motivation to do so. If you still doubt this, test them with some questions about the meanings of terms defined in the Glossary.

I am not convinced that much tailoring of investment strategy to particular needs is required anyway. Most investors fall within one of the four broad categories described in Chapter 11 – retirement saver, purposive investor, lump sum investor and rainy day saver. It is far more important to understand the meaning of risk by reference to these objectives than to explore 'risk appetite' or 'risk tolerance'. Most people have low risk tolerance, when risk is properly defined and understood. Those who don't should be kept well away from the casino or the stock market.

I've given a lot of space in this book to different ways of thinking about risk, and described at length in Chapter 7 the theory I have called SEU. Treated both prescriptively and descriptively, this theory completely dominates quantitative approaches to investment today. Intelligent investors should learn to 'think SEU' – to understand its principles but not to follow them blindly. That means learning to think probabilities and expected values. Such an approach recognises that many different outcomes are possible, and assesses, even quantifies, the likelihood of attractive and unattractive outcomes.

SEU implies detachment in investment decisions. If you are a gambler by temperament, you may enjoy the search for a ten bagger, but the expected value of the search is likely to be negative. If you are concerned principally to minimise the regret that you will feel (or that your bosses will make you feel) with hindsight, then the expected value of your strategy is also likely to be negative. These losses of expected value are the costs of emotional involvement in your investments.

The most important implication of SEU is the 'mind your portfolio' principle. Every investment decision should be judged not just by the character of the individual investment but also by the contribution it makes to your overall portfolio. An incidental, but large, benefit of being your own investment manager is that you are the only person who knows everything you are doing.

Like the efficient market hypothesis, SEU is an illuminating theory so long as you do not make the mistake of believing that it is true: It is not true either as a prescriptive theory – What should I do? – or as a descriptive theory – How do market participants respond to risks and uncertainties? The conventional view is that you, the typical dumb investor, don't think SEU but that markets do. This view is mistaken. Markets don't generally think this way, but you often, though by no means always, should. SEU is a powerful tool for thinking about well-defined risks, the things we know we don't know. SEU can describe the risks you encounter when you play roulette, or wonder what the European Central Bank will decide about interest rates at its next meeting. But SEU helps little when we contemplate uncertainties. The things we don't know we don't know.

The prevalence of uncertainty explains why SEU thinking doesn't come naturally. We didn't experience the complexities of modern financial markets in the long process of evolution that hardwired our brains, or in the schools and playgrounds where we were taught to cope with life. Many, though by no means all, situations we face in financial markets are ones for which SEU methods are relevant. We make mistakes. Sometimes the mistake is not to use SEU principles when they might help us – as with the stockbrokers who could not take a detached view of Robb Caledon. More sophisticated investors sometimes make the error of using SEU principles where they don't help us – as in the banks whose risk modelling failed to describe the events that brought them to their knees.

The sophisticated world of modern finance relies on models and forecasts in its assessment of both risks and fundamental values. Most people who are not professionally engaged in building models or producing forecasts respond to models and forecasts with cynical naïveté – a curious mixture of disdain and credulousness. At a visceral level these people know that no model can capture the complexity of the world of finance, business and politics, yet they treat the output of models with the utmost seriousness. They believe that economic forecasts convey little useful information, and yet they pay almost obsessive attention to them.

Financial analysis without models is impossible. But investment managers and executives of financial services firms who rely on the output of models they don't understand have relinquished decision-making to a black box. Such individuals profess adherence to science, but their behaviour is identical to that of earlier generations of decision-makers who consulted the oracles or employed soothsayers to read the entrails. You don't have to be able to build models yourself, but you do have to understand a little of what the models can do to understand and make best use of the limited but real insights they can provide. Numbers can illuminate, but they can also blind.

You need analysis and models more than you need forecasts. If you were able to see the future, profitable investment would be easy, but you can't. Nor can anyone else. The only useful information that people who predict the level of the stock market a year from now give you when they speak is that you should pay very little attention to anything they say. General knowledge about the future is 'in the price'. Specific knowledge about the future is vouchsafed to very few, and the people who have it are mostly prohibited from trading on it.

Instead of devoting time to speculation about what the future holds, recognise that the future is inescapably uncertain. Equip yourself with what will be a portfolio that will be robust to many different contingencies. Such diversification is the most effective means of coping with a complex world. Knowing what you don't know gives you a considerable advantage over those, amateurs and professionals alike, who don't know what they don't know, or do know what ain't so. A broadly diversified portfolio based on real assets will give you considerable protection against risk and uncertainty with little compromise on return. In a 100 per cent efficient market there would be a trade-off between risk and return, but in a partly efficient market there is not. New investment technology using internet dealing means that the retail investor can achieve a diversified portfolio with relatively modest sums.

Three simple rules – pay less, diversify more and be contrarian – will serve almost everyone well. If you have an established investment portfolio based on advice, you will almost certainly find that a substantial part of your total assets is in open-ended managed funds that are closet-indexed. This costs you too much and is inadequately diversified. You can transfer this money into a group of exchange-traded funds, closed-end funds and real estate investment trusts on substantial discounts. That strategy will give you exposure to a range of countries, types of security and styles of management. It will also give you lower charges, and less risk in your overall portfolio. An emphasis on market sectors at a discount will automatically imply a contrarian stance. You will lose what you have already paid in initial charges to set up your investments, but that money has gone anyway. If you are at an earlier stage of your investment career, you can structure your portfolio along these lines from the beginning.

Modern financial markets are complex, but much of the complexity is for the benefit of providers, rather than consumers, of financial services. If you don't understand it, don't do it. That simple maxim would have saved both amateurs and professionals billions of pounds over the years, and the more recent the years, the larger the savings.

Whether you hire a financial adviser or not, you are on your own. I hope this book can be your companion.

Glossary

Absolute return The total return on a portfolio. Absolute return is
measured without benchmarking or reference to market movements.
26

Acquisition The takeover of one company by another. 69

Acquisition accounting Accounting treatment designed to flatter the
accounts of the acquiring company. 88

Active management (portfolio) Professional asset selection. Contrast
with passive management, which simply follows an index. 44

Agency costs Costs of intermediation, which reduce the returns on
financial investment relative to those of the underlying productive
investment. 188

Allais paradox A problem in behavioural economics devised by the
French economist Maurice Allais which demonstrates a 'Dutch book'.
134, 159, 160

Alpha Outperformance of an investment or investment fund, relative to
a benchmark, adjusted for risk. (The *beta* of the portfolio is calculated
to measure what part of excess return is accounted for by return to
above average risk.) 130

Alternative investment Asset outside mainstream categories of shares,
bonds and property. Traditionally alternative assets were mostly
physical objects (such as paintings and commodities), but more
recently the term is mainly used to refer to private equity and hedge
funds. 178, 207

Amortisation *See* DEPRECIATION.

Anomalies Deviations from the efficient market hypothesis. 52, 69

Arbitrage A strategy to profit from divergences in the prices of similar or
related securities. 177

Arbitrageurs Traders using arbitrage strategies, especially those that trade between an acquirer's stock and that of the prospective acquisition. **177**

Asset-backed securities (ABS) Tradable securities based on a pool of loans. An asset-backed security can have several tranches of security relating to the same asset pool; if the value of the pool deteriorates, the senior tranches will be paid first. **171**

Asset stripping Breaking up a company to realise the value of its underlying assets. **99**

Asset value The value of the assets underlying a security (which may differ from the market price of the security). **44, 98**

Bagger (as in 'ten or twenty bagger') Speculative stock which increases greatly in value. **23**

Basis point Each percentage point of yield is 100 basis points.

Bayesian The view that degrees of belief can be expressed as probabilities updated with new information. **121**

Behavioural finance, behavioural economics Analysis based on empirical or experimental studies of behaviour (especially towards risk) rather than models of rational choice. **71, 134, 145**

Benchmark The index specified to judge an investment manager's performance. **79**

Best execution The obligation to place a trade at the best price available in the market.

Beta The predicted effect on the price of a security of a 1 per cent movement in the benchmark index. **130**

Black–Scholes model The most widely used model for pricing options. **149, 167**

Blue chips Shares in large companies. **107, 136**

Bonds Securities with fixed interest rates and redemption dates. **34**

BRIC Principal emerging markets – Brazil, Russia, India, China. South Africa has sometimes also been included.

Call option The right to buy a security at a fixed price at a future date (*see also* PUT OPTION). **167**

Capital asset pricing model (CAPM) A model that predicts that expected rates of return will be determined by a combination of the risk-free rate and a risk premium determined by the asset category and the asset *beta*. **132**

Carry trade Arbitrage strategies that yield repeated small profits, usually from interest rate differentials (*see also* TALEB DISTRIBUTIONS). 178

Chartist Someone who predicts security prices by identifying trends from charts. 69

Chinese walls Measures (including rules and physical separation) to prevent different divisions (principally buy side and sell side) of a financial institution from exchanging information. 68

Closed-ended An investment fund whose shares can be acquired or disposed of only by selling to another investor. Such a fund may therefore sell at a premium or discount to its asset value. 178, 188

Closet indexation Active management which closely follows the content (and performance) of the benchmark index. 78

Collateral Provision against a liability.

Collateralised debt obligation (CDO) An asset-backed security whose value is based on a (generally) variable pool of debt instruments of specified quality. 171

Commission bias Investment recommendation influenced by the adviser's remuneration. 4

Competitive advantage The ability of a business to produce at lower cost, or to command higher prices, than other businesses serving the same market. 100

Complex systems Social or natural systems whose mathematical description demands dynamic, non-linear relationships. 71

Compound interest Calculation in which returns are increased by interest on reinvested interest. 27

Confirmation bias A tendency to select evidence that supports views that are already held. 143

Consensus forecast The median (or perhaps mean or modal) forecast, a product of the tendency of all economic forecasters to cluster together. 56

Consumer prices index A measure of inflation calculated by measuring the changing price of a fixed basket of goods.

Contract for difference (CFD) An agreement to pay (or receive) the difference between the present and future prices of a security. 165

Contrarian Someone who buys assets not currently favoured by the mind of the market. 210

Conventional investor An investor who applies closet indexation. 19, 183

Correlation Assets are correlated if movements in their prices tend to move in the same direction (*see also* BETA). 55

Cost of capital The cost to a firm of raising capital (typically an average of the cost of corporate debt and the total return required by equity shareholders). 96

Counterparty The person on the other side of a transaction. Market counterparties are institutions trading securities. 165

Credit default swap A derivative contract that pays in the event of the default of a borrower. 171

Credit rating An assessment of credit risk, often by a rating agency.

Credit risk The risk that a borrower will fail to meet the interest or principal on a loan. 38, 147

Day traders Small speculators who buy and sell frequently, perhaps within a single day. 23

Depreciation An allowance against profits for the fall in value of assets through time or use. 92

Derivatives Securities whose value is based on the value of other securities. 165

Diminishing marginal utility A tendency for additions to income or wealth to be valued less by the beneficiary as that income or wealth increases. 124

Discount rate, discounted cash flow (DCF) The process of discounting future revenues to compute a present value. 95

Distressed debt Bonds or loans on which the borrower may fail to make payment. 177

Diversification The process of reducing risk by buying assets whose returns are uncorrelated. 129, 203

Dividend The dividend on a share is the (usually quarterly or biannual) payment declared by the company. 31

Dividend yield The annual dividend per share as a percentage of the share price. 33

Dutch book A sequence of apparently attractive gambles which, if accepted, will leave the taker worse off. 159

Earnings before interest, tax, depreciation, amortisation (EBITDA) A profit figure reported by companies seeking to deliver flattering accounts of their affairs (*see also* PRO FORMA EARNINGS). 91

Earnings guidance The process by which companies influence analysts' forecasts of their earnings. 80

Earnings per share Profits after tax, divided by the total number of shares in issue. 33

Earnings yield (*see also* PRICE:EARNINGS RATIO) Earnings per share, as a percentage of the share price. 87

Eat what you kill The practice in professional firms of rewarding partners by reference to the revenues the individual partners themselves generate. 91

Efficient market hypothesis (EMH) The proposition that all relevant information about the value of a security is reflected in its price. 6, 50

Emerging market Country outside the principal developed economies (e.g. BRIC countries). 44

Enhanced bonds A structured product that uses derivatives to provide a higher yield (and risk) than the underlying bond. 174

Equity An equity interest is the right to receive what is left after prior claims have been met: e.g. ordinary shareholders receive the residual after debts and preferred shareholders have been paid. The owner's equity in a house is its value less the value of any outstanding mortgage. 17

Equity premium, equity risk premium The expected difference between the return on shares and the return on a safe asset. 28, 96, 132

Exchange-traded fund (ETF) A fund traded on a stock exchange whose value is linked to an index. 45

Execution only The service offered by a broker who will deal but not advise. 185

Exercise price The price at which you can buy or sell a share under option (*see also* STRIKE PRICE). 168

Expected value The average outcome of a gamble, calculated by multiplying potential pay-offs by their probabilities. 114

Expiry date The last date at which an option can be exercised. 168

Fat tails A phenomenon in which extreme events happen more frequently than a standard statistical distribution (e.g. binominal or normal distribution) allows. 151

Financial engineering The attempt to create value by repackaging investment products. 172

Financial investment, productive investment Financial investment is investment in securities; productive investment is investment in the activities that give these securities their value. 17

Fractal A geometric shape, each part of which resembles the whole. 152

Free cash flow Net cash from operations after deducting necessary investment. 92

Fundamental indices Market indices in which the weights of different securities are derived from economic indicators other than their market values. 217

Fundamental value The expected value of the cash flows generated by an asset. 84

Futures The right to buy or sell a security or commodity at a fixed price on a future date. 166

General knowledge Publicly available information. 56, 154

Generally accepted accounting principles The principal US accounting standard. 89

Going concern basis The assumption (for valuation purposes) that a company will continue in business.

Gross redemption yield (GRY) The total return from a bond, including any decline or increase in capital value between the present and maturity. 37

Halo effects The tendency to give high ratings to all characteristics of a favoured item or individual. 143

Hedge An asset whose price is expected to move in the opposite direction from the price of the asset it hedges. 128

Hedge fund An adventurous, open-ended investment company charging high fees. 176

High-net-worth Rich. 10

Hot hand Persistence of strong performance (*see also* SERIAL CORRELATION). 145

Independent Two variables are independent if their movements are unrelated. 129

Index fund Fund whose value follows that of a benchmark. 190

Index-linked stocks Securities on which interest and principal increase in line with inflation. 69

Information asymmetry Characteristic of markets in which the seller knows more about the goods than the buyer. 56

Initial public offering (IPO) The first offering of stock in a company to the public. 30, 75

Insider trading Dealing by corporate executives or their advisers (or their agents) on the basis of information about the company not yet publicly disclosed. 51

Insolvent A company or individual is insolvent when liabilities exceed assets.

Intangible assets Assets other than property, plant and investments: e.g., brands, patents, reputation. Sometimes called 'goodwill'. Figures for intangible assets reported in balance sheets mainly refer to overpayment for acquisitions and mean little. 92

Intelligent investor Someone who defines their own investment strategy by reference to fundamental value, thinks total return and minds their portfolio. 195

Interest rate risk The risk that a bond will fall in value owing to interest rate rises. 36

International financial reporting standards Accounting standards applied in most countries outside the United States. 91

Investment banking Traditionally, banking focused on securities issuance and corporate advice (principally IPOs and acquisitions). Modern investment banks also undertake (principally undertake) market-making, trading and asset management. Most are now part of financial conglomerates with corporate and retail banking operations. 9, 190

Junk bonds Bonds below investment grade. 171

Know your customer The regulatory obligation on a financial adviser to base recommendations on specific knowledge of the investor's circumstances. 3

Lemons Goods that the seller, but not the buyer, knows to be of inferior quality. 57

Leverage The process of increasing risk and potential return on an asset through borrowing. 40

Life insurance Insurance policy which pays on the death of the insured. Often packaged with savings products – such a package is called life assurance. 16

Likelihood The degree of belief in a narrative. 113

Long The opposite of short: a positive position in a security. 164

Long/short fund A fund that takes short positions as well as long. (A 130/30 fund will own shares worth 130 per cent of its value and have short positions equivalent to 30 per cent.) 176

Mark-to-market The practice of revaluing assets in line with current market values. 47

Market capitalisation The total value of the shares of a company. 33

Market risk The risk profile created by general market movements. **130**

Mean reversion A tendency for variables to return to their long-term average. **56**

Mental accounting An inclination to compartmentalise a portfolio rather than to mind a portfolio as an aggregate. **162**

Merger The combination of two firms.

Momentum The tendency for price movements to continue in the same direction (*see also* SERIAL CORRELATION). **55**

Monoliners Financial services firms that specialise in a single product or product group. **15**

Moral hazard The tendency for average product quality to deteriorate when there is information asymmetry. **59**

Mutual fund The US term for a European OEIC (*see* OPEN-ENDED INVESTMENT COMPANY). **43**

New issues The sale of new shares for cash by a company (*see* IPO). **8**

Noise Short-term price movements not justified by changes in fundamental value. **35**

Noise traders Frequent traders who act on noise (*see also* DAY TRADERS). **35**

Non-recurring items Costs that a company does not want to charge against profits. **91**

Normal distribution The most common – bell-shaped – statistical distribution. **114**

Open-ended investment company (OEIC) A European fund that creates or redeems shares or units in line with investor demand (cf. MUTUAL FUND). **43**

Option The right to buy or sell securities at a price agreed in advance. **167**

Overweight Holding a larger proportion of one's portfolio in a particular security than the share of that security in the relevant index. **79**

Passive fund, passive investment A fund or investment strategy that tracks an index. **45**

Payment-in-kind securities Bonds on which the interest rate increases as the creditworthiness of the borrower declines. **125**

Payment protection insurance Retail product which may meet loan repayments during sickness or unemployment. **16, 93**

PE ratio See PRICE:EARNINGS. **84**

PEG ratio The ratio of the price:earnings ratio and the growth rate of earnings. **84**

Penny shares Shares whose value is only a few cents per share (even though there may be many millions of shares). Often issued to appeal to noise traders. 23

Personal probability (subjective probability) An estimate of the probability of a particularly outcome of a single event. 121

Price:earnings ratio The ratio of the market price of a security to earnings per share after tax. 84

Principal The amount outstanding on a loan. 96

Private equity fund A fund that takes large stakes in unquoted companies. 44, 179

Pro forma earnings The profits companies would like you to think they have earned. 91

Productive investment *See* FINANCIAL INVESTMENT. 17

Proprietary trading ('prop desks') The internal hedge funds of banks. 24

Put option An option to sell a security at a price agreed in advance (*see also* CALL OPTION). 167

Quant Someone who specialises in mathematical modelling of investment questions. 5

Quantitative easing The purchase of debt securities by a central bank. 207

Random walk A process in which each change is independent of all previous changes. 49, 56

Rational expectations The assumption that individual expectations reflect all potentially available information. 64

Real estate investment trusts (REITs) Closed-ended funds which invest in property and enjoy a special tax regime. 44, 226

Real return Investment return after allowing for inflation. 27

Redemption date The date on which a loan will be repaid.

Reflexivity A characteristic of a process in which expected outcomes of a process affect the outcomes themselves. 78

Relative performance Investment performance relative to a benchmark. 28

Retained profits Profits that are not distributed as dividends. 31

Revenue recognition Anticipation of revenues not yet received in cash. 91

Risk-averse Disposed to value risks or gambles at less than their expected value. 125

Risk premium, equity risk premium The difference between the return on a risky asset and the yield on a safe one. 28, 96

Running yield The income yield on a bond whose market price differs from its redemption value (*see* GROSS REDEMPTION YIELD). 37

Scenario planning A mechanism for reviewing plans by positing several different scenarios of the future. 143

Secured loans Loans secured against specific assets. 18

Serial correlation The relationship between price movements in successive time periods. Short-term positive serial correlation is when price movements continue in the same direction (momentum). Long-term negative serial correlation is the tendency for long-term movements to reverse (mean reversion). 55

Sharpe ratio The ratio of standard deviation (variability) to the return from an asset. 120

Short seller A negative position established to benefit from the fall in value of a share. 61, 165

Short-term positive serial correlation The expectation that short-term price movements will be followed by other moves in a similar direction (*see also* MOMENTUM). 211

Specific risks Risks that are specific to the investment concerned and unrelated to movements in the general level of share prices. 130

Spread betting Betting on the rise and fall of a security or index (*see also* CONTRACT FOR DIFFERENCE). 165

Statistical arbitrage Computerised trading systems for exploiting short-term discrepancies between prices of similar securities. 177

Stock options The right (often given to senior executives) to buy the company's shares at a future date at a favourable price. 80

Strike price The price at which an option is granted. 167

Structured product Security with complex relationship to the underlying assets and liabilities. The result of financial engineering. 172

Subjective expected utility (SEU) A theory that individuals should or do approach risk by maximising the expected value of pay-offs using subjective (personal) probabilities. 111

Subprime borrower Subprime borrowers have poor credit ratings and the loans they take out in turn attract the adjective subprime. 143

Survivor bias Misleading generalisation about performance based on analysis of a population from which poor performers have been removed. 146

Sustainable competitive advantage A competitive advantage that a business can successfully maintain over time. 101

Swap, swap rates (generally of interest rates). A swap rate defines the terms on which fixed and variable rate obligations can be exchanged. The transaction is a swap. 165

Synergies Alleged benefits from mergers. 93

Taleb distributions Processes in which frequent small gains are punctuated by occasional large losses. 146

Technical analysis What chartists do. 69

Time preference The 'exchange rate' between present and future consumption. 18

Total return Investment return as a percentage of assets, including both income and capital gain. 22, 196

Tracking error A measure of how closely an index fund follows the benchmark index. 45

Trading floor Traders in investment banks typically work at desks and screens in one trading room. 7

Underweight *See* OVERWEIGHT. 79

Value at risk In risk modelling, the anticipated loss at some low percentile of the risk distribution. 115

Variability, volatility Measures of how much and how rapidly a security price goes up and down. 120

Winner's curse The tendency for assets to be bought by the person who makes the highest assessment of their value. 58

Yield curve The relationship between interest rates and bond maturities. 37

Bookshelves and Bookmarks

The Economist, Financial Times and *Wall Street Journal* all offer guide-books that cover most investment topics. If you plan to buy individual stocks, you should have a book on how to read accounting statements, such as Bob Parker's *Understanding Company Financial Statements*. And you should learn basics of corporate strategy. There are many books written on corporate strategy and for investment analysts, but not many target readers of this book would want to finish them. Dick Rumelt's *Good Strategy, Bad Strategy* is witty and perceptive and has lessons for investors as well as corporate executives. I'm bound to recommend my own *The Hare and the Tortoise*, a distillation of *Foundations of Corporate Success*. The world of business and finance is notorious for writing that luxuriates in jargon and complexity. John Lanchester's *How to Speak Money* is an excellent antidote and guide. Peter Bernstein's *Against the Gods*, on risk, is an exemplar of how to make complex concepts appear simple.

Do you want a book that contains the secrets of how to be rich? I hope not. But you might want advice from Soros and Buffett. The most relevant of George Soros's several books is *The Alchemy of Finance*, while Lawrence Cunningham offers an entertaining collection of extracts from the essays Buffett writes in his annual reports to Berkshire Hathaway shareholders (which are available on the company's web site). *Snowball*, by Alice Schroeder, is an exhaustive biography of the sage of Omaha.

If you want a small shelf of books about the industry that are fun to read, you might consider: from the 1980s, Burrough and Helyar's *Barbarians at the Gate*, an account of the last days of RJR Nabisco, and *Liar's Poker*, by Michael Lewis, set in Salomon in its heyday; and John Cassidy's account of the New Economy bubble, *dot.com*, best read in parallel with J. K. Galbraith's account of *The Great Crash, 1929*, which is beautifully written; its lessons are all still relevant.

The best narrative account of the global financial crisis is Andrew Ross Sorkin's *Too Big to Fail;* Michael Lewis's *The Big Short* is a highly entertaining account of one aspect of its origins, and the same author's more recent *Flash Boys* is an introduction to some of the issues raised by the absurd world of the high-frequency trader. I do not recommend the self-congratulatory memoirs of those who claim to have saved the world from the crisis for which they themselves were largely responsible; but Mervyn King's *The End of Alchemy* instead tries to draw lessons for finance and economics in relatively detached manner.

A comparison of Tom Wolfe's *The Bonfire of the Vanities* and Anthony Trollope's *The Way We Live Now* reveals that, while the actions and the instruments change, the fundamentals of financial follies do not.

The inspiration for a book like this one, which aims to provide practical advice with a rigorous intellectual basis, is Burton Malkiel's *A Random Walk down Wall Street,* which has been for years what I recommended to the encouragingly numerous people who sought such a book. *Random Walk* has been through eleven editions since it was first published in 1973, but its age shows, and the institutions and products it considers are American. So are the jokes, which are not to European taste. Still, it remains a classic. The permanent classic is Benjamin Graham's *The Intelligent Investor.*

Other academics who have written popular books on investment are Jeremy Siegel, whose *Stocks for the Long Run* is an unashamed paean to the virtues of equity investment, and Robert Shiller, who had the good fortune to publish *Irrational Exuberance* just as the New Economy bubble was bursting. Similar books you might consider are William Bernstein's *Seven Pillars of Investing Wisdom* and either of David Swenson's volumes, *Pioneering Portfolio Management* and *Unconventional Success.* Swenson, Yale's much-fêted investment manager, adopts a rather similar approach to the one described here, but Swenson invests better than he writes.

Do you want to pursue some of the more philosophical issues that have arisen in the course of this book? Quants and risk managers in the financial world make constant case of probabilities without much thought about what the numbers they readily deploy mean. Ian Hacking's *An Introduction to Probability and Inductive Logic* provides a good introduction to the underlying complexities. Questions about the nature of explanation – What does it mean to say a theory is illuminating but not true? – are at the heart of this book. People of a philosophical bent will appreciate the influence of Richard Rorty, whose related ideas are best set out in *Philosophy and the Mirror of Nature*. I found Wade Hands's *Reflections without Rules* an invaluable introduction to the central relevance of this sort of approach in modern economics.

Whatever books you put on your shelves, you will want to add some bookmarks to your computer. The internet gives you easy access to both products and information. All financial services organisations use web sites to market and give access to their products, and competitive pressures ensure that most are easy to locate and use. But good web sites cost money to build and maintain, and, one way or another, he who pays the piper at least influences the tune. While comparison sites listing financial products are invaluable, bear in mind that comparison sites are financed through commission.

The internet also makes access to information much easier. Most companies have an investors relations section on their web site, from which you can obtain annual reports and other financial information. Your stockbroker's site will probably have a research section that summarises these data and gives you other data about the company. Bulletin boards, which are a forum for title tattle about individual stocks, are amusing, but both the information and opinions on them should be treated with great caution.

Bibliography

Allais, M., 1953, Le Comportement de l'Homme Rationnel devant le Risque: Critique des Postulats et Axiomes de l'Ecole Americaine. *Econometrica*, v. 21, no. 4, p. 503, doi:10.2307/1907921.

Bachelier, L., trans. M. H. A. Davis and A. Etheridge, 2006, *Louis Bachelier's Theory of Speculation: The Origins of Modern Finance*. Princeton, NJ: Princeton University Press.

Bayes, M., and M. Price, 1763, An Essay towards Solving a Problem in the Doctrine of Chances. By the Late Rev. Mr. Bayes, F.R.S. Communicated by Mr. Price, in a Letter to John Canton, A.M.F.R. S. *Philosophical Transactions of the Royal Society of London*, v. 53, pp. 370–418, doi: 10.1098/rstl.1763.0053.

Bernoulli, D., 1954, Exposition of a New Theory on the Measurement of Risk. *Econometrica*, v. 22, no. 1, p. 23, doi: 10.2307/1909829.

Biggs, B., 2008, *Wealth, War, and Wisdom*. Hoboken, NJ: John Wiley & Sons.

Black, F., and M. Scholes, 1973, The Pricing of Options and Corporate Liabilities. *Journal of Political Economy*, v. 81, no. 3, pp. 637–54, doi: 10.1086/260062.

Bowden, M., 2012, *The Finish: The Killing of Osama bin Laden*. New York: Atlantic Monthly Press.

Cunningham, L., 2002, *How to Think Like Benjamin Graham and Invest Like Warren Buffett*. London: McGraw-Hill Education.

Dimson, E., P. Marsh, and M. Staunton, 2002, *Triumph of the Optimists: 101 Years of Global Investment Returns*. Princeton, NJ: Princeton University Press.

Fama, E. F., and K. R. French, 1992, *The Cross-Section of Expected Stock Returns*. Chicago, IL: Center for Research in Security Prices, Graduate School of Business, the University of Chicago.

Friedman, M., 1976, *Price Theory: A Provisional Text*. Chicago, IL: Aldine.

Friedman, M., and L. J. Savage, 1948, The Utility Analysis of Choices Involving Risk. *Journal of Political Economy*, v. 56, no. 4, pp. 279–304, doi: 10.1086/256692.

'H. W. M.', 1933, Review of J. M. Keynes, *Essays in Biography. Journal of the Royal Statistical Society*, v. 96, no. 3, p. 512, doi: 10.2307/2342137.

Harrod, R. F., and J. R. Hicks, 1939, Value and Capital. *The Economic Journal*, v. 49, no. 194, p. 294, doi: 10.2307/2225091.

Hicks, J., 1939, *Value and Capital; An Inquiry into Some Fundamental Principles of Economic Theory*. Oxford: Clarendon Press.

Kahnemann, D., P. Slovic, and A. Tversky, 1982, *Judgment under Uncertainty: Heuristics and Biases*. Cambridge: Cambridge University Press.

Kay, J., 2009, *The Long and the Short of It: A Guide to Finance and Investment for Normally Intelligent People Who Aren't in the Industry*. London: Erasmus.

Keynes, J. M., 1920, *The Economic Consequences of the Peace*. New York: Harcourt, Brace and Howe.

Knight, F. H., 1921, *Risk, Uncertainty and Profit*. Boston, MA: Houghton Mifflin.

Lo, A. and MacKinlay, A., 2002, *A Non-Random Walk Down Wall Street*. NJ: Princeton University Press.

Malkiel, B., 1973, *A Random Walk down Wall Street*. New York: W.W. Norton.

Markowitz, H., 1952, Portfolio Selection. *Journal of Finance*, v. 7, no. 1, p. 77, doi: 10.2307/2975974.

Pigou, A. C., and J. M. Keynes, 1921, A Treatise on Probability. *Economic Journal*, v. 31, no. 124, p. 507, doi: 10.2307/2223083.

Sharpe, W. F., 1964, Capital Asset Prices: A Theory of Market Equilibrium under Conditions of Risk. *The Journal of Finance*, v. 19, no. 3, p. 425, doi: 10.2307/2977928.

Shiller, R. J., 2000, *Irrational Exuberance*. Princeton, NJ: Princeton University Press.

Soros, G., 2003, *The Alchemy of Finance* (2nd edn). London: John Wiley and Sons Ltd.

Taleb, N. N., 2001, *Fooled by Randomness: The Hidden Role of Chance in the Markets and in Life*. New York: Texere.

Zweig, J., 2008, *Your Money and Your Brain*. New York: Simon & Schuster.